FILTERED

Café culture is flourishing in cities across the world. From London to Seoul, Melbourne to Shanghai and many cities in between, people are flocking to cafés. A recent phenomenon, café culture has made its reappearance only since the end of the 20th century. What is the appeal of the café for urban dwellers? And why now? 'Having a coffee' might be a daily ritual, yet it is more than coffee that draws us to the café. Cafés are vital social spaces, technically connected work-spaces and businesses that are forging design and food trends.

The café is the lens through which this book explores major changes occurring in everyday life in cities across the world. Urban regeneration has fuelled the growth of urban amenity and social consumer spaces. The impact of technology, social and workplace transformation, and the ascendency of the design and food industries all find expression in the spaces of the cafe. The specialty coffee movement is a thriving, global presence, uniting café staff and customers across geographical borders, with a shared commitment to the connoisseurship of coffee.

In the book's global sweep, it examines the development of café culture in China, Japan and Australia as significant and interesting departures from traditional European café culture. Australia is a world leader and successful exporter of its unique style of coffee and food. Interviews with café patrons and staff illuminate why the café has become a meaningful place for many people in the 21st-century city.

Emma Felton is Senior Lecturer in the Creative Industries Faculty at Queensland University of Technology. She has written widely about urban experience from interdisciplinary perspectives, including gender and design approaches. She is co-author and editor of the book *Design and Ethics: Reflections on Practice* (Routledge, 2012).

'In Filtered, Emma Felton shows us how the café – and café culture – is entwined with urban development across place and time. Despite variations across continents and populations, cafés have made an indelible mark on our cities. Felton explains how the café is a window into our changing urban culture, work habits and social spaces. She details their uneasy relationship with broader issues including neighbourhood change and displacement, and their role in networks of global trade. This book is a must read for anyone with an interest in urban cultural studies.'

– Carl Grodach, Professor and Director, Urban Planning and Design, Monash Art Design & Architecture, Monash University

'The author shows the historical and global continuities of the café as a social site. Her study employs observation, interviews and analysis of cultural texts. The interpretations are illuminating and the narrative entertaining. Felton shows how the café, and the act of having a cup of coffee, are at the centre of dilemmas related to how we now live, work and consume. Drawing on historical, cultural and sociological approaches, the study moves between the local and global scales, aesthetic and political dimensions. Along the way, *Filtered* helps us understand the ubiquity of the café and the centrality of coffee in our cities and cultures.'

– Ian Woodward, PhD, Professor, Consumption, Culture and Commerce, Department of Marketing and Management, University of Southern Denmark

'An intriguing brew of the social life of café culture and how it relates to dynamic urban transformation. By presenting historical and contemporary expositions that intricately plait café culture with economics, aesthetics, culture and technology, Felton's book will appeal to both specialist and general readers.'

– Kelvin E.Y. Low, PhD, Associate Professor and Deputy Head, Department of Sociology, National University of Singapore

FILTERED

Coffee, the Café and the 21st-Century City

Emma Felton

LONDON AND NEW YORK

First published 2019
by Routledge
2 Park Square, Milton Park, Abingdon, Oxon OX14 4RN

and by Routledge
52 Vanderbilt Avenue, New York, NY 10017

Routledge is an imprint of the Taylor & Francis Group, an informa business

© 2019 Emma Felton

The right of Emma Felton to be identified as author of this work has been asserted by her in accordance with sections 77 and 78 of the Copyright, Designs and Patents Act 1988.

All rights reserved. No part of this book may be reprinted or reproduced or utilised in any form or by any electronic, mechanical, or other means, now known or hereafter invented, including photocopying and recording, or in any information storage or retrieval system, without permission in writing from the publishers.

Trademark notice: Product or corporate names may be trademarks or registered trademarks, and are used only for identification and explanation without intent to infringe.

British Library Cataloguing-in-Publication Data
A catalogue record for this book is available from the British Library

Library of Congress Cataloging-in-Publication Data
Names: Felton, Emma, author.
Title: Filtered: coffee, the café and the 21st century city / Emma Felton.
Description: Abingdon, Oxon; New York, NY: Routledge, 2019. |
Includes bibliographical references.
Identifiers: LCCN 2018037492| ISBN 9780415787574 (hardback) |
ISBN 9781138367920 (pbk.) | ISBN 9781315225869 (ebook)
Subjects: LCSH: Coffee–Social aspects. | Coffee shops–Social aspects. |
Coffee industry. | City life.
Classification: LCC GT2918 .F45 2019 | DDC 647.95–dc23
LC record available at https://lccn.loc.gov/2018037492

ISBN: 978-0-415-78757-4 (hbk)
ISBN: 978-1-138-36792-0 (pbk)
ISBN: 978-1-315-22586-9 (ebk)

Typeset in Bembo
by Deanta Global Publishing Services, Chennai, India

To Kevin

CONTENTS

FIGURES

ACKNOWLEDGEMENTS

This book has had a long gestation, and a relatively short writing period. Lots of coffees (soy flat white and piccolos), conversations, and friendly interest among friends and colleagues have contributed to its completion. Thanks are due to Imogen Hayes, whose excellent research skills and Mandarin were a valuable asset in Japan and China. Patrick Hayes created the book cover and provided information about café culture in Indian cities, assuring me of the phenomenon's global reach. As always, I'm grateful to Kevin, a critical reader as well as an enthusiastic wingman. His support is much appreciated.

I am most grateful to Sandra Hogan for her work on the manuscript. And to Susan Johnson whose enthusiasm for the project has been sustaining. Many thanks to the skilful artists who generously contributed their talent, Xin Xin Wen for her China photographs and Tricia King, photographer in Australia. Also gratitude to my colleague Caroline Heim at Queensland University of Technology, whose encouragement helped to re-boot the project from an earlier Australian-only version of the book.

Gillian Swanson and Xin Gu also provided valuable support.

Thanks to all the people who generously gave up their time to talk with me about either running a cafe or their experience of visiting cafes. In particular, Ralf Ruller in Berlin, and Chrissie Trabucco and Mark Dundon in Melbourne.

This book would not have appeared in its present form without the patience and backing of my commissioning editor Gerhard Boomgaarden at Routledge. Many thanks to Gerhard, who was very accommodating at a critical stage of the project, and also to assistant editor Mihaela Diana Ciobotea at Routledge.

INTRODUCTION

> The cafe is a shape-shifter. Its persistence is due to its malleability.
>
> *Merry White*[1]

Anyone living in a city at the beginning of the 21st century couldn't fail to notice the remarkable escalation in the number of cafés popping up across many urban neighbourhoods. This was the prompt that began the investigation which eventually led to this book. What are the factors driving this growth? And why now? As research tends to do, my subject drew me into an intriguing web of relationships and diversions, which stretched far beyond the many cities and cafés I visited; and the people I met who worked in and patronized cafés. When I first proposed the idea of a book about the café and the city as a lens through which to examine contemporary urban socio-cultural change, I soon realized that I had not calculated the extent of the contemporary café's global reach – café culture is thriving in cities across the world, not just those in the West. In places such as Shanghai, Seoul and Bangkok, café culture is a recent phenomenon, but it is booming. As a global phenomenon, café culture piqued my curiosity even further.

Another discovery was the complexity and depth of the coffee industry itself. The book began by looking at cafés in the broad sense – any type of café located in a city and where people congregated – but it soon became apparent that the specialty coffee movement is one of the most dominant types among the recent wave of cafés, particularly in Australia and Asian cities where café culture is relatively new. Specialty cafés are everywhere. Distinguished by their artisanal approach, from sourcing origin beans to how beans are roasted and to the multiple ways coffee is brewed, these cafés all share a dedication to the entire process of the beverage. The specialty coffee movement is a globally connected community of café staff and aficionados, whose dedication is shared via technology through a multitude of blogs and social media apps. Yet for specialty coffee enthusiasts, concerns about sustainability and ethical consumption sometimes sit at odds with coffee's growing status in the pantheon of elite, gourmet food and drink cultures.

For a book with such a broad reach, each chapter's topic by default has to be highly selective and idiosyncratic. So for instance, in choosing to include café culture in Japan, China and Australia, many countries with equally interesting and relevant genealogies of café culture are left out. At the same time, allotting one chapter per country hardly taps beneath the surface of café and urban culture in places with rich cultural traditions and urban histories. Perhaps those books are yet to be written.

The book's exploration of café culture, whether specialty, independent or franchise cafés, is the city near the beginning of the 21st century city. How we live in cities is transforming dramatically, and in a very short period of time. Technological innovations, changes to work, population mobility and the growth of urban amenity and consumption as lifestyle practices are factors that all shape the types of cities and urban experience we encounter today. Each of these influences intersect, and in their various ways are supported in the café, making it an important place for many urban inhabitants – and a fascinating site to explore contemporary social and working life. Merry White, in her book *Cafe Life in Japan* (2012), refers to cafés as 'shape shifters' whose historical endurance is due to their malleability and ability to adapt to the changing needs and roles of urban citizens. This appears no more evident than in today's metropolitan areas.

What has occurred in the last two decades that has contributed to the growth of café culture everywhere? While technology has certainly played a major role in distributing global trends occurring across food, drink and design industries and uniting communities of interest, many other elements are at play. Chapter One outlines major developments that are occurring globally and how they have impacted on metropolitan life, each explored in greater detail in subsequent chapters. For several decades, the processes of urban revitalization have been occurring in many cities across the world. Urban planning strategies have been alert to the appeal of culture and amenity, and the café is firmly embedded within this nexus. Chapter Two departs from the material city to investigate the social aspect of café life, of why people are drawn to cafés. Historically, cafés were embedded in the social and economic relations of the city, and in interviews with café patrons and staff it is clear that sociality is still a major drawcard. But the world is a very different place today than it was during the café's historical ascendency. Who would have predicted even ten years ago that you might find and meet your life partner via an app on your smart phone, and with whom you first meet in a café? In cities of increasing cultural diversity, cafés are important – and safe – places to get to know others who are less known to us. If living in cities is about living among strangers, then cafés are vital meeting places for strangers or those less familiar.

While the story of café culture and coffee is representative of globalization, its history shows us that coffee has always been a global product *par excellence.*

Originating in Ethiopia, coffee was transported across to Yemen in the 16th century, and on to Europe in the 17th century. The Dutch were first to farm it en masse in their colonies in Ceylon and more successfully in Java, Indonesia. In the 18th century, French colonists took it to the Caribbean, then Mexico and Brazil, which now remains the world's largest producer. Coffee agriculture was closely tied to sugarcane, and plantations relied heavily on slave labour. Today, coffee's colonial legacy is still evident in the disparity between its production by low-waged agricultural workers and its consumption by people in affluent countries.

The business of coffee and cafés is multidimensional, situated in a complex network of global relationships and supply chains. Several excellent books have been written on this topic, so Chapter Three presents only a summary of some of the major conditions of both coffee agriculture and the contemporary café industry. For greater depth, books such as Mark Pendergrast's *Uncommon Grounds: The History of Coffee and How It Transformed the World* (2010) and Anthony Wild's *Coffee: A Dark History* (2004) are entertaining and thoroughly detailed accounts of coffee's history. James Hoffman's *The World Atlas of Coffee* (2014) provides a delightfully visual account of coffee production and producing nations, brewing, roasting and other current features of the industry. Coffee's colonial history is also evident in corporate colonization; the global behemoth Starbucks has cornered the market in China and is expanding in India, establishing shrewd partnerships with powerful local corporations. As well as looking at conditions of agricultural workers, Chapter Three identifies some of the less equitable conditions for café workers in affluent countries.

Coffee culture in Australia, Japan and China is the subject of the following three chapters. I use Australian café culture and cities as one of the book's central reference points, while also discussing cafés in a range of cities across the world. One of the main considerations here is the exponential growth of café culture in Australia and its contribution to the global specialty coffee movement; Australia's café culture is an export success story. The other reason is an autobiographical one. Living in an Australian city, I've witnessed major transformations occurring over the course of two decades, and this has equipped me with a range of experiences and observations. I am no coffee aficionado, and while I enjoy a daily strong soy cappuccino, my interest in cafés was triggered by observing their rapid growth firstly in my own neighbourhood during a period of urban renewal, and subsequently elsewhere.

While much has been written about the café's origins in 16th-century Constantinople, then westward to Europe, less has been written about café culture elsewhere. Historically, Asian populations are known for their tea consumption rather than coffee, but it might surprise readers to know for instance, that Japan was the first country in the world to establish a café chain in 1907, opened by the Paulista group in Tokyo and Osaka. National histories of cafés and coffee unearth unique cultural practices and unusual entrepreneurial endeavours; they have much to say about the forces of colonialism, immigration and cultural identity. Australia's enjoyment of the espresso was due to its introduction by post-World War II Italian and Greek immigrants, something of an inroad considering the Anglophone population at the time, and whose attitudes to foreigners were shaped by a White Australia policy. And yet Australia has gone on to be leaders in the world's specialty coffee scene, exporting not only barista and entrepreneurial skills, but a unique style of café culture.

People are drawn to cafés for the coffee, the people, a reprieve from the daily grind. But there are discernible reasons why we choose one café over another, and this has much to do with its ambience, aura and the 'sense' of the place it conveys. The café is a sensual, immersive experience – even in the digital age – and many elements work together to create enjoyment: staff attitude, décor, music, location and the less tangible quality of atmosphere. Chapter Seven unpacks what it is that constitutes a café's ambience and its significance in our attachment to place and community. In speaking with people about their favourite cafés, I encountered some surprising hierarchies on their lists of importance. In any discussion of design – whether the café interior, or the dizzying array of coffee equipment currently available – it is impossible to ignore the ascendency and increased public awareness of design and the design industries.

And finally, the book ends with the largest and most complex topic of all – the impact of technology on our cities and our lives. Technology's influence is registered in cafés in the way we communicate and work, enabled by Wi-Fi, laptops and smart phones; how we access information about coffee and cafés through a plethora of blogs, social media apps and digital maps; and how a café promotes itself. I could not have undertaken the extensive research I did without the internet, a minefield of current and historical coffee information, with articles, blogs and scholarly research at my fingertips. My trusty smartphone proved invaluable for tracking down cafés in lesser-known parts of unfamiliar cities, making the task even simpler by mapping transit routes, times and costs.

Technological innovations have rapidly reshaped our lives and continue to do so in ways that are still occurring and hard to predict. The nature of work, communication, mobility and travel have been totally transformed. Nothing is immune from technology's reach, including what was once a totally embodied, sensual experience in the café.

Note

1 White, Merry. 2012. *Coffee Life in Japan*. Berkeley, CA: University of California Press, p. 12.

1

THE CAFÉ AND THE CITY

> Coffee changes people. Moreover, it changes the way they interact with their friends, their fellow citizens and their community. The proliferation of coffee-house drinkers and the establishment of coffee-houses were the first signs of change.
>
> *Markman Ellis*[1]

Cafés and coffee culture are flourishing in cities across the world. From Melbourne to Shanghai and to Tokyo, Berlin and London, café culture is firmly embedded in the fabric of contemporary urban life. The growth and popularity of the café since the late 20th century is phenomenal and is tightly linked to profound socio-cultural and technological change. The crucible of that change is the city. While 'having a coffee' might be a ritual of everyday life, it is more than coffee that draws us to cafés.

The coffee bean is the world's fourth most traded agricultural commodity and the coffee industry is a (US) $100 billion global industry. Worldwide we drink over 500 billion cups of coffee a year. An abundance of blogs and social media is devoted to the topic, and an array of specialist equipment and accoutrements supports a thriving global industry. Coffee is now a connoisseur's playground, from ethical sourcing of origin beans and direct trade between roasters and plantations to a variety of specialty coffee styles, all of which suggests it is analogous to wine-making or fine dining. Coffee tastings or 'cuppings', artisanal roasting and blending, and international barista and latte art competitions are all hallmarks of coffee and a café's distinction.

Finland, The Netherlands and Norway vie for the title as the highest consumers of coffee. Asian countries, mostly known for their tea cultures, are the fastest growing consumers of coffee, with the biggest uptake occurring in the highly populated countries of China and Indonesia where coffee consumption has grown steadily by around 15% annually from 2012. But the story is similar the world over; in 2017, the American specialty coffee market grew by 20%. It is no surprise that cafés are the fastest growing segment of the thriving hospitality industry, given the context that has helped to fuel their growth.

Fifteen years ago, in my inner-city neighbourhood in Brisbane, Australia, I could count the number of cafés on one hand. Now there are over sixty in a radius of about three kilometres. My neighbourhood, like many inner-city areas across the world, has been transformed through urban renewal processes and population growth. Cafés and restaurants have become an integral part of the transformation and subsequent appeal of the area. Some cafés appear in unlikely places, wedged in between buildings and scattered throughout semi-industrial or commercial precincts, but wherever they are, they are busy. In Australia, often credited as a world leader in specialty coffee and the invention of the flat white (a fact contested by New Zealanders), independent and specialty cafés outshine global chain coffee shops. It is the only country where Starbucks made a hasty retreat, closing down 60 of its 87 cafés when it first rolled them out at the beginning of the 21st century. Australia has also been credited with exporting its particular style of coffee and café culture to cities across the world – to Singapore, London, Paris and New York. The ubiquitous presence of cafés, whether independent or chains, has transformed the streets of many urban precincts across the globe.

It is impossible to talk about the café without foregrounding its relationship with the city. What has changed about metropolitan life and the way we live now that has produced a flourishing café culture in cities across the world? What is the café's relationship to the contemporary city's social and economic life? Historically the café has a well-established connection to the city as an important gathering place in the social life of cities, a critical role that the café still occupies today. But there are also major differences. Today's cities are characterized by unprecedented technological developments, highly mobile populations, social change and globalization, making the experience of quotidian urban life highly distinct from previous eras.

The café's origins

Since its 16th-century origins in Constantinople (today's Istanbul), café culture has been entwined with the economic fate and social fluctuations of the metropolis. But prior to coffee's arrival in Constantinople, legend has it that coffee was first discovered in Ethiopia by a goat herder who noticed a change in his goat's behaviour when it nibbled red cherries, which contained the raw coffee bean, from a bush. The goat herder, noticing the energizing effect on the goat after eating the cherries, tried them himself. From Ethiopia, coffee beans were exported to Yemen, where the first recorded account of coffee appeared and where it was used by Sufis in their all-night devotional practice to help them stay awake. Coffee was widely consumed throughout the 15th century in the Middle East in Persia, Egypt, Turkey and North Africa, where it was often consumed communally, being passed around in a cup and shared. Coffee's Middle Eastern origins have earnt it the title of the 'wine of Islam'. For historian Wolfgang Schivelbusch this is an apt descriptor, the logic of coffee drinking for Arab-Islamic civilization being indisputable:

> As a non-intoxicating and non-alcoholic, indeed even sobering and mentally stimulating drink, it seemed to be tailor-made for a culture that forbade alcohol consumption and gave birth to modern mathematics. Arabic culture is dominated by abstraction more than any other culture in human history.[2]

According to legend, Mohammed was cured of narcolepsy with coffee and there is evidence that it was used medicinally for a range of ailments. Coffee became a lucrative trade item and its popularity invoked the ire and suspicion of various Arab rulers and was banned periodically. Coffeehouses were considered to harbour improper activities; as Ralph Hattox notes in his history of coffeehouses, these ranged from "gambling to involvement in irregular and criminally unorthodox sexual situations".[3]

During the 16th century, coffee made its way to Constantinople. As the Ottoman Empire's seat of power, the city was a ferment of artistic and architectural achievement; it also attracted a large influx of immigrants. Among them were Greek, Armenian and Jewish people seeking religious freedom and social rights. Constantinople became a centre for cultural integration and its cafés were an amalgam of cultures, because of its denizens but also because of its coffee; the beans originated from the Arabian Peninsula, were brewed in Constantinople and were sipped from cups imported from China. Cafés sprung up all over the city in various modes, from takeaway-style coffee stalls to coffee shops and coffeehouses, the latter the most spacious and enduring. They were foremost social places where men met to converse, play games and conduct business. Within fifteen years of coffee's first appearance in the city, there were over 600 coffeehouses.[4]

Just under a century later from their establishment in Constantinople, cafés made their first appearance in another empire – this time the British. Britain was just beginning to reap the harvest of its colonial expansion. In London, the first café was established in the centre of the financial district of the city by Pasqua Rosee, a Greek Orthodox servant. It was sponsored by merchants from the Levant Company, the trading house that organized and regulated trade with the Ottoman Empire. The merchants had acquired the taste for coffee during their lengthy excursions to the Ottoman cities.[5] The café's popularity in London grew quickly and soon there were between 300 and 500 of them in the city.

As places that are entwined with the city's fortunes, the café as a symbol of economic power is no better demonstrated than in the case of London's Lloyd's Coffee House, which opened in 1688. Established by Edward Lloyd, it quickly became a meeting hub for insurance brokers and people in the maritime occupations who visited to hear the latest trade news. The café was popular as a place primarily for men to meet and conduct business, a common use of the early coffeehouse. Over the years Lloyd's cafés grew in number and business activity and eventually, Lloyd's relinquished its coffeehouse role altogether and became the world-famous insurance brokerage, the largest in the world for many years.[6]

The cafés of London, and later Vienna and Paris, were renowned as places where people gathered to discuss art, politics and literature. In Paris, many cafés became hubs of cultural and intellectual activity, where the distribution of ideas and debate went hand in hand with the distribution of coffee, fuelling the intellectual life of the city. A visitor to Vienna in the 1700s wrote that it was full of cafés 'where those novelists who busy themselves with newspapers delight to meet'.[7] European cafés were more inclusive than their Middle Eastern antecedents, they offered a public place where men and women could gather and converse. In Britain cafés become known as 'penny universities' because for the price of a cup of coffee you could sit for a long time discussing or listening to 'extraordinary discussions' on politics and other matters.

And so the history of the café and metropolitan development – culturally, socially and economically – is similarly marked in cities across the world where a vibrant café culture has been established: in 19th-century Tokyo, early 20th-century Shanghai, and mid-20th-century New York, Melbourne and Sydney. These histories are too complex and numerous to detail in this book, but they all share common patterns of growth, from the arrival of immigrants, the development of trade or industry and, frequently, a renewed support for cultural development.

The café's ascendency: Why now?

The early cafés were places of intense sociality and conviviality. Today's cafés are still places of sociality, but technology, social change has increased the range of what people do in cafés – and how. In a mobile, socially fragmented world, cafés more than ever provide spaces to connect with people. Or in Robert Hughes's elegant phrase, they are places 'where solitudes might lie together', somewhere to sit and watch the world go by, to work or read. It is hardly surprising that people seek out places to meet or be alone in public, given the social changes that have accelerated since the latter part of the 20th century. We are living in a period of profound social, technological and political change. The way we live our daily lives has been transformed, most notably through internet technologies, globalization and population mobility, whose consequences are most acutely experienced in the city.

It's widely remarked that, for the first time in history, the majority of the world's population lives in cities. The tipping point occurred just after 2009 and growth has been rapid, this statistic is put into perspective when we consider that less than 25% of people lived in cities in 1950. As populations swell into metropolitan areas, their demographics are changing. Highly mobile populations have produced cities of greater cultural and ethnic diversity. The global north–south division, referred to throughout this book, aligns roughly with the distinction between the world's most advantaged and least advantaged economies. Cities in the global south, where the majority of the world's urban populations live, are getting younger. In the global north, populations are ageing, and single-person households are on the rise. This is due in part to affluence, gender equality and longevity. In Australia 25% of the population lives alone, and in other Western countries such as Denmark, Sweden, France, Italy and Germany, the numbers are even higher.[8] City skylines dotted with cranes are a common sight, signalling the rapid expansion of apartment dwellings. In Western cities in particular, a shift from lower-density housing to apartment-style living has been accompanied by the parallel growth of urban amenities such as restaurants, cafés and bars, which have become the de facto social living spaces of apartment dwellers. With its hospitable ambience and buzz of humanity, the café is a quick fix to human connection if you're living alone, or a social lounge room if your apartment is small.

By far the most significant catalyst of quotidian change is technological innovation or 'digital disruption' whose scale of impact on people's lives is comparable to the Industrial Revolution of the 18th century. In a period of just over twenty years, technology has completely transformed every aspect of our lives. Whether this is experienced most directly in the way we work and communicate, or indirectly in in a way that nonetheless affects us, the impact has been profound. Every industry has been transformed. And although service industries such as the café appear to offer primarily a sensual, embodied experience, technology has brought changes which make the 21st-century café very different from its historical antecedent. From the sophisticated technology of espresso machines, roasters and the fine calibration of coffee making and roasting, to the impact of social media, the café industry has not escaped the impact of technological change. Moreover, the spaces of the Wi-Fi-connected café are also working spaces for a growing number of freelance and contract workers.

Defining café cultures: The dominance of specialty cafés

This book is a general investigation of café cultures, but I soon discovered that the explosion in cafés is predominantly among the independent style of café. Independent cafés vary in style and approach, across cities, regions and countries. So while I discuss a range of café types, including chains such as Starbucks, most are independently owned cafés. A sub-sector of independently owned cafés are known as specialty or sometimes 'third-wave' cafés. Occasionally they are referred to by the more pejorative term 'hipster' cafés. The latter term is used because these cafés are often distinguishable by a standardised aesthetic: minimalist décor, raw timber and white tiles, as well as their association with bearded male baristas. Independent cafés sit on a continuum, where at the specialty end, the quality of the coffee bean and artisanal approaches to roasting and brewing is the priority. Along the continuum are cafés where the coffee quality is important but the focus is not artisanal. Independent cafés are located everywhere – in bookshops, laneways, cafés, hole-in-the-wall cafés, converted houses, warehouses and purpose-built spaces.

I use the terms 'specialty' and 'third-wave' interchangeably throughout the book. However, specialty is more aptly applied to coffee, as in the specialty coffee movement, which denotes an artisanal approach to coffee production. Foremost in specialty cafés is a dedication to the connoisseurship of coffee, from sourcing the beans to the artisanship and expertise of the coffee roaster and the barista. Café proprietors who roast and blend their beans present an artisanal edge, and the roastery provides a primary or secondary income stream. Throughout my interviews

FIGURE 1.1 Artisanal approaches to coffee. Photo credit: © iStock.

with café owners, it became clear that not at all cafés that *look* like specialty cafés – that is, through a common aesthetic – share the same dedication to the connoisseurship of coffee. Several café owners were quick to emphasize this point. In fact, specialty coffee is distinguished by an international standardised grading process. The Specialty Coffee Association (SCA) grades coffee on a scale to 100. Coffees that grade 60 or above are considered 'commercial' and those that score over 80 are graded as 'specialty' coffee. As we will see in Chapter Three, the production of specialty coffee is dependent on careful cultivation in small-lot pastures, specific microclimates and soils. Specialty cafés have sprouted like mushrooms across cities in areas that are usually in the process of gentrification or in existing gentrified areas. They've made a particular impact in cities whose café culture has emerged from the European café tradition or have had traditional tea drinking cultures, for example in Australia and Asian countries such as China and Korea.

Café culture has experienced exponential growth in Australia, which has been credited as the country where the first 'flat white' milky style of coffee was developed, although it's a fact contested by New Zealand, where the same claim has been made. But as British coffee specialist James Hoffman notes:

> while the argument continues over whether the flat white was invented in Australia or New Zealand, it undeniably came from Australasia and has been spread by those who travelled to Europe and North America to open businesses there.[9]

There are different views on the origin of specialty cafés, but it is generally accepted that the west coast of the United States is where it first made its appearance. However, both the United States and Australia are credited with spearheading and developing the movement, transporting it around the world. Its ascendency began in the late 20th century, running in parallel with the most recent period of global urban revitalization. The café's emergence at this time places it at the centre of the new urban amenity, where it is aligned with the growth in consumer and aesthetic cultures. Media reports are quick to claim the relationship between urban renewal and café culture in headlines such as 'How third wave cafés are transforming high streets' and 'Gentrification means the world is one big flat white'.[10]

Cafés appear to be everywhere, but the penetration of third-wave cafés varies across cities. Third-wave cafés exist in Britain and the United States and throughout European countries, although in the traditional café culture countries of Europe such as Italy and France, their growth appears less vigorous. In Asian countries such as Japan, Singapore, Korea, Thailand and India, third-wave café culture began a little later, in the first and second decades of the 21st century, where it appears to be flourishing. Cafés existed in many Asian countries prior to the 21st century, but in general they were not of the 'third-wave' variety.

THE CITY

> The coffee-house helps manage lives. It supports the various schedules of city-dwellers, provides respite and social safety in its space, and offers refreshment and the demonstration of taste, in several senses.[11]

Cities have been undergoing momentous change since the end of the 20th century. Some commentators believe we are just on the cusp, and that far greater changes lie ahead. Our cities are ever more dense, diverse and complex than any other period in history, and many have been subject to the process of urban revitalization. Café culture is synonymous with urban revitalization and while this section explores the influences that shape the 21st-century city in broad terms, café culture itself is predominantly about the people who visit cafés and work in them. In the same way, while we can talk about the city's infrastructure and amenity, the metropolis is first and foremost a place where large numbers of people dwell – increasingly in close proximity to one another. Cities are about people – and it is the 'soft city', the city of lived experience that is the main focus of the book. Historically the city is central to human activity and endeavour, a place that has generated most of our art, culture, commerce and technology.

Cities are enormously complex places and each one is distinct. Every place is unique, shaped by its own historical, socio-cultural and geographical specificities, its practices and institutions. Cities can differ markedly from one another, even when they are located within countries with shared cultural backgrounds. Yet while the processes of urbanization are contingent on locally produced factors such as urban governance policies and investment, cities are increasingly subject to global processes and flows of capital. How the global impacts on the local is complex and will be different in each location, but there are also shared similarities. So while it is not within the scope of this book to explore each urban

FIGURE 1.2 Melbourne, Australia Laneway cafés. Photo credit: © iStock.

context presented throughout, I seek out the commonalities through the book's main themes, identified in each chapter. In this way, the café is used to explore broader social, technological and industrial changes which are occurring globally and affecting the world's cities in various ways.

In defining what I'm referring to as a city throughout the book, I mean the urban conglomeration that is the both the urban core and its suburbs. Each city has unique patterns of habitation; for example, while Australia is highly urbanized with approximately 75% of its population living in cities, most people live in the suburbs in low-density, single dwellings. In the United States the pattern of urban/suburban living is similar. In China and India this is not the case, where high-density apartment dwellings are required to house massive populations. However, the cafés discussed throughout the book, tend to be located in inner-city precincts, because this is where they are most numerous and where much of urban revitalization is occurring. Cafés do appear across suburbs, outer suburbs and country areas, and are popular for much the same reasons as their inner-city counterparts. That is, part of their appeal is that they're filling a human need to gather, connect and conduct the complex business of 21st-century living.

Global influences

In Western cities, the current period of accelerated urbanism began with the gradual decline or relocation of the manufacturing industries from urban centres from the 1970s. In manufacturing's place came the growth of other industries, – of the finance sector, the service industries and more recently the knowledge and cultural industries. Along with economic globalization and the roll-back of state responsibilities in the global north, these shifts have contributed to reshaping urban economies of the 21st-century city.[12] Other factors have also come into play which connect cities in the northern hemisphere more closely to those in the southern hemisphere. In his account of globalization's impact on cities, James Spencer (2014) argues that the unravelling of colonial power since 1945, and more latterly the end of the Cold War from the 1990s, have untethered cities from the sovereignty of nation states: 'New fault lines of global economic, social and cultural connectivity' have enabled urban conglomerates to form alternative alliances and bases of power.[13]

The global economic structure that defines the current period is frequently referred to as neo-liberalism. In the global north, neo-liberalism is defined broadly by reduced state intervention and services, with a concomitant emphasis on private investment and the promotion of a free market economy. Neo-liberalism advocates small government and is underpinned by the belief that economic freedom and, in particular, the system of private property is essential for other forms of freedom. It is a process which has contributed to the intensity of urban development and is implicated in growing spatial divisions and inequality in cities across the world. In the urban context, neo-liberalism promotes private sector investment to produce revenue for the city or reduce its budget. Geographer David Harvey argues that the type of urbanization we see today, with the escalation of commercial and domestic buildings and developer-led land speculation, is the inevitable outcome of the neo-liberal practices of capital accumulation. Urban growth is propelled by concentrations of surplus product, that is, capital, which is mobile and seeks out places for investment, creating allies of capitalism and urbanization. In this febrile environment, urban authorities have adopted strategies whereby cities compete with each other for investment, fostering development. For Harvey and others[14] this is invariably a class phenomenon, 'since surpluses are extracted from somewhere by somebody, while control over their disbursement typically lies in a few hands.'[15]

There are many consequences of private capital investment in cities, not the least of which leads to gentrification. This aspect of urban life is a significant part of the story of contemporary café culture.

Urban revitalization or gentrification

Ink! Coffee in Denver, Colorado, placed a sign on the footpath outside which read: *Happily gentrifying the neighborhood [sic] since 2014.* The other side read, *Nothing says gentrification like being able to order a cortado.*[16]

Contemporary cafés have become leitmotifs of urban revitalization. Urban revitalization is no longer confined to the global north; it's something of a global phenomenon. What do we mean by urban revitalization, regeneration or gentrification? Urban revitalization or regeneration are terms which broadly refer to a 'rebirth or revival in the character and conditions of a place that has endured a period of decline'.[17] Gentrification more specifically refers to the transformation of a working-class or vacant area of the central city into middle-class residential and/or commercial use. This phenomenon might occur on an individual level, with people buying old houses and renovating, or be part of a larger urban planning strategy. One of the outcomes of gentrification is that, because of the increased investment into an area, property values are driven up. Poorer residents, particularly those who rent, are frequently pushed further out of the city centre as they can no longer afford to live in their old neighbourhoods. Revitalization is advocated by urban authorities who are alert to investment opportunities and may provide a host of incentives and subsidies for development. The desirable outcomes here are cities or city precincts that are promoted as attractive spaces for people, businesses and tourists, thus attracting further investment.

For example, cities publicize their attractions such as commercial and lifestyle activities on dedicated websites. This is the case with London's Seven Dials neighbourhood, which sits behind Covent Garden and the slowly gentrifying Soho. For several centuries it was renowned as an unsavoury district, home to the urban poor in the 18th and 19th centuries and immortalized in the works of Charles Dickens. Now it's a hip drawcard for locals and tourists, and fiercely branded. On the day I visited, outside the well-regarded Café Monmouth a line of people several metres long was queuing to get into the small café. The neighbourhood has all the hallmarks of classic gentrification: a plethora of food and drink outlets, niche boutiques and upscale shops. All cities typically undergo periods of decline and revival, but one of the major differences now is that they are more deeply connected through globalization – transmitting cultures, money, goods and services across the planet at lightning speed. This has resulted in similarities in patterns of development in cities across the world, despite their location in countries with distinctive characteristics and culture.

FIGURE 1.3 Ink coffee! Sign and graffiti response. Photo credit: © CBS.

There are legitimate reasons why the term 'gentrification' has become politically charged, and the alternative terms of 'urban revitalization' or 'urban renewal' are commonly employed. Urban renewal or gentrified areas are identifiable not only by renovated and new buildings, but also by the increase in urban amenity in a place. Third-wave cafés have become a symbol of urban renewal, because they form a significant part of the expansion of amenities, along with shops, bars and restaurants.

It is easy to see why Ink! Coffee's boast, quoted at the beginning of the section, was divisive. Situated in Five Points, an historically and culturally significant neighbourhood of Denver, the area was once home to a dynamic African American culture. An influx of tech companies changed the economy of the area, introducing a new class of urban professionals, part of the forces of gentrification. The sign resulted in five days of demonstrations by local African American residents for the implied racism in the comment. This isn't the first time long-term residents of gentrifying neighbourhoods have taken to the streets. In Berlin's eastern district of Friedrichshain, thousands of protestors rioted in the streets as squatters were evicted from their homes in 2016. In random attacks throughout the city's gentrifying areas, luxury cars such as Porsche, BMW and Mercedes have been set on fire by leftist radical groups protesting the restructuring of low-income neighbourhoods, which has forced out poorer residents. Anti-gentrification protests have also occurred in London and in Los Angeles, indicative of the level of aggrievement caused by displacement and economic shifts.

The press has been quick to identify cafés as signifiers of gentrification and sub-editors exercise their imaginations with catchy headlines. Lamenting the gentrification of Soho, London, the *Guardian* headlined an article about changes to the inner-city area, 'Gentrification means the whole world is a giant flat white – we have to stand up for sleaze and old dives'.[18] In Singapore, the *Straits Times* ponders the same problem with the similar metaphor when referring to the Tiong Bahru district, 'Do Singapore neighbourhoods risk death by *Cappucino*?'[19] Satirical headlines like these both entertain and underscore the public concern over gentrification of urban neighbourhoods. In Australian political discourse, cafés and coffee have come to symbolize both urban gentrification and class-based political allegiances. The derisive use of the term 'latte sippers' is routinely invoked by typically rural-based politicians, when it stands for those voters who live in wealthier inner-city areas, and whose politics usually lean toward the progressive. In a similar caffeinated geographical division, areas of Sydney and Melbourne that are demarcated by what some people refer to as the 'latte line' represent the division between wealthier suburbs and lower socio-economic suburbs.

Cafés as barometers of gentrification is something that British blogger Sam Floy cheekily highlighted in his 'investment heat map'. Floy published a series of heat maps correlating coffee shop density with those London neighbourhoods classified as 'up and coming'. Tongue in cheek, he recommended that a homebuyer's best bet for a return on investment was an area with a high density of chicken shops rather than cafés, because house prices had yet to explode in those areas.

Historians are often quick to point out that the café has long been a marker of gentrification. In 17th-century London for instance, coffee houses were indicative of the growth of colonial prosperity and the trade boom of the era. We have seen in the earlier example of Constantinople, where the café was first established, that its development occurred in a city with unprecedented growth, financially, culturally and demographically.

Yet the jury remains out on the impact of cafés on a neighbourhood. Urban scholars are divided over whether cafés contribute to, and lead, a class shift in a neighbourhood, or whether they follow in the wake of rising house prices. Studies in the United States have supported both sides of the argument[20] Nevertheless, a vigilant observer will note that when a spate of new cafés appears in a neighbourhood in a short period of time, other changes are being ushered in. And although coffee is an affordable drink for most people, sitting in café and paying around (AU) $4.00 for a cup of coffee on a regular basis requires a combination of monetary resources, time and cultural know-how. While the patterns of renewal are distinct from city to city and country to country and vary in scale, typology and impact, the processes which underlie global urban renewal are similar. They shape the kind of city we inhabit today: a vital, consumer-focused metropolis with an abundance of amenities and the unprecedented rise of the service and hospitality industries.

Urban dwellers: Demographic shifts

Although definitions of cities vary according to scale, services, administrative area and population size, there is a general agreement that over 100,000 people constitute a city. This book uses population as a definition for what makes a city rather than geographical measures, because my focus is on the city of people, who they are and how they live. And although we keep hearing about the growing urbanization of the world, it is nonetheless useful to bear in mind that more than 70%of the world's population lives in urban areas with fewer than 500,000 inhabitants, relatively small for an urban conglomeration.

Yet the upward trajectory of megacities cannot be ignored either; these are urban areas of over ten million inhabitants. Megacities are increasing, most notably in Asian countries. Indeed, Asia dominates world urbanization with 54% of the world's cities with populations over 500,000. Tokyo-Yokohama's urban conglomerate has remained the most densely populated urban area in the world, at 37.9 million, for the last six decades, followed by Jakarta in Indonesia at 31.8 million and New Delhi, India at 26.5 million.[21] In the West, North America has the second largest share of urban area population at 12.5%. Today, only five of the twenty largest cities are in the high-income world and their average population is 21.5 million. These are Tokyo, Osaka, Los Angeles, New York and Seoul.[22]

FIGURE 1.4 Tokyo Urban Café. Photo credit: © Emma Felton.

The way we live in cities has changed – for some countries more than others. The most pronounced shift has occurred in many Western cities. Growing populations mean that urban dwellers are living in the denser housing styles of high-rise apartments and town houses. The rapid pace of urbanization in China has produced the most spectacular changes; from rural life to intense high-rise living in less than forty years. There are less visible factors – such as the types of employment, services and housing affordability that have affected the way urban dwellers live. The demography of global cities is rapidly changing too. In countries in the global south, the mean age is under thirty-two (with the exception of China at thirty-eight), compared to cities in the global north who are facing ageing populations of around forty-three plus. And movement to cities, an historical trend, has increased exponentially since the latter part of the 20th century, creating cities that are more ethnically diverse than previous urban periods.

On the move: Population mobility

Urban population growth is typically the result of increased birth rates and the movement of people to cities. People move to urban areas for a variety of reasons—seeking employment, seeking asylum from conflict, to study, to reconnect with family and loved ones, and for leisure travel. But what has defined population movement of the late 20th century is its scale and intensity. As Sheller and Urry point out:

> All the world seems to be on the move. Asylum seekers, international students, terrorists, members of diasporas, holidaymakers, business people, sports stars, refugees, backpackers, commuters, the early retired, young mobile professionals, prostitutes, armed forces, these and many others fill the world's airports, buses, ships, and trains.[23]

The sheer scale of movement can be seen in global demographic statistics. In 2016, 3.7 billion air passengers flew back and forth across the planet; 65 million refugees were displaced from their homes, a figure which has doubled in the last ten years; and 244 million migrants moved from their homeland to another country. The majority of people moving around the planet end up in urban areas, whether for short or extended periods or settling permanently.[24]

Such 'hyper-mobility' and advances in technology have altered everyday life in the city, with the scale and pace varying across locations and contexts. But the cumulative effect has prompted social scientists to describe this current period as 'the new mobility paradigm',[25] an era which intensified from around 1990. Mobility refers not only to the movement of people, but also to objects, ideas and information, the latter assisted by technological innovations. Mobility is both a defining characteristic and a crucial aspect of social transformation, with our current period occurring from the beginning of the technological revolution and deregulation of global markets in the 1980s. Mobility is a double-edged sword, depending upon its causes. For those with the resources, mobility can be experienced as freedom, privilege and pleasure, while for others mobility is thrust upon them, experienced as displacement and potential hardship as a result of war, poverty and other upheavals. Whatever the cause, mobile populations along with economic developments have resulted in greater social stratification and the loosening of traditional social networks.[26] Yet while traditional social ties are diminishing in some places, new and emergent forms of sociality are developing. The city, with all its complexity of human habitation, is the microcosm for new ways of living.

Technology

> Networked digital information technology has become the dominant mode through which we experience the everyday.[27]

One of the most significant features of the contemporary city is the impact that technology has delivered. Information and communication technologies (ICT) have completely transformed the experience of everyday life, with particular consequences for urban living. ICTs are integrated throughout all aspects of life: in the communication sphere, across the public sector and in commerce and industry. Cities are now instantly navigable - digital maps, transport timetables, and urban information can be readily accessed via a smartphone and satellite navigation. Technology infrastructure as much as physical infrastructure is changing urban experience. While many cities struggle with maintaining their physical infrastructure, it's likely that they're well serviced by wireless and technology networks. Digital-parking apps, bike-sharing apps and ride-sharing companies such as Uber are relatively recent developments, with greater innovations on the horizon. Driverless cars and roads which generate solar energy are already in existence and set to change the way we move around cities in profound ways.

The impact of technology on people's working lives is influenced by the industries and roles in which they're involved, but the transformation is profound; this is the subject of Chapter Seven. Technology has spurred on flexible work arrangements, providing the means by which people can work outside a dedicated place or office, with the accessibility of internet connectivity. At the same time, the growth of contractual and project-based work has produced a demand for non-traditional work spaces. Enter a café during the day and it is a common sight to see people working at laptops, and while some cafés encourage this, others do not. The café's ambience is subtly shifted by the replacement of the former analogue activities of reading and writing to the same activities that are now mediated via computers, laptops and word processing. In traditional European cafés, newspapers and journals were a central part of the café's appeal, as a source of current information and daily news. Walk into a café today, the activity is the same, it is just the medium that's changed.

The ubiquity of technology since the end of the 20th century has produced social, cultural and economic transformations across all dimensions of life. Such change is mapped out across the spaces of the city and in the ways in which urban dwellers live their daily lives. While much of the world's population accesses technology on a daily basis, the digital divide – uneven access to internet-based technologies – creates a barrier to full civic participation. Older people, people from low-income backgrounds and women are those most at risk.

Urban cultural development

Cities historically, are the crucible of culture. Culture refers here to both artistic expression and the culture of everyday life. Today culture is used as a major strategy for urban revitalization: since the late 20th century, culture and cultural life have become a basis on which to develop local economies and revitalize urban centres. Thus one of the common signs of urban revitalization is the appearance of large-scale cultural and lifestyle precincts in cities. The facilities are often located along waterside areas which have been redeveloped from decommissioned industrial and port sites such as in London, Marseilles, Melbourne, and Brisbane's Southbank. Cultural precincts are typically funded and regulated through a combination of private and public partnerships. Frequently the location of major art and cultural institutions, these precincts are also the sites of innumerable dwellings, – apartment blocks and offices, entertainment facilities, parklands and, in some cases controversially, casinos for high rollers. In the instance of Sydney's Barangaroo, a 22-hectare harbour side redevelopment, approval for a casino and hotel was granted, despite opposition from high-profile politicians and businesspeople for its lack of appeal to the majority of people. Similar waterside revitalization precincts can be found in Hong Kong and Singapore, which have established cultural and entertainment areas in Kowloon and in Singapore's Marina Bay Gardens area. In redeveloped waterside localities, decommissioned warehouses are converted to 'New York'-style loft living, targeted at young professionals. Around the new dwellings and precincts, an abundance of urban amenities service residents and tourists, among which cafés and restaurants are intrinsic to the flourishing hospitality economy.

Cultural precincts might be given added distinction with iconic buildings that house cultural institutions, and are designed by 'starchitects', architects whose buildings have become so widely acknowledged that the buildings acquire celebrity status. The Guggenheim Museum in the port city of Bilbao, Spain, set a benchmark and precedent for iconic cultural buildings in 1997. Designed by American architect Frank Gehry, the building and the gallery it housed was highly successful in drawing people to the city, which had declined through the collapse of the shipbuilding industry. A striking, multifaceted building of titanium and stone, its success at helping to revitalize the city became known as the 'Bilbao Effect' and other cities followed the model. The building attracted so many visitors that its cost was recouped within three years after construction.

In the early 2000s the concept of the 'creative city' emerged and took hold. The United States-based author Richard Florida became influential in transporting creative city ideas across countries. Mobilizing the relationship between culture and urban revitalization, Florida came up with the term the 'creative class' to describe those people who worked in technology and creative industries and were attracted to cities because of their 'talent, technology and tolerance', which he coined 'the three T's'. One of his claims is that cities with 'bohemian enclaves' which supported social inclusivity and ethnic diversity were a major drawcard for the growing army of professionals in the technology and cultural industries. The apparent economic benefit of these industries and 'talent' was widely promoted and policies supporting them were adopted throughout many global cities. The slogan of the 'creative city' became something of a global phenomenon in the early 21st century, and Florida advised many city administrators across the world. Despite critiques to his claims as flawed, too simplistic and elitist, the creative city retains something of a legacy as a method of economic revitalization. Time has confirmed the critics' concerns: it is the wealthier middle class who have benefited from rampant property speculation and social inequality in cities has widened in many places.

The ways in which cultural amenities have developed in parallel with the growth of commercial spaces, for some urban critics, have resulted in an unsuccessful balancing act between nourishing and destroying the city's distinctive cultures.[28] The argument here is that urban culture and cultural precincts share increasingly similar features in cities the world over, with the result that urban environments become homogenized. While some cities may be more successful than others at retaining a sense of their local culture and distinction, the proliferation of lifestyle consumption, from niche galleries to experiential activities, delivers a particular ubiquity and homogeneity of urban experience.

It is certainly the case that when I visited various cities and cafés throughout Australia, Europe and Asia, the third-wave style of café was often identifiable by its appearance alone and the café experience was to some extent analogous. Yet, despite this, the local influence was quite evident. You could not mistake a third-wave café in Berlin, for instance, for one in Shanghai. Moreover, culture is good at asserting itself; it is complex – both material and symbolic – and works in intangible ways. It's about people, language, rituals, values and a way of life – each varying from place to place. A place's culture matters moreover because it is a 'domain of life which is different from but always related to…our *social existence*'.[29] The social dimension of urban cultural life is explored in Chapter Two, and I argue, has much to do with the popularity of the café in the contemporary city.

City, culture and consumption

Cities of the 21st century are places of prodigious consumption, although the city as a site of consumption is nothing new. The history of the city is the also the history of production and consumption. From as early as 206BC, traders travelled across the extensive network from the east, in what is known as the Silk Roads, where goods were produced and traded in cities such as Xi'an, Samarkand, Aleppo and Damascus and many more. Around cities where traders gathered, places to eat and drink first appeared. It wasn't until the 18th-century Industrial Revolution that production and thus consumption were propelled to another level through the processes of mass automation. The next development occurred in the 20th century with mass employment, the growth of wage equity and the greater levels of affluence it produced.

Today our consumption choices are turbo-charged. We are confronted with a plethora of purchasing options – we can buy products, services and experiences to cater to every whim and peccadillo, if we have the resources. The face of consumption is dominated by modes of lifestyle and culture that have become the mainstay of the urban economy.[30] Food and drinking cultures are a major force of the urban experience and the hospitality sector has become a 'vital space in which taste and lifestyle are produced and consumed through food and drink, music and décor, ambience and service style'.[31] An abundance of shops, services, bars, restaurants, cafés, galleries and cinemas line the streets of urban centres. Urban historian Lewis Mumford in his landmark book *The Culture of Cities* (1938) talked about cities as either predominantly 'producing cities or consuming cities'. In the contemporary city, it appears that the balance has shifted towards consumption as a fundamental function of urban life.

Culture, broadly defined, is a significant part of the consuming experience; it is the culture of everyday life such as the places we visit and where and what we eat and play, as well as the traditional forms of culture housed in galleries, museums and theatres. Culture has been a major focus of urban revitalization, a strategy to attract economic investment, talent and tourists. The aesthetic industries – those concerned with food, art, fashion and design – have flourished as never before, providing a multitude of sensory experiences for the urban citizen and tourist. Food cultures, which require both high levels of innovation and expertise on the part of the producer, as well as the cultural knowledge of the consumer, have become a major force of the urban experience. Their range and variety are growing, with phenomena such as 'gastro-tourism', 'drinkatainment', themed bars and craft beer outlets all relatively new additions in the life of cities. Cities such as Melbourne in Australia, Barcelona in Spain and London in Britain among other places have become known for their innovative, gourmet cuisine; their restaurants are stops on the foody tourists' itineraries. 'Authentic' culinary experiences such as foraging parties, farm to table and Chef's Table experiences are what foodies seek. As attractions for visitors to a city, the development of the aesthetic industries is part of the shift in urban economic development. The café sits alongside this global growth in restaurants, boutique bars and the parallel production of niche and gourmet food and drink products. Cafés provide their own unique type of aesthetic experience – they are more affordable than gourmet restaurants for instance, and therefore more democratic, and they also function as a place of respite to recoup, for the relatively low cost of a cup of coffee.

How we engage with our cultural environment has become ever more invested with meaning as products and services proliferate. Trends in styles in food, drink, clothing, music and other consumer items are signals of personal and collective affiliations, differentiation and distinction. Now we have greater mechanisms of self-identity, with a plethora of consuming and lifestyle practices, rapidly transmitted via media and the internet. In former traditional societies, roles and expectations of behaviour were much more clearly defined – and limited. Whereas in the contemporary world, we have to work out our roles for ourselves, as sociologist Anthony Giddens puts it: What to do? How to act? These are all questions we have to answer on some level even if they don't register consciously.[32]In the city, this confusion can be even more fraught, because our identity is somewhat fragile, more prone to flux and changing fashion, due in part to the greater inputs and influences available to us. Urban scholars have been making these claims about the city for a long time. In 1903, eminent urban sociologist Georg Simmel, writing at the turn of the 20th century as urbanism was developing in Europe, declared that individual assertion through forms of distinction is an act of self-preservation. Simmel's argument is similar to contemporary sociologists: that the necessity to declare one's uniqueness is an urban-based phenomenon, and comes from being thrust among the large, diverse throng of humanity, in which it's easy to lose oneself.

The act of consuming, whether the purchase of a product or experience, links our identities by association to markers of taste, distinction and lifestyle practices, which the product provides through its symbolic dimension.[33] Thus consumer culture can work to maintain or re-negotiate social and class divisions and can create greater divisions between those who have more resources to consume than others. Even a relatively affordable product such as coffee is loaded with meaning. Indeed, in 17th-century European court society, coffee afforded the opportunity for the 'display of elegance, grace, and high refinement. The porcelain that was created expressly for drinking at the court was what mattered most'.[34] Now it is not so much the porcelain but the coffee itself – its provenance, how it is roasted and brewed – which serves as a form of social distinction in third-wave cafés. The simple act of going to a café has a host of attendant associations. Which café you frequent regularly sends a signal about what type of person you might be, what sort of affiliations you have. Someone who drinks their coffee at a franchise café such as Starbucks will be judged differently from a person who insists on buying coffee from a specialty café. The knowledge of beans, roasting and technical equipment is essential armoury for connoisseurs of coffee and cafés today. A myriad of social media enables the acquisition and distribution of coffee and cafés' information through reviews and photographs from both consumers and professionals working in the industry. Moreover, the cost of coffee varies widely, depending on the style of café and the particular city and country. When it is calculated relative to the average wage of the country, coffee can be a luxury product. For instance, in Shanghai, China it is common to pay between (AU) $6 to $8 for a cup of coffee, which places coffee in a luxury market for the average wage earner. In a country such as China, this challenges the argument that the café is egalitarian because of its relative affordability compared to other lifestyle consumption. Yet the picture is far more complex than this, and while the specialty café movement is strong in cities across the world, there are many other types of cafés that don't command the same sort of prices and prestige.

Consumer culture is central to the experience and function of city life and the café sits within an economic network and culture of consumption. But there are other reasons besides the desire to appear distinctive or 'in the know' about coffee that draw people to cafés. The café's history tells us much about its social function; and its current global popularity points to a raft of other factors that underpin its ascendency in urban life.

Notes

1 Ellis, Markman. 2004. *The Coffee House: A Cultural History*. London: Weidenfeld and Nicolson, p. 24.
2 Schivelbusch, Wolfgang. 1992. (Translated David Jacobsen.) *Tastes: A Social History of Spices, Stimulants and Intoxicants*. New York: Random House, p. 417.
3 Pendergrast, Mark. 2010. *Uncommon Grounds: The History of Coffee and How It Transformed Our World*. New York: Basic Books, p. 6.
4 Hattox, Ralph. 1985. *Coffee and Coffeehouses: The Origins of a Social Beverage in the Medieval Near East*. Seattle, WA: University of Washington Press, p. 81.
5 Ellis, Markman. 2008. "An introduction to the coffee-house: A discursive model." *Language and Communication* Volume 28, Issue 2, April, pp. 156–164 (p. 158).
6 Schivelbusch, Wolfgang. 1992. Ibid., p. 49.
7 Pendergrast, Mark. 2010. *Uncommon Grounds: The History of Coffee and How It Transformed Our World*. New York: Basic Books, p. 9.
8 Chamie, Joseph. 2017. "The rise of one person households." *Interpress Service*. http://www.ipsnews.net/2017/02/the-rise-of-one-person-households, February 22. Ret. 30.8.17.
9 Hoffman, James. 2014. *The World Atlas of Coffee: From Beans to Brewing – Coffees Explored, Explained and Enjoyed*. London: Hachette, p. 111.
10 Moore, Suzanne. 2015. "Gentrification means the world is a giant flat white – we have to stand up for sleaze and old dives." *The Guardian*. https://www.theguardian.com/uk-news/commentisfree/2015/nov/18/gentrification-world-giant-flat-white-stand-up-sleaze-old-dives-london, November 8. Ret 30.8.17.
11 White, Merry. 2012. *Coffee Life in Japan*. Berkeley, CA: University of California Press, p. 14.
12 Huse, Tony. 2014. *Everyday Life in the Gentrifying City: On Displacement, Ethnic Privileging and the Right to Stay Put*. Farnham, UK: Ashgate.
13 Spencer, James H. 2014. *Globalization and Urbanization: The Global Urban Ecosystem*. New York: Rowman and Littlefield.
14 Zukin, Sharon. 2010. *The Naked City*. New York. Oxford University Press.Peck, Jamie and Tickell, Adam. 2002. "Neoliberlizing urban space." *Antipode* Volume 34, Issue 3, July, pp. 380–384.
15 Harvey, David. 2008. "The rights to the city." *New Left Review* Volume 53, September–October, pp. 23–40 (p. 24).
16 Brown, Nick. 2017 "Colorados Ink! Coffee apologizes for gentrification focussed marketing." *Coffee News*. https://dailycoffeenews.com/2017/11/24/colorados-ink-coffee-apologizes-for-gentrification-focused-marketing/, November 24. Ret. 3.02.18.
17 Grodach, Carl and Ehrenfeucht, Renia. 2016. *Urban Revitalization: Remaking Cities in a Changing World*. New York. Routledge, p. 17.
18 Moore, Suzanne. 2015. Ibid.
19 Pow, Choon Piew. 2015. "Do Singapore neighbourhoods risk death by cappuccino?" *The Straits Times*. https://www.straitstimes.com/opinion/do-singapore-neighbourhoods-risk-death-by-cappuccino, January 30. Ret. 3.10.17.
20 Kilkenny, Katy. 2017. "A brief history of coffee shop as symbol of gentrification." *Pacific Standard*. https://psmag.com/economics/history-of-coffee-shop-as-symbol-for-gentrification, July 26. Ret. 14.1017.
21 Cox, Wendell. 2017. The 37 megacities and largest cities: *Demographia World Urban Areas*: 2017. *New Geography*. http://www.newgeography.com/content/005593-the-largest-cities-demographia-world-urban-areas-2017, April 21. Ret. 3.10.17.
22 Cox, Wendell. 2017. Ibid.
23 Sheller, Mimi and Urry, John. 2016. "The new mobilities paradigm." *Environment and Planning A: Economy and Space* Volume 38, Issue 2, pp. 207–226 (p. 207).

24 Haas Institute. 2017. "Moving targets: An analysis of forced global migration." Research Report. http://haasinstitute.berkeley.edu/sites/default/files/haasinstitute_moving_targets_globalmigrationreport_publish_web.pdf. Ret. 13.10.17.
25 Sheller, Mimi and Urry, John. 2016. Ibid.
26 Bauman, Zygmunt. 1998. *Globalization: The Human Consequences.* New York: Columbia University Press.
27 Greenfield, Adam. 2017. *Radical Technologies: The Design of Everyday Life.* London: Verso.
28 Zukin, Sharon. Ibid.
29 Byrne, David. 2001. *Understanding the Urban.* London: Palgrave, p. 25.
30 Foley, Malcom, McGillivray, David and McPherson, Gayle. 2012. *Event Policy: From Theory to Strategy.* London and New York: Routledge.
31 Bell, David. 2007. "The hospitable city: Social relations in commercial spaces." *Progress in Human Geography* pp. 7–22 (p. 17).
32 Giddens, Anthony. 1991. *Modernity and Self-Identity: Self and Society in the Late Modern Age.* Stanford, CA: Stanford University Press, p. 70.
33 Bourdieu, Pierre. 1984. *Distinction: A Social Critique of the Judgement of Taste.* London: Routledge.
34 Schivelbusch, Wolfgang. 1992. Ibid., p. 19.

2

THE CAFÉ

Sociality and community from both sides of the counter

> When I'm down, and when I'm up, I go to a cafe. I've gone to write, to read, to see friends or to get away from friends, to have strong feelings and to escape strong feelings, to pursue a crush or because of loneliness, because of inertia, because of dependency.
>
> *Benjamin Aldes Wurgaft*[1]

Sociality, the city and the café

Mikey owns and operates a café in inner-city Brisbane, Australia. He is known for his friendliness and wide-ranging conversation. He knows what coffee his regulars drink and, if possible, will start preparing their coffee as soon as they appear in the café. A lot of regulars drop in for their morning coffee and chat. The chat is important. Some of Mikey's customers who would typically be unfamiliar with the topics regularly discussed in the café, such as football or American politics, make sure they're sufficiently familiar to participate in discussions.

Lots of social interaction occurs in cafés, including casual conversations between staff and customers, meeting friends, first dates, job interviews, tourists getting their bearings, students studying, business meetings, interest group meetings and people using technology to communicate or read. The enthusiastic adoption of café culture as a social space is indicative of changes in how people network and meet, and more broadly of transformations occurring at a structural level. It's hardly surprising that people seek out places to meet others, given the changes in social and familial relations wrought by globalization and mobile populations. It's no coincidence that, historically, the café's ascendency in the city has occurred during periods of significant social and economic upheaval. While the history of the café is allied with the economic fortunes of the city, it is also allied to developments in sociality and cultural life.

On the one hand, cafés are consumer-focused places that require resources, but they are of course, much more than this. As well as the cup of coffee, we frequently expect a less tangible, more affective experience than simply drinking coffee entails. As places of hospitality, the café offers 'ways of being with others', which encourages behaviour such as reciprocity and civility, tacitly encoded into the café's spaces. In cities of increasing scale and cultural diversity, places to be with others, to be alone or work, are in growing demand. How café patrons utilize the space is highly contingent, but, as I explore in this chapter, it is clear that the café has become a meaningful place for urban inhabitants. This chapter looks at the café as a social space, starting with its historical antecedents through to its role and phenomenal growth in the contemporary city. It includes extracts from numerous interviews I undertook with both café patrons and staff in cafés in Australia, England, Hong Kong and Germany. First though, what is it that is unique about the café as a public or semi-public place?

Urban hybrid places

There are two essential features of city life that have an impact on the everyday life of citizens. One is the consumer-focused nature of urban life, and the other is that in cities we live in close proximity with strangers. The café, as a hybrid place, has the capacity to link these two ontologies in useful ways. While diversity is a leitmotif of the contemporary city, living among strangers demands particular skills and tolerances. People living in cities, especially densely populated cities, need places outside the spaces of the home and work to gather and to get to know one another. Or simply to be alone. Walk down the street, past an urban park or square and usually there are people congregating, walking together, talking or sitting by themselves. More latterly markets, cafés, restaurants, bars and shopping centres and malls are the semi-public gathering places of modern cities. The café is a semi-public space because it supports civic life and social engagement. Along with parks, squares and streets, the café characterizes 'different senses of being with others in public'.[2] In contemporary, secular societies it is hardly surprising that the café has gained greater relevance as a place that supports sociality. With the decline of institutions that were once the locus of sociality and community such as the church and voluntary and sporting organisations, the café is one of the few semi-public places that welcomes a diversity of people to meet. In the face of the decline of traditional institutions, the café promises a cultural cosmopolitanism, encounters with people who we don't know or don't know very well.[3]

Cafés are sometimes referred to as 'third places' or hybrid places because they support informal social interaction in the same way as pubs, markets and shopping centres. Ray Oldenburg (1989) coined the term 'third place' to refer to what is essentially a social space, an informal public gathering place. First and second places are home and work.[4] For Oldenburg, third places are all about the development of community and social interaction and the vital role they play in urban life.

FIGURE 2.1 Contemporary café culture Istanbul. Photo credit: © iStock.

This book refers to cafés as 'hybrid' places rather than third places because, although cafés share many features of third places, that definition's exclusive emphasis on community building precludes other aspects of contemporary café culture. Today, the café's hybrid spaces support not only social interaction, but also a range of other activities. While meeting face-to-face is common in cafés, so is the mediated interaction of internet technologies and mobile phones. It is not uncommon to see people sitting alone with their laptops, reading, perhaps working or communicating with others online. Cafés are also used for solitary purposes, with the express intention of leaving home to be alone. In Japan, many Japanese people visit the café as a place to be 'private in public', alone without being lonely. The café offers freedom from a highly structured form of social obligation and a precious respite from the pressures of work and family life.[5] This isn't a phenomenon confined to Japan; millions of urban inhabitants in densely populated cities all over the world live in small apartments, and a hybrid place outside the home and workplace provides a similar type of reprieve. Moreover, we don't have to be escaping obligations to enjoy the release of time spent in a café, it's a place to simply escape the confines of a small apartment, the growing complexity of contemporary urban life, and be amongst the throng of humanity.

Historical grounds

There is a well-established history of the café and its role in the development of sociality. The café as a social gathering site has been thoroughly documented from its first appearance in 16th-century Cairo and Istanbul during the Ottoman Empire, across to London and the continental coffeehouses in 17th-century European cities such as Paris and Vienna, and in other parts of the world.[6] This aspect of the café's history then, though fascinating, requires only brief mention here. The Ottoman coffeehouses were first and foremost social gathering places where a diversity of men such as government officials, scholars, tradesmen and artisans assembled to converse. They became so popular so quickly that according to a Turkish historian of the time, Ibrahim I-Pecevi, they 'multiplied insensibly'.[7] Coffeehouses soon became the locus of other social activities. Ralph Hattox in his history of the early Middle Eastern coffeehouses describes how gaming was also a vital part of coffeehouse life. Games such as chess and backgammon were popular, and later various forms of live entertainment were introduced into some coffeehouses.

The addition of entertainment was prompted by proprietors attempting to gain a competitive edge, and included the employment of storytellers, musicians and, in some larger establishments, puppeteers for shows, tumblers and performers. However, despite the range of activities on offer in many coffeehouses, the principal reason that people visited was for conversation, as Hattox points out:

> the coffeehouse was above all a place for talk: serious or trivial, high-minded or base, that place more than any other seemed to lend itself to the art of conversation. Amid the relaxing surroundings and atmosphere of leisure afforded by the grand metropolitan coffeehouse, caffeine-stimulated talk thrived ....[8]

FIGURE 2.2 Interior of Constantinople Coffee House, 16th century. Photo credit: Jean-Pierre Dalbéra [CC BY 2.0 (https://creativecommons.org/licenses/by/2.0)], via Wikimedia Commons.

Communication, conviviality and conversation were also the principal draw-cards of the 17th-century London coffeehouses, the first of which was opened in 1652 by Pasqua Rosee, a Greek immigrant. They rapidly became vibrant centres of news and business dealings, and, as newspapers had yet to be established, early coffeehouses were the main source of news and information. Journalism and literature were soon a fundamental feature of 17th- and 18th-century coffeehouses. By the early 18th century, London had a number of weekly journals such as *The Tatler* and *The Spectator* which began their lives in the coffeehouse, and whose editorial offices were located there.

From the outset, coffeehouses encouraged inclusivity, and were places where a range of social classes mingled. In London, the Rules and Orders of the Coffee House from 1674 state that 'First Gentry, Tradesman, *all* are welcome hither, and may without affront sit down together'.[9] However, inclusivity here only extended to classes of men, because it was unacceptable for women at that time to appear in public alone. A woman would be considered of ill repute or morally questionable if she were unchaperoned in a public place such as the coffeehouse. The only female presence was the 'coffee woman' who took care of the daily operations of the business, but she also helped to establish the type of sociability in place, where her conversation was also a valued part of the café business.[10]

By the beginning of the 19th century, coffeehouse culture in Britain declined and the coffeehouse had been transformed into gentlemen's clubs or restaurants. British colonies were abundant with tea, bringing their harvests home, and the changeover in drinking habits was swift. While café culture languished in Britain, it gained a foothold across the channel in continental Europe. In Paris and Vienna and later in Germany, Russia and Sweden the café in Europe soon became synonymous with the continent's intellectual and artistic history. A refuge and gathering place for artists and bohemians, the café occupied a central role in European literary development as well as artistic movements such as Impressionism and Expressionism. Parisian cafés are renowned for the writers they nurtured, through gatherings of intellectuals such as Baudelaire, Rousseau and Voltaire. Cafés also played a key role in the various revolutions throughout Europe during the 19th-century Napoleonic and Romantic eras, and at various times throughout history became hotbeds of sedition and outlaws.

Wherever cafés first appeared, they were always notable as places of conversation and debate. Philosopher Jurgen Habermas describes how early 18th-century cafés and other public gathering places were critical to the development of reasoned debate and discussion, which had broader significance for the wider public sphere. The café was the first convivial place that enabled people to gather and discuss society's problems and, through discussion, were able to influence political action. Conversational techniques were practised and café society, according to Habermas, encouraged a mode of social interaction which was distinguished by its 'open and inclusive character' and the expectation of a 'patient, willing comprehension of sympathetic fellows'.[11] Though not all was reasoned conversation in the café. Markman Ellis provides another account of sociality; while the early coffeehouses were places where you could expect polite conversation, some were also known for their raucous patrons and occasional criminality.

Over a century later, the coffeehouse morphed into the espresso bars and cafés of the 1950s in Europe, North America and Australia. While located in cities which had radically transformed over the century, these cafés were similarly known for their mix of customers from a diversity of classes, races and cultures. With more liberal attitudes towards the genders, women were among their patrons. It is interesting to note that such was the notoriety of the espresso bar's diverse customer base that *Architectural Digest* magazine claimed the new coffee bars were 'the greatest social revolution since the launderette in 1954'.[12] In Australia, café culture was introduced during this period principally through post-war migration from Italy and Greece and like the Greek kafeneion, the café became the social hub of Australian country towns in areas where there was little social infrastructure or few places that offered opportunities to gather.[13]

Today, cafés in the global north are more socially inclusive than those of any other period in their history. Certainly, they are more hospitable to women than hybrid places such as the pub or bar, whose social life traditionally revolved around masculine relationships and interests and where alcohol can fuel unwanted attention and behaviour. Gender inclusivity is a large part of the cafés current evolution; it is a benign, neutral social space in which women feel comfortable. It's interesting to note that while the café has yet to replace the pub as a popular venue, in Britain the number of pubs is declining while the number of cafés is on the rise. In the five-year period between 2011 and 2016, the number of town centre bars and pubs fell by about 6,000 while cafés and restaurants rose by 6,000. It's a testament to the importance of cafés for communities and the appeal of their adaptable, inclusive spaces.

Sociality in consumer spaces

While the café's history is steeped in accounts of sociality and its popularity today is clearly related to its role as a social gathering place, its other role as a consumer space implies a certain tension. Part of this is simply to do with the costs of consumerism, but it is the politics of consumerism, discussed in the previous chapter, which has long been a topic of scholarly debate. Consumerism is one of the hallmarks of the contemporary city and its critics point to the ways in which it reinforces social divisions, creates forms of social distinction and exacerbates inequality. Consuming, whether a product or an experience, requires not just resources, but also knowledge and skills that often have their basis in class.

Indeed, one of the criticisms of the recent crop of third-wave or specialty cafés, with their focus on an artisan product, is that customers require high levels of connoisseurship and knowledge, and this sets them apart from regular coffee consumers. There are charges of elitism about a product which is basically an everyday beverage; and that specialty cafés tend to privilege middle and upper-class consumption and lifestyles. The argument follows that in the broader context of the city, urban amenity is becoming increasingly homogenised, so that the same sorts of amenity and experiences appears everywhere across the globe. It is true that third-wave cafés in cities across the world tend to be recognisable by a shared aesthetic, but this does not diminish the significance of their social role; nor indeed are all cafés third-wave. There are many styles of cafés and, as I elaborate later, varied styles of cafés appeal to a range of different people.

Another way of thinking about our concern with consumer-based lifestyle, taste and social distinction is not simply about mindless exploitation or self-indulgence. Rather it can be seen as 'an existential search for distinction in a deeply secular culture'.[14] The proliferation of hospitality and entertainment industries – in the form of cafés and restaurants – are the consumer-based social places where new forms of sociality and attachment are being nurtured and sustained. Cities are as much about being with others as they are about consumerism; how we use spaces and places is a determinant of our social lives.

What occurs in hospitality spaces is transforming the broader public culture and ways of living in the neighbourhood, creating 'new solidarities and new collectivities' with the capacity to produce a 'convivial, hospitable ecology.'[15] Today, people connect in many different ways– through shared lifestyles, sub-cultures, tastes and mutual interests and in a way that is often mediated by technology. The city's amenities provide opportunities for increasing modes of sociality. Shops, cafés, parks, restaurants and other public and semi-public spaces are the contemporary *agora* or meeting place.

Contemporary social groupings might be regarded as 'tribes', which are types of 'emotional communities' because they are primarily based in affective experience. Embedded in the rituals and performances of everyday life, we belong to any number of tribes – membership is fluid and open – but what unites them is the power of basic sociality. Proximity, emotion, everyday interactions and a collective feeling of shared joy are the elements that bind people together. The spatial dimension to tribes is important: neighbourhood is the site of social networks, where local amenities such as the café allows social groupings to be cemented by neighbourly practices.[16]

While it is not straightforward to quantify the important role that cafés play in the development of sociality and community, it is readily visible when entering any café and in conversation with café patrons. Ferriera's study (2017) into the role of the café conducted across five British cities found myriad social activities occurred inside its spaces, some driven by the businesses themselves. From gathering places, to places where people can be 'alone in public', the study highlighted the significance of cafés for the social and cultural life of local communities. Some café businesses go to great lengths to support their local communities, including activities such hosting books clubs, craft groups and entrepreneur meet ups. The quotation from a café proprietor in Ferriera's study below echoes many of the sentiments expressed in my interviews with café staff:

> The most important thing for us is that we are looking after people that come through the door...we have created this atmosphere with a really nice space and somebody can come in and have a bit of time, have a nice tasting coffee that isn't going to cost them the earth, then that's hugely important for this community.[17]

The community aspect of café life is paramount, but urban living with its incessant demands and distractions also requires time to be alone, to regenerate, reflect or simply to perform a range of activities by oneself. The home or workplace might not always be the place where being alone is most optimal. Congested and crowded living- and workspaces are a common feature of cities. More people are living alone in cities than in previous eras, creating the conditions for social isolation and loneliness. Being alone but among others, amidst the 'warmth of sociality', can be experienced by proxy, a feeling which is generated by the environment and people in close proximity. As Rita, a regular café user, explains:

> Well, I think it's important as a way to get out of my apartment, to be less isolated. So even though I'm not socializing very much, it's still a social thing, because I'm with people.[18]

Similarly, the blogger Katie explains what she enjoys about being alone in a café, which is related to her working day:

> I regularly spend pockets of time alone in cafes, for lunch or a quiet cup of tea or chai, with a book or my journal or simply my own thoughts for company. It feels less cloistered, less monastic, than eating lunch in my office with the door shut, and yet there's a sheer curtain of privacy between me and the rest of the world. In bustling Boston, where I cram into the commuter train with hundreds of strangers and walk to work among dozens more, it feels deeply restorative to carve out an alcove of space for myself during the workday...Some days do call for total solitude, and as near silence as I can get. But on many others, I love feeling that tug, that connection to the beat of whatever city I happen to be in.[19]

An urban gathering space for people to gather and/or do things together was what spawned the non-traditional café chain that doesn't charge for coffee but rather charges by time. Café Ziferblat was first established in Moscow in 2011 by a young Russian Ivan Mitin. Based on the principle of a 'free space' where people can get together or be alone, it is run along the lines of a social enterprise, where the café charges by the minute, and the coffee and cakes are free. The cafés also rely, to some extent, on donations. The idea arose from a group of people who used to write poetry together, and the cafés caught on quickly and are now franchised in twelve cities across Eastern Europe, Russia and Britain. Ziferblat's website lists its varied uses, pointing out that it's not a co-working space but is sometimes used as

FIGURE 2.3 Sociality: alone among the group. Photo credit: © iStock.

a place for musical concerts, lectures and other kinds of hobby activities – providing 'different opportunities for sociality and other forms of social engagement'.

The convivial or hospitable city

As an affordable place to meet with people in the city, the café seems to be without peer. But it's among those less familiar to us that the café is particularly useful. In getting to know someone, whether a work colleague or potential partner, the common ritual of meeting for coffee enables a comfortable negotiation with people we don't know very well. The café's hospitable codes facilitate a sociality that is not so easily navigated in other spaces of the city. It also removes the burden of hosting. As David Bell describes, the ways of relating to each other which are practised in bars, cafés and restaurants can be seen as 'potentially productive of an ethics of conviviality that revitalizes urban living'.[20]

From its outset, the coffeehouse was quickly established as a place that lifted the burden of home hosting. Turkish historian IbrahIm Pecevi tells of how the well-to-do citizens in 16th-century Istanbul would, prior to the coffeehouse, lavish large amounts of resources giving dinners at home for their friends. With the establishment of the coffeehouse, new regimes of hospitality became available. The city's elite could entertain their friends for only a few coins, a radical departure from how aspects of social life were previously conducted. Hospitality was no longer the exclusive domain of one's home, with all the possessions, wife, children, slaves and symbols of proprietorship that had always been present when extending to the guest the full resources of his household. The act of hospitality could now be transferred to a public place where one's responsibilities, and perhaps prestige, as host were more limited. This implied a subtle shift in the relationship between host and guest, and a break, if only symbolic, with old values.[21]

The gesture of having coffee with someone is essentially a hospitable gesture. Such behaviour has particular importance today, particularly in cities of increasing social and cultural diversity. For Roland Barthes, the distinctive feature of the city is that it's a place where 'we meet with the other'. In contrast to life in provincial towns and villages where people could be known for generations, the anonymity of the city provides greater freedoms, as well as thrusting us among large throngs of strangers. Urban growth has produced ever more diverse cities and if Barthes's statement was apt in the 1980s, it is ever more so now, nearly forty years later. How strangers live together in cities of unprecedented scale and density raises compelling issues to do with social cohesion and the civil life of cities.

As well as offering spaces for sociality, café culture also encourages civility. The gesture of 'having coffee' is hospitable; it requires mutual give and take – conversation and dialogue. The techniques of conversation—of listening, responding and sharing information – are civil gestures. Civility and generosity are straightforward in the café because it has pre-established codes of conduct and is an environment that's focused upon hospitality. Paying for another's drink, although not a great expense, is a simple act of hospitality; 'taking someone to coffee' has become part of the lingua franca of workplace and business culture. Cultivating friendships is easy in the café; in Bookman's 2014 study, Jessica, a university student, notes:

> It's just a nice place to meet with other people cause you're kind of on neutral territory, you can arrive when you want, you can leave, you're not at someone's house so you don't feel obliged to be host or the guest, play either of those roles.[22]

As Jessica's observation shows, the café's neutrality as a meeting place is predicated on its role as a transitional or liminal space; it's neither domestic, work, nor wholly public space. It's regulated temporally by its function as a place of food and beverage consumption, providing a finite period to meetings, where the length of encounter can be determined by the time it takes to consume a coffee or snack. In this way, the possible complexity or ambiguity associated with meetings with people less known to us in the more intimate spaces of the home is avoided and may relieve the onus that can be associated with entertaining. In this capacity, the café offers a safe testing ground for new relationships.

Cafés are well utilized for Tinder and other first dates organized online. Decisions about whether to pursue a relationship beyond the semi-public spaces of the café and elsewhere or into the more intimate spaces of the home can be comfortably negotiated. Cafés that are well integrated into their local communities will have staff who know their regulars, a relationship that's developed by daily routines and regularity. A sense of familiarity helps to generate interactions and introductions with other café patrons, whether while chatting at the café bar or through more strategic efforts. For instance, in the case of Nick who I interviewed in Sydney, Australia, it was the proprietor of his local café who introduced him to his partner:

> Marc, the current proprietor asked me about four years ago if I was interested in meeting someone who had asked him if he knew any decent blokes. I said yes and he said he'd try to arrange something. Heard nothing more. I was on RSVP at the time as was Claire. One day in Jan or Feb 2015 Claire was coming out of the café with a bloke as I was going in… I recognized her as someone whose profile I had seen on RSVP and saved as a favourite but not yet contacted. I asked Marc who she was and he said it was Claire who had asked him about decent blokes. I asked him to give her my number. Later at home I looked for her on RSVP but she had removed her profile. Several days later in Feb she phoned me and we met at the café and the rest as they say is history. I asked her about her disappearing profile. She said she had had enough of RSVP and decided to give it a break on or around the day we passed in the café (she says seeing me had nothing to do with that).

The fact of being a regular at a café and getting to know the staff helps to create a sense of trust that enables this sort of introduction. Nick and Claire felt sufficiently comfortable with Marc and trusted his sense of judgement, which resulted in the connection – and some serendipity gave the relationship greater odds of working out.

But while the café supports civil encounters, this does not necessarily translate to tolerance or understanding of difference. There is an historical, literary tradition of romanticism and the city, whereby the freedoms the city offers and encounters with strangers provide myriad opportunities for interesting connections and self re-invention. This tradition overlooks the reality of antipathies between people. Some studies show that contact or exposure with strangers or 'the other' is often not enough to generate genuine respect and understanding of difference.[23]Tensions exacerbated by factors such as unemployment, cultural difference, acts of urban terrorism and social inequality are hard to overcome. The city's spaces and its amenities are mapped out through processes which are inscribed with relations of power, communicating hierarchies and meaning about who belongs and who doesn't. As a result, socio-spatial inequalities can feed fear and mistrust. How sociality works in the city is complex and diffuse.

The café itself, although a relatively neutral space, isn't immune from subtle forms of inclusion and exclusions, its own hierarchies of power. We intuit who belongs in the space which communicates meaning via visual elements such as the interior design, furniture and its arrangement, the staff, music and the type of coffee served. In cafés, as in any consuming space, cultural capital, that is, specific knowledge and skills, are required to navigate through the transaction process. Such social hierarchies cut across other divisions such as gender and class. Something as seemingly innocuous as knowing the difference between a macchiato and a piccolo could save a customer potential embarrassment and demonstrate their level of connoisseurship. Yet, despite this, the relatively low cost of obtaining entry into the café through the purchase of a drink gives it greater accessibility than many other consumer places.

How inclusive can cafés be?

If cafés are the new meeting places, they need to accommodate a wide range of people and some cafés are more socially inclusive than others. But different café styles appeal to different people and demographic groups. There are people who prefer chain style cafés, while others prefer independent and third-wave cafés. Paradoxically, despite the socially progressive associations of third-wave cafés, with their focus on ethical practices and agricultural sustainability, studies have shown that minority groups tend to feel more at home in chain cafés.[24]

During the course of researching this book, I visited cafés in a host of locations in several countries and cities. Due to the variety of cafés I encountered, overall the patrons were a diverse lot, depending on where and what style of café I happened to be in. If any generalized observation can be made, it's that many of the specialty style cafés – on superficial appearances – had the most distinctive groups of patrons. In these cafés, irrespective of where they were located, customers were predominantly youthful to middle-aged, and tended to appear somewhat culturally homogenous. However, many of the cafés I visited, including specialty styles, did appear to accommodate a diversity of people. Indeed, the café in my Australian neighbourhood that I regularly visit provides excellent specialty coffee and is patronized by a very eclectic group – from the local 'ambos' (ambulance and paramedic workers), police, local mothers, hipster types, office workers and so forth.

It is interesting that chain cafés such as McDonald's, Starbucks and Costa (in Britain) tend to be more socially inclusive than other types of cafés. This could have something to do with the standardisation and homogeneity of their layout and their predictable menus and aesthetics, which make it possible for a wider range of ethnic and social classes to project their own meanings onto them. Predictability is an important element, creating ease with the environment, as Jones' study into chain cafés observes:

> The regularity and standardisation of corporate cafes allow them to function as 'open' to *confident* use in a way that more boutique, specifically 'ethnic' or intensely 'local' consumption spaces may not.[25]

The 'light touch' of sociality expected in the chain café, where staff display courtesy but limited attention – are non-intrusive – to the clients, recalls Goffman's (1963) notion of 'civil inattention' that's required for people to feel comfortable in its spaces. In Jones' study, one of the researchers observes the social diversity of Costa café's patrons, clearly at ease in the café:

> A Muslim woman…chats to one of the two staff behind the counter and two young women—both South Asian, about 18 or 19—debate what to have to drink. As I look round I see people reading newspapers, an older white (English?) man on his phone, a black woman (African/African-Caribbean?) is busy on her laptop and there are a young white (English) couple talking on one of the squashy sofas. There is music on and the atmosphere is one of general comfort.[26]

Starbucks introduced a cosy, home-style seating arrangement in its first shop in San Francisco, which included comfortable leather lounge couches that encouraged sitting and chatting. The idea of a lounge room is that it generates a sociality: the company's website features a declaration where this is made explicit:

> We believe that a coffee lounge must be a place that creates links. We believe that a coffee lounge should be a place of connection—with others, with oneself and with our environment.

On the occasions I visited chain cafés in London, my observations of the clientele were similar. Social inclusion was expressed in a particularly arresting manner when I visited the café chain Pret a Manger in Paddington. Here I observed a scene between a customer and staff member which spoke volumes of the social diversity and inclusivity of that particular café. It was the first café chain shop I'd visited for some time, and I was alert to the demography of its customers, alert to the data about chain cafés and minority groups.

In Pret a Manger, the customers were an eclectic lot, more so than in the third-wave cafés I'd been frequenting at the time: women in hijabs, Asian men, elderly Caucasian women and men, a disabled woman and children were among the wide array of customers there. A middle-aged disabled woman in a wheelchair entered the café alone and placed her order. She then wheeled herself over to a table and began to address no-one in particular in a loud voice, in a random fashion. Most people looked away or ignored her but, undeterred by the lack of response, she continued to make the occasional comment rather loudly. After she'd been sitting there for a while, one of the café staff, a young woman, approached her with her coffee. She then stayed, chatting to the woman and standing close to her chair. She was clearly familiar with her (I assumed at this point that she was a regular) as she'd put her arm around the woman and was asking familiar questions about (I think) her apartment and her dog. I suspected this vignette was something that was unlikely to occur in a third-wave café. For a start, this particular disabled woman might feel that she didn't belong in a café with a more homogenous culture, and quite possibly the staff at an independent café – where overheads might be leaner – would be too busy to spare the time to chat in the manner of the Pret a Manger staff member. The appeal of chain cafés for a broader range of people is about their neutrality as a social space, which no one particular group lays claim to.

Convivial, semi-public gathering places such as the café, food halls and plazas can be seen as what Elijah Anderson refers to as 'cosmopolitan canopies';[27] these spaces provide a protective umbrella, where the only obligation is to be civil towards one another. People might usefully engage in 'folk ethnography', in other words, 'people watching', a sense-making activity which is helpful in building understanding about the strangers we live among, particularly those people who are different from ourselves. It's also of course an activity that can feed either prejudices or truths, and, regardless of the reality of our perception, is a process that helps to define a place. It is easy to overlook the ways in which the city's spaces are testing grounds for democratic and civil behaviour. For example, everyday acts of 'mundane friendliness' with people we don't know in cities, such as holding doors, sharing seats, talking with shopkeepers and taxi drivers and chatting to regulars at cafés all represent a 'baseline democracy that might be fostered'.[28]

The sense of welcoming generated in cafés is embedded in their operations, as we can see in Mikey's behaviour discussed in this chapter's introduction. Starbuck's training includes attention to the friendliness of its staff, making sure that people feel welcome. Indeed, all the café proprietors I spoke with stated that they try to instil a welcoming attitude in their staff, some – as we have all experienced – to greater effect than others. Susie, a barista who works at the Barn in Berlin, talks about the importance of welcoming café patrons and her enjoyment of the host's role:

> I think yeah I've always been taught that you should always…it's the idea of the host and the hosted…like pretty much if you walk into a café you should always be welcomed.
>
> One of the first things I was ever taught when I started working in the service industry, they wanted to put across to us how the panic sets in when you walk into a space you're not familiar with. I think it's one of the greatest things I've ever been taught. The owner got behind the counter and

> got us to walk in as customers and then ignored us for a minute. And just did what he was doing and then he asked us how long it felt. It felt much longer. I really enjoy the customer side of it.

This sense of welcoming and procedure help to fuel the convivial life of the café, and staff training and management is critical to achieve it.

Café, place and community

Cafés are located in physical communities, and as such, the café can be an important place for community development and place attachment. The idea of community is complex; it's both imagined and real. Communities are welcoming as well as restrictive, defensive and exclusive of the stranger. In the traditional use of the term, community implies that some people are allowed in and others are not. Hospitality, on the other hand, requires welcoming the stranger, and the café is one of the few places that enables this.

We become attached to places through regular attendance at these venues and through the types of social interaction we encounter there. Consistency helps to nurture a sense of belonging among co-located people. We patronize certain cafés over others, become regulars and get to know the staff. It's the elements of a café – its ambience, service, the types of coffee or tea, the food – that help forge a relationship with the local community. Sometimes the owner or barista is crucial to the community generated, as is the case with a neighbourhood coffee cart, situated in a courtyard adjacent to a neighbourhood centre in inner-city Brisbane. Meg, a retiree, is a regular at the coffee cart, which is a drawcard for a diverse mix of locals, particularly on a Friday morning when musicians sometimes perform. I quote Meg at some length because she points to an important serendipity and informality about catching up with people in her neighbourhood, whom she might not otherwise see:

> Sandy Tsu walked in…She used to tutor my daughter in Chinese and has just got married and we embraced and caught up with news. And as I left I had this lovely sense of connectedness and I thought this is what a coffee shop is to me. A focal point for my community, where I catch up with people who are more than acquaintances but not the level of friends…just people from my life who I care about and am interested in and can bump into in a lovely informal way and hear their stories. I would never think to seek out Sandy, but she is a real sweetie…That place (the café) has really come to mean a lot to me. I had been at a bit of a loose end today and couldn't really think of anyone to arrange to meet…everyone's away or working, but the neighbourhood centre café provided me with interaction and friendship.

Meg's description of the other café patrons as 'more than acquaintances, but not quite the level of friends' characterizes an essential aspect of community – that it's a group of people whom we move among with varied levels of interaction, from the intense to casual. Casual encounters with people we don't know very well help to generate the sense that we belong to a community, regardless of one's role. The sense of feeling, or 'the warmth of the collective' is what Michel Maffesoli refers to when he talks about this function of social tribes.[29]

Ralf, the owner of three cafés in Berlin, is equally passionate about the idea that his cafés are vital community hubs. He talks about the responsibility that staff play in making people feel welcome:

> If you have strong servers and hospitality people working for you, they connect everyone…the Little Barn (café) is like a hub not only for foreigners but for the whole neighbourhood to really come every day and they'll maybe have a second home in Berlin or they live here for a while. And we know their names and their coffee preferences.

It is one thing for customers to enjoy a sense of belonging when the café is an anchor in their neighbourhood, but to what extent does community extend to those we don't know? While aspects of urban life such as sitting in cafés thrust us in close proximity with strangers, this does not necessarily mean we engage in meaningful encounters with people we don't know. Do strangers strike up conversations in cafés? I asked Ralf if he sees evidence of this:

> Yeah totally. That I think is the beauty about coffee, it's really connecting people to talk about the product. We also made it a point not to have music in the space in the Little Barn…Just to talk to the baristas. Talk to each other. Also have a space where you can read or write or have a meeting with someone and so if everybody would be on a laptop that's really weird.

Ralf's reference to technology as a distraction is echoed by other café owners, with some regarding it as death to the café's role as a conversational space. Some cafés actively discourage the use of technology such as Birch Café in New York, which makes Wi-Fi available only after 5pm as a strategy to encourage conversation. For a period, the café provided laminated letter signs to take to your table with conversational prompts such as *A life changing book I should read*….While the response to the prompts was mixed, some people did take up the prompts and chat to strangers.

Sociality and connoisseurship: From the other side of the counter

People who work in cafés, as in the service industry in general, are often attracted to the industry because they like to work among people. The staff are important in helping to generate sociality among clients and creating a happy, pleasant 'vibe'. In discussions with third-wave or specialty café staff, two things became clear quickly. One was that café entrepreneurs and their staff are a highly connected, often international group who appear to enjoy the conviviality and community that the specialty coffee movement can offer. Assisted by technical apps such as Instagram, Facebook and blogs, the specialty coffee world is a small one. This played out in positive ways for the people I spoke with, in terms of finding jobs, mentoring and getting to know like-minded people. Susie, quoted above, is an Irish barista who moved to Berlin after she was offered a job by Ralf Ruller of the Barn. As a stranger to a new city, where she wasn't a native language speaker, Susie found it easy to lock into the local specialty coffee community. Regular coffee events and barista, latte art and other competitions are forums where café workers meet and get to know each other.

The second common characteristic was how passionate, almost obsessive, people working in the specialty coffee movement are about the industry. The capacity to connect with people through coffee was paramount. When asked why she thought this was the case, Susie offered this explanation:

> I only started drinking coffee a few years ago and then I got obsessed...the idea that there was all these really short-term rewards and then long- term rewards...So you had your short term rewards of giving someone a coffee and them really liking it and telling you. Then seeing yourself getting better every day the longer you were on the machine or in the shop – you were getting quicker every time. But there was these long-term things where you realized that you started to build and it was very obvious as you were building. Because some people would come to you to look for advice. People would ask you questions...people knew you.

For Australian specialty café entrepreneur, Talor Browne, who has become an advocate for people working in the coffee industry, it's the social connection that's paramount for her work in cafés. She expresses this poignantly:

> I think the modern world that we live in can be excruciatingly lonely, so the thing that I enjoy most about coffee is the relationships that form around it. I grew up in my mother's hairdressing salon, talking to the ladies with their heads in dryers. So I was constantly talking to strangers and sharing things about theirs and my own life. I loved the sense of family you got from the regular clients that met at the salon. It wasn't a massive leap when I started working in cafes. People are trying to find meaning and a place to belong - customers and staff alike.[30]

Melbourne-based café entrepreneur, Chrissie, echoes similar sentiments to Talor when asked about her relationship with her customers at her café, Assembly:

> Our regulars are everything...they are the reason this business sustains all the workers. And I have so much...and everyone who works here has so much genuine appreciation for them choosing to come here. And they're such good people.

The appreciation clearly works both ways as Chrissie tells how one of her regular customers invited her to her 70th birthday party. Her specialty-style café in inner-city Carlton, a gentrified neighbourhood which still retains some of its traditional working-class origins, defies the stereotype of a predominantly hipster clientele. The café attracts a diversity of customers from local office workers to long-term local residents in social housing.

There's a strong sense of belonging that the specialty coffee movement seems to engender, which Ralf, Susie and Chrissie and other café entrepreneurs I spoke with repeatedly refer to. The sense of community is clearly a drawcard, but what is it about specialty coffee in particular that generates such passion and dedication? The answer might lie, in part, in the communities of practice forged by the dedication to connoisseurship and the artisan skills of specialty coffee staff. The connoisseurship of the café operator, a topic developed in Chapter Three, refers to the artisanal practices and expertise used to produce high-quality coffee where the focus is on continual improvement. All stages of coffee production from plant growing, harvesting, roasting and brewing are carefully attended to in order to produce subtleties of flavours and varietals, as in the production of wine.

FIGURE 2.4 Informal seating outside Assembly Café Melbourne, invites locals. Photo credit: © Patrick Hayes.

The concept of authenticity is a part of the specialty coffee movement's appeal – understood by its connection to traditional and non-mechanized agricultural methods, direct relationships with farmers, and the pursuit of a pure brew. Authenticity is associated with contemporary food and drink cultures, and is highly valued among discerning foodies. Yet while certain foods and beverages might be perceived as authentic, authenticity is not necessarily inherent; rather it's somewhat relational. That is, authenticity is measured only by its relationship with other foods, particularly say, inauthentic foods. For beverages such as coffee, when measured against instant varieties, specialty coffee appears more authentic. Characteristics that add to a product's appearance of authenticity are geographical origin (Ethiopia, Colombia and so forth for coffee), 'simplicity' (hand-picked and sorted beans) and links to historical traditions. Authenticity, like connoisseurship, endows status and social distinction for those with the knowledge and cultural practices.

Yet, as with consumerism, the pursuit of distinction is not simply about the desire to be above the pack. Like foodies, coffee connoisseurs are caught in a tension between charges of elitism and a genuine thrust for democratic values, – the rejection of corporate culture (i.e. chain cafés), a recognition of the inequality between coffee consumers and producers and efforts to close this gap. Measures such as direct trade with coffee farmers, cutting out the middleman to encourage sustainable wages to farmers, a focus on agricultural sustainability and involvement in schemes which assist underpaid workers are all part of the democratic push. Chrissie sums up this paradox in general about the specialty coffee movement:

> Definitely the response though has been like, 'This is a hipster café'. Or, 'I don't belong here. It's too pretentious'. Or, 'I'm not comfortable in my space'. *That is my worst nightmare. And that is I think the industry's worst nightmare as well.* Because we're trying to present quality but we're being accused of pretentiousness. Because people just want an accessible drink. They don't want to know here it's from. So I think we've got to slow it down really. Win people's trust back and focus on service.

It is easy to see how authenticity and connoisseurship in the specialty coffee industry form the basis of a shared set of practices and values which bind people together. As values, they're formative in community and identity, working in a way that helps to unite people across cities and countries, with their shared beliefs and values. Unbounded geographically, technology plays a crucial role in promoting the latest information, trends and knowledge and connecting communities of practice and consumption. But the coffee connoisseur's allegiances towards distinction and democracy are complex and paradoxical. Inequality and exploitation are also evident among workers in cafés in affluent countries, with insecure and poorly paid conditions for casual, vulnerable workers. Moreover, despite the attempt to address inequities amongst agricultural workers and farmers in the global south, the legacy of coffee's colonial relationship is still firmly embedded in its global flows of trade.

As cities grow in density, complexity and social diversity, citizens are adapting and acquiring new techniques of urban living. The café's spaces have become important in the lives of urban citizens, allowing for a wide range of interactions: from enjoying the company of people we know, to getting to know those who are less familiar to us. At the same time, technology has changed the nature of sociality through internet-based communication, and its impact is felt in the café. At a broad level, the café supports the growth of networks of sociality, and in facilitating civil encounters its hospitable milieu encourages behaviour such as reciprocity and consideration. The widespread take-up of café culture encourages a mode of interaction, a social ethic, which at its optimum has the capacity to foster conviviality, respect and tolerance.

Notes

1 Aldes Wurgaft, Benjamin. 2015. "Writing in cafes." *The Los Angeles Review of Books*. https://lareviewofbooks.org/article/writing-in-cafes-a-personal-history/, September 9. Ret. 3.2.17.
2 Tonkiss, Fran. 2005. *Space, the City and Social Theory: Social Relations and Urban Forms*. Cambridge, UK: Polity.
3 Laurier, Eric. 2008. "Drinking up endings: Conversational resources of the cafe." *Language and Communication* Volume 28, pp. 165–181 (p. 166).
4 https://www.pps.org/reference/roldenburg/ 21.8.17
5 White, Merry. 2012. *Coffee Life in Japan*. Los Angeles, CA: University of California Press.
6 Hattox, Ralph. 1985. *Coffee and Coffeehouses: The Origins of a Social Beverage in the Medieval Near East*. Seattle, WA: University of Washington Press. Pendergrast, Mark. 2010. *Uncommon Grounds: The History of Coffee and How It Transformed Our World*. New York: Basic Books. Wild, Anthony. 2005. *Coffee: A Dark History*. New York: W.W. Norton and Company Ltd. Ellis, Markman. 2004. *The Coffee House: A Cultural History*. London: Weidenfeld and Nicolson.
7 Ellis, Markman (ed.). 2006. *Eighteenth-Century Coffee-House Culture*. London: Routledge, p. xxv.
8 Hattox, R. 1985. Ibid., p. 100.
9 Schivelbusch, Wolfgang. 1992. (Translated David Jacobsen.) *Tastes: A Social History of Spices, Stimulants and Intoxicants*. New York: Random House, p. 52.
10 Ellis, M. 2004. Ibid.
11 Habermas, Jurgen. *The Structural Transformation of the Public Sphere: An Inquiry into a Category of Bourgeois Society*. Cambridge: Polity Press, 1962.
12 Ellis, M. 2004. Ibid., p. 234.
13 Alexakis, Effy and Janiszewski, Leonard. 2014. *Selling an American dream: Australia's Greek Café: A Nationally Touring Exhibition*. Sydney, NSW: Macquarie University.
14 Chaney, David. 1996. *Lifestyles*. London: Routledge, p. 17.
15 Latham, Alan. 2003. Urbanity, lifestyle and making sense of the new urban economy: Notes from Auckland, New Zealand. *Urban Studies* Volume 40, 1699–1724 (p. 1719).
16 Maffesoli, Michel. 1996. *The Time of the Tribes*. London: Sage.
17 Ferreira, Jennifer. 2017. Cafe nation? Exploring the growth of the UK cafe industry. *Area* Volume 49, Issue 1, pp. 69–76 (p. 5).
18 Bookman, Sonia. 2014. Brands and urban life: Specialty coffee, consumers, and the co-creation of urban café sociality. *Space and Culture* Volume 17, Issue 1, pp. 85–99 (p. 91).

19 Gibson, Katie Noah. 2012. Hanging out in cafes alone. https://katieleigh.wordpress.com/2012/08/22/hanging-out-in-cafes-alone/, August 22. Ret. 25.2.18.
20 Bell, David. 2007.The hospitable city: Social relations in commercial spaces. *Progress in Human Geography* pp. 7–22 (p. 12).
21 Hattox, Ralph. 1985. Ibid., p. 98.
22 Bookman, Sonia. 2014. Ibid., p. 93.
23 Valentine, Gill. 2008. Living with difference: Reflections on geographies of encounter. *Progress in Human Geography* Volume 32, Issue 3, pp. 323–337.
24 Jones, Hannah, Neal, Sarah, Mohan, Giles, Connell, Kieran, Cochrane, Allan and Bennett, Katy. 2015. 'Urban multiculture and everyday encounters in semi-public, franchised cafe spaces.' *The Sociological Review* Volume 63, pp. 664–661.
25 Jones et al. 2015. Ibid., p. 657.
26 Jones et al. 2015. Ibid., p. 654.
27 Anderson, Elijah. 2004. "The cosmopolitan canopy." *The ANNALS of the* American *Academy of Political and Social Science* Volume 595, September, pp. 16–30.
28 Thrift, Nigel, quoted in Bell, D. Ibid. 2007, p. 20.
29 Maffesoli, Michel. 1996. Ibid.
30 Browne, Talor. 2016. "Smart girls make coffee." blog:http://smartgirlsmakecoffee.tumblr.com/post/142235392500/talorbrowne, April 4. Ret. 26.8.17.

3

COFFEE BUSINESS

Coffee is money....

Drifting in a lazy, autopilot trajectory, in my own cloud of unknowing, down Bethnal Green Road towards the pop-up shopping hub by the London Overground station at Shoreditch, I register a notice in a window that says: 'No coffee stored overnight.' Once upon a time, white vans (for white men) were nervous about their tools and ladders, but now the value is in coffee, barista coffee, gold dust: the marching powder of the shared-desk classes who are hitting it hard in recovered container stacks and bare-brick coffee shops glowing with an occult circle of pale screens and fearful concentration.

Iain Sinclair[1]

Global consumption of coffee is nearly 10 million tons a year and since 2000 has risen by 38%.[2] It's one of the most traded agricultural commodities, constituting a significant part of the world economy. It is big business, principally for coffee entrepreneurs in the global north. Coffee's production and consumption echoes its colonial relationships: it is mostly consumed by people in affluent countries and produced by agricultural workers in less affluent countries. Over 82% of the world's coffee comes from 17.7 million small-scale coffee farmers, many of whom struggle to make a decent living. Only a minority are able to plan beyond supporting themselves and their families and are able to invest in the future. It is an incredibly labour-intensive crop, and the average daily wage for an agricultural worker is sometimes less than the price of a latte in an artisanal café in the global north. Coffee is roasted and brewed in cafés all over the world where customers can pay up to $US8 a cup.

As this snapshot of coffee's production and consumption unfolds, it is clear that coffee's colonial origins have left its imprint on the contemporary global industry. And while globalization has sped up the flows of labour, services and products, in a sense this is nothing new. Nowhere is this more apparent than in the history of coffee.[3]

This chapter follows the business of coffee from its agricultural production through to its consumption in cafés. It's a multifaceted and complex industry of transnational producers, suppliers, value chains and consumers. While the links between coffee and colonialism are well established, from the 17th-century Dutch East India Company to the purchase of present-day ownership of large-scale plantations by multinational corporations, this chapter will only touch on some of coffee's neo-colonial relations. A globally traded commodity across a range of political regimes and national borders, tracing the neo-colonial relations between multinational companies, small upscale boutique roasters, plantation owners, coffee bean co-ops, regulatory bodies and workers is highly complex. Rather, I look at broad issues of concern that emerge from the agricultural business of coffee in the global south, and from the café industry in the global north. These include how coffee is produced and labour conditions in coffee-producing countries and to a lesser extent, in affluent countries. Here the growth and professionalization of the industry through the rise of the specialty coffee movement is representative of the bean's growing status in the pantheon of gourmet food and aesthetic cultures. The role of global players in the café chain market such as Starbucks, and the rise of specialty coffee business models, add further layers to a highly complex, multibillion-dollar industry. Not least is the issue confronting all agricultural production and consumption: environmental sustainability.

The contemporary coffee terrain

Coffee production and cafés are multifaceted businesses. The number of producers, consumers, brands, coffee shop outlets and clients, as well as those who work in the farms and its different distribution and processing channels, produces a dizzying array of stakeholders unmatched by other businesses.[4]

Over 90% of coffee's production occurs in the global south, and the biggest producers are Brazil, Vietnam, Indonesia and Colombia. There are around 100 species of coffee beans, but the world drinks two main types of coffee, Arabica and Robusta. About 75% of the world's coffee production is Arabica and 25% Robusta, the latter a more heavily caffeinated bean. Although it doesn't grow its own coffee, Switzerland is one of the world's largest exporters and exports more coffee than Swiss chocolate or cheese. This is largely because of the location of food giant Nestlé in Switzerland, the company that produces Nescafé and Nespresso, both very popular coffee products. While a scan of urban neighbourhoods across the world might indicate a flourishing café culture, supply fluctuates, and coffee is a highly volatile commodity. Its production is greatly affected by weather and more recently by climate change patterns. It is susceptible to disease and rising costs due to changing agricultural methods.[5]

Coffee is shipped via distribution companies and into cafés and roasteries throughout the world. The United States is the largest importer of coffee, followed by France, Germany and Japan. However, these statistics don't reflect the amount of coffee drunk per capita, as Finland and Norway are the biggest coffee drinkers at 12kg per capita per year and 9.9kg respectively. Although specialty cafés have grown exponentially since the end of the 20th century, spearheading the world coffee growth, only 5% of coffee grown passes the specialty coffee Q grading tests. Asian countries are leading the upsurge in coffee, where their traditional tea-drinking cultures are being challenged by coffee's growing popularity. In a five-year period from 2012, coffee demand increased in Asia by a record 34.3%. In Hong Kong, specialist coffee shops were the fastest-growing category of beverage outlets increasing by 10% in 2016. In the same year, Indian cafés/bars registered growth of 11%. The specialty coffee market in Australia has been strong for over a decade, with an average growth rate of 5% annually. Declines were recorded in some countries such as France, Greece and Israel, which is to do with local competition in the food and drink industry, as well as the economic conditions of those countries.[6]

Cafés are part of the hospitality or service industries and, as such, are subject to cultural trend-related influences which can make them volatile businesses. They are nonetheless a growing sector of many economies. Cafés, restaurants and bars have been thriving since the late 20th century in many cities across the world. The subsequent development of food and drink cultures has been dramatic, accompanied by increasingly levels of skill of people working in the industry. In gourmet restaurants, third-wave cafés and micro-breweries, the careful attention to food and drink preparation using a combination of experimentation and artisanal approaches has created generations of connoisseurs or 'foodies' across both sides of the counter. Franchized television shows such as *Masterchef* and *My Kitchen Rules* have helped to promote the thriving foodie and drink culture. While these programs are typically about the amateur pitting their skills against a panel of experts, rarely can the contestants hope to reach their level of expertise. Food and drink, once mainly the province of the amateur, is now in the hands of professionals.

Niche markets: The ascendency of specialty coffee and third-wave Cafés

There are many types of independent cafés, but a growing sub-sector is specialty coffee and its distribution in third-wave or specialty cafés. Specialty coffee has become a significant player in the food and beverage industries. These cafés exist on one end of a continuum of independent cafés. While most independent cafés offer good-quality beans and skilled baristas, the specialist café's distinction is that the proprietor has a comprehensive knowledge of the entire process of coffee production ('from crop to drop'), from the bean's origin, ethics of production and varietals of coffee, to the skills of roasting, brewing and latte art.

Not all cafés follow such rigorous practices, and this attention to the entire process is a recent development. In earlier iterations of the café, the owner rarely roasted their own beans, nor would they make it their business to know much about the process of coffee farming. Interestingly, several British, American and Australian breweries sharing similar artisanal approaches to craft beer have expanded into the café industry.

It's generally agreed that the specialty coffee movement emerged from a small cluster of coffee shops in American cities, from the 1970s and 1980s, and gained traction during the 1990s. Seattle is often pinpointed as the place where third-wave cafés began, with its origins and consumption closely associated with fundamental changes in the cultural and economic fabric of the city. However, it wasn't long before the movement was accelerated in Australia, Japan, Britain and Scandinavia.

If we are at the 'third wave' of coffee and cafés, then what are the first two? To appreciate the impact and development of specialty coffee, it's useful to outline the genealogy of coffee consumption. 'First-wave' coffee is attributed to the emergence of coffee drinking from the 1800s through to the early 20th century, in which several companies were successful in promoting coffee as an everyday beverage in the home. Effective marketing and the innovation of air-tight lids and later vacuum packaging contributed to coffee's take-up in the home via companies such as Maxwell House and Folgers in the United States. The 'second wave' was in part a reaction to the low-quality, mass-consumed coffee of the first wave, and involved a change to a more refined type of coffee with some attention to roasting and brewing. Companies such as Starbucks are seen as pioneering second-wave coffee, with the opening of their first store in Seattle, United States, in 1972. However, in other countries such as Australia, as we discuss in Chapter Four, espresso machines serving quality coffee were introduced into cafés from the early 1960s, with the arrival of Italian and Greek migrants.

Third-wave or specialty cafés' approach of connoisseurship means that all the elements of coffee production are carefully attended to. Specialty café proprietors source their own beans or use a reputable supplier who works directly with farms. Many prefer ethically sourced coffee and use direct-trade or fair-trade schemes from producer to roaster, an arrangement aimed to be mutually beneficial for producers and buyers. The type of bean, the temperature and skill of roasting, the temperature of milk and how the coffee is brewed are all important to ensure the maximum flavour of the bean itself. The expertise of the barista is critical in producing a quality cup of coffee and a plethora of worldwide barista competitions exists in which baristas test and display their skills at coffee brewing, 'latte art' (creating images on frothy milk) and expertise at coffee tasting. Coffee and café culture have developed levels of expertise and distinction which were previously non-existent in the industry.

Specialty coffee has spawned new and revival forms of coffee making. Using methods other than the espresso machine extraction such as the pour-over, the process is aimed at producing the best possible taste from the coffee bean

FIGURE 3.1 How coffee is made, Excelsior Café Tokyo. Photo credit: © Emma Felton.

itself. For coffee purists, milk is an unwelcome distraction from the pure taste of the coffee, sullying its flavour. Brewing processes can be time consuming, as with Cold Drip and Cold Pressed coffee, which can take up to twenty-four hours depending upon the size of the equipment. In the Cold Drip method, the ground coffee sits below a flask of iced water which drips slowly onto the coffee. Similarly, with Cold Press the ground coffee brews for hours in cold water and is then strained through an unbleached filter such as muslin or calico. The advantage of this method over the traditional iced coffee, which uses heated coffee but adds ice blocks and cold milk, is that the beans' acidity is reduced.

Despite the growth of independent or third-wave cafés, coffee chains such as Starbucks (US), McDonald's McCafe (US) and Costa (UK) continue to dominate the sector. The values associated with specialty or third-wave cafés tend to be in opposition to large corporate business models such as Starbucks and Costa Coffee. Their focus is on small, sustainable businesses, whose point of difference from chain store cafés is their artisanal practices, ethical focus and appeal to local communities. Their resistance to corporate models helps to establish their distinctive presence in the global coffee market. The specialty coffee industry is built on the ethos to serve high-quality coffee that's produced by fairly paid farmers, with a positive impact on all elements of the supply chain. However, even while roasters pay premium rates for quality coffee, and producers experiment with fermentation and improve infrastructure to access better-paying markets, it is an ideal that is not always reached for every coffee farmer.

While specialty coffee operators might reject the corporate model of businesses and cafés chains such as Starbucks, many are nonetheless alert to growth opportunities, such as value adding through developing economies of scale. So it's not unusual for a successful café proprietor to establish several small cafés across the city in which they began. Mark Dundon founded the Seven Seeds café in Melbourne, from its precursors in 2000, and is credited with leading the third-wave café movement in Australia. He operates four cafés in that city, works directly with coffee farmers and has a wholesales coffee distribution network. Moving into farm ownership or shareholding is the next step for specialty coffee pioneers, and Dundon recently bought a 50% share in an Honduras coffee farm. An adventurous business proposition, several coffee proprietors in the global north have adopted this model.

Expansion has been most evident among specialty cafés in the United States. The boutique roasting company Blue Bottle, established in 2002 in San Francisco, increased its number of stores to forty by 2016, across the country and internationally to Japan. Blue Bottle went one step further than most specialty café owners who might limit themselves to a handful of cafés. They recently sold their majority share (68%) to Nestlé in 2017, which raised concerns among some customers about the continued integrity of their product.[7] Blue Bottle is not alone in seeking out investment from larger transnational companies. Small coffee operators such as Stumptown in the United States and Veneziano in Australia are among the few who have sold majority shareholdings to large corporations.[8] While Starbucks is often referred to as the first specialty coffeehouse, established in 1971, it serves styles of coffee that are far removed from the artisanal approach of contemporary specialty coffee. But that's changing now and the company is edging in to capture some of the market. Starbucks has rebranded a sector of its business, naming it Starbucks 'Reserve', which promotes artisan coffee with labelled provenance. There are 1,000 Reserve stores across the United States, with their design plucked from the aesthetics of specialty cafés; Starbucks maintains its grip as the world's leading café chain.

Starbucks is a thriving global business which continues its growth trajectory especially since moving into China. In 2017 its revenue was (US) $22.39 billion. China's coffee consumption is increasing by 16% per year and Starbucks now has 2,500 coffee shops there. At one stage it was opening a café a day. In 2012, Starbucks partnered with Indian behemoth Tata in a 50/50 partnership and has cafés throughout India branded as Tata Starbucks Alliance. Starbuck's first store outside the United States opened in Tokyo in 1996; now the company owns 27,339 stores in seventy-six countries and is spread across six continents. It seems the only country where Starbucks hasn't flourished is Australia, where a strong independent café culture, and perhaps resistance to American commerce, saw sixty-seven stores closing down over a five-year period.

The bean: Coffee farming

The story of how coffee gets from the bush to your cup is a lengthy one. It's surprising that the cost of a cup of coffee has remained so low for so long, considering the numerous stages of agricultural production and the increasing awareness of the economic challenges faced by coffee farmers. The coffee industry is divided into three segments: the growers, the roasters and the retailers, and in each segment there are many variables that control the cup of coffee that people enjoy. The export and import aspects of the industry are drivers in the amount of coffee that's produced daily. The production of coffee is enormous – 11 million hectares of the farmland in the world are utilized for coffee farming. Brazil is the most significant Arabica producer and Vietnam produces the most Robusta. Arabica has a reputation as the higher-quality bean, one which is naturally mild and aromatic, with rich, rounded flavours. It is shade grown at high altitudes of over 600 metres and is therefore harder to cultivate than the more bitter but more disease- and insect-resistant Robusta, which can be cultivated at lower altitudes and is easier and less labour intensive to harvest. Although Arabica is generally higher quality, the best Robusta can be superior to low-end Arabica.

Coffee bushes grow in subtropical and equatorial regions, optimally in high altitudes. Coffee production is an inherently volatile business which has an impact on those who rely on the industry for a living. Annual yields can vary enormously depending on weather conditions and disease such as rust, making it hard for growers to predict their income. Speculation on the stock market, and large harvests from major origins such as Brazil, also effects the price paid to coffee producers. As the majority of the world's coffee trade is supplied by Brazil, any change in their supply has an enormous effect on coffee prices and on the industry.

In recent years, the global popularity of specialty coffee mainly in the north is having an impact for producers of specialty coffee, with some yields earning record prices. In July 2017, a world record was set for the price of premium coffee when fifty-one lots of naturally processed Geisha sold for $US601 a pound. The coffee, planted in high altitudes, came from Canas Verdes Farm, part of the renowned (to those in the industry) Hacienda La Esmeralda in Boquete, Panama.

FIGURE 3.2 Coffee berries. Credit: © Jonathan Wilkins [CC BY-SA 3.0 (https://creativecommons.org/licenses/by-sa/3.0)], via Wikimedia Commons.

It was purchased by Jason Kew of Kew Specialty Coffee Company in Hong Kong. The majority bidders at this auction were from Asia, whose burgeoning café scene has been developing over the last decade.

The process

Farming coffee requires significant manual labour. Agricultural workers' wages are the costliest part of farming for the producer. From planting, the coffee bush takes about four to five years to bear fruit, with most farms harvesting annually. The coffee bean is actually the seed of the plant which is referred to as the cherry. Once the cherry is ripened and ready for picking, the coffee production entails several stages: picking, processing, drying, milling (including hulling and polishing), sorting, grading and exporting the bean. Every stage of the process is impacted by weather, duration and other factors. In most countries, coffee labourers pick the cherries by hand because they grow in small clusters and the plants are bushy. The trees are often planted in tropical rainforests, making mechanical harvesting rarely an option. But farmers in some countries such as Brazil are able to mechanize this part because the coffee fields are relatively flat

FIGURE 3.3 Colombian coffee farmer preparing beans (https://commons.wikimedia.org/wiki/File:Coffee_Farmer.jpg).

and large scale. The remaining process of extracting the bean from the cherry, drying it and sorting, is lengthy.

Once picked, the beans are dried out before milling. The coffee then goes through either a wet process or dry process. In the dry process the cherries are dried in the sun and turned and raked regularly throughout the day, which can take several weeks. Alternatively, the wet method requires specific machines and uses lots of water to separate the good beans from the bad ones and remove the mucilage that surrounds the bean. While resting in the tanks, naturally occurring enzymes will cause this layer to dissolve. However, this method is often seen as ecologically unsound because the wastewater is considered a pollutant. The final steps involve milling, which is removing the last layers of dry skin and remaining fruit residue from the dry coffee, and cleaning and sorting. Milling is done with the help of a machine and the green beans are sometimes polished. Sorting is a manual or mechanized process and is worked out by bean density, size and colour. Grading is the categorizing of the bean for the market, and occurs at their point of origin, set by the standards of that country. It is based on criteria of botanical variety, density and weight of the bean, place and altitude of growth, as well as preparation and taste. The bean is tasted or 'cupped' throughout several stages. Beans are also required to meet a number of internationally recognized standards, which meet defects and moisture content as well as altitude standards.

Problems for coffee producers

There are many well-known challenges faced by coffee producers and agricultural workers. Low wages, job insecurity and agricultural volatility are top of the list. Coffee production provides a living for around 125 million people who are directly involved in coffee agriculture, and many of these are migrant workers. Wages can be as low as $(US)3 a day, sometimes in flagrant disregard of local labour laws which typically set minimum wages of around $6 an hour, depending on the country. Other difficulties for agricultural workers can be lack of contracts, precarious and poor housing conditions and child labour. At the same time, coffee producers are navigating a volatile and risky market in which factors such as climate change, pest-related diseases, and political conflict effects their crop yields and incomes. Paying even minimum wages can be difficult in some circumstances.

The challenges faced by small-scale coffee farmers means there is a danger of being reduced to a cycle of poverty. Consistently low and volatile income can leave little for investment in the farm, which results in decreasing yields and lower income; thus, the cycle continues. It is astounding to think that when adjusted for inflation, commodity futures for coffee have remained mostly static for forty years even though costs of production have increased dramatically. And while there has been much work pushing for sustainable production, the coffee industry's understanding of the role coffee plays in farmer livelihoods remains elusive. Ensuring a healthy, sustainable coffee supply is directly related to farming families earning an adequate income.

In addition to the more common problems outlined above, coffee growers can face several other trials. Among them are food insecurity, ageing farmer communities and migration, with young people leaving for the cities. Low productivity, ageing coffee trees, expensive fertilizers, lack of market information and poor direct market access all impact on coffee yields and income. On top of all that are common environmental challenges such as soil erosion and degradation, changing climate conditions (small lot farming is carried out in equatorial zones) and poor waste water management among many other factors.[9]

The vulnerability of agricultural workers has been identified by non-government organizations (NGOs) such as Fair Trade, Dan Watch and a host of others. Practices such as debt bondage, confiscation of identity papers and wage theft are not uncommon in some countries. Agricultural workers with low levels of literacy or an inability to read are vulnerable to exploitation and they may have signed contracts which agree to insufficient wages. Workers' health might be compromised too, by the unsafe use of pesticides.

Coffee can be big business for a country's economy. The Vietnamese government's decision in 1986 to grow coffee has helped transform the country's economy. The coffee industry now employs 2.6 million and during the 1990s production grew by 20%–30% every year. The industry has produced some compelling statistics: in 1994 some 60% of Vietnamese lived under the poverty line; now less than 10% do. However, coffee agriculture is not without its hazards in Vietnam, as a large number of unexploded bombs remain in the ground after the Vietnam War during the 1970s. Moreover, as in many coffee-growing regions, environmental devastation is occurring through deforestation, which could mean the potential depletion of land for coffee cultivation.[10]

Addressing inequities in coffee trade

Several movements and organizations exist to help address coffee agriculture's many inequities. Driven by the global prominence of coffee as a daily brew, a growing demand for specialty coffee and an increased concern about sustainable food practices, a host of strategies have been established. Some of these involve coffee distributers and café operators who work directly with farmers. Additionally, a range of organizations, from NGOs, governments, multinational companies to development specialists, has helped to shine a light on sustainability issues in the industry, as well as the more inequitable labour practices of coffee production.[11] Yet while localized and international strategies exist to build resilience among coffee producers to generate more equitable and sustainable outcomes for coffee labourers and the environment, success is highly contingent on local conditions and circumstances. For example, the award-winning coffee estate which garnered the record for the highest price paid for coffee in 2017, Hacienda La Esmeralda, pays their labourers three times the average wage to help to ensure a good quality product, and are able to do this because the profitability of their coffee is extremely high on a regular basis.

Women workers, who can comprise up to 70% of the agricultural workforce, face additional challenges. Gender inequality manifests in exclusion from training, education and lack of land ownership. It is difficult for many women to gain loans, diminishing any opportunity to progress beyond labouring and realize their potential. While such problems exist in other agricultural sectors, each place requires unique solutions based on the environment and local cultural–social norms. Today, due to raised awareness of gender disparity a growing number of gender equity-focused projects are occurring in many coffee growing countries. For example, Bloomberg Philanthropies recently committed (US) $10 million dollars to women's economic development through coffee initiatives in Rwanda and the Democratic Republic of Congo. In Costa Rica, the co-operative The Association of Organized Women of Biolley (ASOMBI) operates the country's first women-run micro-mill. The organization International Women's Coffee Alliance (IWA) operates chapters around the world, finding regional-specific solutions to helping women in coffee production. The IWA in collaboration with the UN and the International Trade Centre (ITC) has set out to build networks of women in coffee throughout growing regions. It is not uncommon for coffee import companies such as the United States-based Cafe Imports and BD Imports to work directly with farmers to establish philanthropic schemes which are aimed at empowering female workers. Some specialty cafés in affluent countries with an ethical focus donate to women co-operatives. For example, Seven Seeds café in Melbourne holds weekly cupping sessions, the proceeds of which go to charities such as Water Wise Coffee and Women for Women in Africa.

One of the most well-known NGOs working with agricultural workers is Fair Trade, which was established in 1988 to promote greater equity in international coffee trade. Fair Trade covers thousands of different types of products and many countries, but it began with Mexican coffee farmers fighting for a fairer price for their coffee. In Fair Trade agreements, a minimum price is determined according to the industry and region, which applies to most certified products. The aim is to ensure that producers can cover average costs of sustainable production and help to combat poverty among poorly paid workers. An abundance of analyses of Fair Trade's economic and social impact presents a very mixed picture. While studies agree that Fair Trade certification initially helped to raise awareness around the injustices suffered by farmers, it is not effectively addressing all the problems it set out to solve. Improvements in the conditions of farmers, workers and to some extent the environment have been documented in several regions, but major challenges remain, particularly in the organization's governance structures.[12] Other studies are downright critical, claiming that Fair Trade actually exacerbates inequality.[13]

One area of agreement is that when coffee prices are high, Fair Trade has less of an impact. During recessions or economic downturns, farmers and workers have benefitted from Fair Trade arrangements. A big part of the challenge for coffee markets is that their prices are more or less set by commodity markets, known as the "the C market." That price was set about a hundred years ago to help stabilize the price of coffee for coffee roasters, which had historically been fairly volatile.

Over the last fifteen years, since the advent of artisan coffee, roasters have pioneered an alternative international trading model. With similar principles to Fair Trade, roasters engage directly with farmers in direct trade agreements. This cuts down the middleman or third parties with its certification criteria. Direct trade is aimed at building 'mutually beneficial and respectful relationships' with individual producers or co-operatives in the coffee-producing countries. The idea is that building sustainable, long-term relationships allows prices to be personally agreed upon so that they cover the cost of production and provide an additional premium for high-quality coffee, with no additional cost to the farmer for certification. Coffee specialists do it because they want more control over the quality of the coffee and can also have an input into social or environmental concerns. Dissatisfaction with the third-party certification programs is another reason. Direct trade is concerned only with small-lot farming or micro lots – the growing, selling and buying. Micro lots are small amounts of coffee grown within a farm, and on tiny amounts of land, as small as half an hectare.

Intelligentsia, Stumptown Coffee Roasters and Counter Culture Coffee in the United States and Union in Britain were pioneers of direct trade with farmers. Union invests money in Rwanda's coffee industry through the purchase of a centralized coffee-washing station and provides workshop training in Guatemala to train farmers to evaluate their coffees effectively and select for complex sensory attributes. These types of initiatives benefit both the coffee roaster's business and the coffee producers by raising the standards of coffee and increasing farmers' incomes.

Specialty coffee's ethos of sustainability is supported by an army of aware consumers, whose concerns about food sources are germane, particularly for the generation whose food supplies may become less predictable in the future. It is not surprising that selling an ethical cup of coffee has become a profitable venture, with the growth of certified coffee one of the biggest recent success stories of the ethical consumer movement. Fair Trade retail sales of coffee beans grew by 250% in the decade from 2004 to 2014. This period has also seen a proliferation of other ethical coffee accreditation schemes, including Rainforest Alliance and UTZ.

Coffee workers in affluent countries

Labour conditions for those working in the coffee industry in cities in affluent countries can barely be compared to those of the global south. Minimum wages exist, even though in countries such as the United States, hospitality workers rely heavily on tips to ensure a reasonable standard of living. In Australia, because specialty coffee is so popular and the average wage is relatively high, good baristas are among the highest paid in the world. However, it is not all good news. In many countries, the hospitality industry is staffed by casual workers, meaning there is little job security and fewer of the benefits paid to full-time employees such as paid sick leave and holiday pay. Although the casualization of the workforce has been occurring for some time, hospitality workers have long been at the forefront of casualization. Moreover, while wages appear to be robust enough, in many cities where coffee culture has taken off the cost of living is extremely high. Cities such as New York, San Francisco, London, Sydney and Tokyo are in the top twenty list of most expensive cities to live in.

Gender inequality is a problem that cuts across geographical boundaries. Injustices in all industries exist, despite decades of industrial relations policies and strategies to improve the working conditions of women and minority groups. Because of the unique characteristics of service industries, casual staff are vulnerable to the vagaries of commercial priorities – and occasionally personal whims. Several women have gone public about the unfair treatment they've experienced in the café industry, and the international coffee community has taken notice. One of their grievances is the over-representation of male baristas, despite the fact that hospitality is statistically a majority female workforce. As in most other industries, the top leadership positions are held by men. The World Barista Competition is dominated by male contestants and, since it began in 2000, has only produced two female winners, as is the case for coffee roasters and other competitions. At the time of writing, Poland's Agnieszka Rojewska is the second female to win the World Barista Competition. But participation has always been low, under 25% female representation and there are systemic reasons for this: it is expensive to enter competitions because competitors have to practise with the best coffee and the best machinery to perfect their skills. Because of the dominance of male baristas, this is easier to achieve for male competitors.

The women café workers or owners I spoke with, some of whom had entered competitions, expressed little interest in competing. This might be because of the perception that competitions were something of a boy's club. Yet winning competitions, gaining a profile can have major benefits for the winners who gain in stature and influence and are able to attract higher wages and positions. On national levels, competitions may be more accessible arenas for women. In Germany for instance, Erna Tosberg has won the German championship twice.

Discrimination plays out at the personal level and can make working conditions uncomfortable for women. Chrissie, the thirty-three-year-old owner of Assembly café in Melbourne Australia, tells me that when she first started working in cafés, she experienced several incidents where the behaviour of male co-workers or bosses made her job difficult. This helped convince her to run her own café, and in an inclusive manner. To attract more female staff, she advertised the position with an emphasis on customer service, with the result that about 80% of her applicants were women:

> I just kind of reworded the ad. The existing skills of the person, [were] potentially less of an importance than the kind of staff I wanted to hire. Someone who is genuinely interested in customer service. And I made it clear that there's no hierarchy here of barista and server. We all do everything...On Instagram with the ad I posted a photo of Phoebe working here...but it took longer to hire someone. I just think there's less women who have had coffee experience. And there's countless people I know who have been doing the same job as their male co-workers and they get less shifts behind the coffee bar. They get less promotions. Less responsibility.

Another Melbourne based café, Handsome Her, has gone one step further and applies an 18% surcharge to male customers to address the gender pay gap. The funds are donated to women's charities. Women are also given priority seating and the café's dishes are given famous female names such as 'Frida Kahlo cheese and bacon bagel'. Inequality in specialty cafés isn't a one-way street, and sexism can occur on both sides of the counter. Both employers and customers can be offenders. Helena Holmes, a barista with many years' experience, has witnessed inexperienced men given shifts over more highly skilled and experienced women, and management hiring more male baristas instead of training the existing female staff. But the gender divide also comes from the customer; Holmes says that 'nine times out of 10' customers will overlook her when she is standing behind the coffee machine, and instead congratulate her male co-workers on the coffee.[14] And conversely staff can get up to sexist tricks with their customers. A Tumbler blogger revealed that she was asked by a barista whether she'd like a 'normal strong latte' coffee or an 'inappropriate strong latte'. When she expressed confusion, he mumbled 'oh never mind' and eventually returned with her coffee complete with phallus latte art.[15]

A specialty coffee industry figure, Talor Browne, has spoken out about mental health issues and gender inequity in the café industry. An internationally sought-after coffee specialist originally from Melbourne, Browne nonetheless found working conditions in some cafés intolerable for the pressure and lack of care towards staff. Browne has appeared at international forums, highlighting the mental health hazards that can afflict people working in the industry. While there is little formal support or organizations for women working in the industry, women have taken to social media, which has provided a forum for informal networking and support via blogs, YouTube and other video channels.

The global coffee and café industry and its industrial relations is highly contingent on location, regulations and a host of other factors. There are numerous other issues faced by those working in the industry, beyond the scope of this chapter. To some extent, many of the challenges faced by employers and employees are found across all industries in a competitive, precarious, market-driven global economy. The hospitality industry itself is an arena of insecure work with a high staff turnover and transient workforce. There is little protection for workers, male or female. It is a volatile and demanding industry for both owners and workers.

Despite this, many specialty café proprietors and increasingly café chains, as I have outlined, pursue their focus on sustainable coffee practices to a more general concern with equality and charity, often targeting the local communities in which they are situated. There are myriad examples of café proprietors the world over giving back, or supporting initiatives which contribute to equality measures or social enterprises in their own cities as well as in coffee-producing regions. These range from helping street people by training them as baristas, employing people with physical disabilities and running events in which the paid proceeds go to local charities.

Coffee's environmental impact

While this book is about the relationship between the café and the city, it would be negligent to overlook important questions circulating around the environment, coffee agriculture and the industry. The sustainability of all agricultural production is a mounting concern, given climate change, population growth and priorities of nations to secure food futures. For many, it is the biggest challenge humankind is facing at the beginning of the 21st century.

The coffee industry relies on the production of millions of smallholder farming families, whose livelihood is vulnerable to climate change, but who also have limited capacity to cope and adapt. With rising temperatures and decreasing rainfalls, more extreme weather events, it is predicted that coffee production will take a hit. In Ethiopia, the native birthplace of Arabica coffee, researchers predict that as much as 59% of the country's current coffee production area could become unsuitable for coffee growing by the end of this century due to the effects of climate change.[16]

The global demand for food and drink is at an unprecedented level as the world's population, at 7.6 billion in 2017, continues to rise at just under 2% per year. More land is cleared for agricultural production each year; this and certain agricultural practices are not without serious consequences. Environmental degradation occurs particularly through large-scale clearing and farming. Traditional coffee farming has less environmental impact than large-scale mechanized farming of the type carried out in Brazil. Cultivated in small lot farms of under two hectares, under the shade of a canopy of trees in rainforest regions, the shade provides a natural habitat for animals and insects, keeps soil erosion in check and helps to sustain the biodiversity of the rainforest. It provides side benefits to the farmer such as fruit, because they grow other crops such as bananas, and firewood. Traditional farmers used a compost of coffee pulp rather than chemicals and fertilizers.

However, today, more and more coffee is being grown in direct sunlight on larger-scale farms. The number of coffee farms using traditional shade-growing methods has dropped significantly from 43% to 24% between 1996 and 2010. Over 41% of coffee farmland contains no shade trees at all.[17] These plantations replaced their shade-grown methods with sun cultivation techniques to increase yields, and it worked. Yields improved dramatically. But like all industrialized agriculture, it also had negative environmental impacts. The full-sun coffee farms are similar to large monoculture crops, making land more susceptible to erosion and climate change. Apart from deforestation and its known impacts, contaminated waterways and loss of topsoil are two of the well-documented problems associated with this type of farming. Subsequently, more pesticides and fertilizers are used to compensate for the loss of natural insect-killing birds and bats, and for the loss of the trees' soil-fertilizing leaves and roots. It is the Robusta bean which is farmed in this method because it is better at tolerating full sun. Robusta is used mainly for instant coffee or combined with Arabica into blends.

The change in farming practices was partly to do with the growth of the coffee industries in Brazil and Vietnam, the first- and second-biggest producers in the world. It is also the result of efforts to increase coffee yields for farmers during the 1970s when agronomists believed that growing coffee in direct sunlight would increase photosynthesis, prevent disease and allow greater planting. The United States' Agency of International Development encouraged farmers to adopt new methods during this period through investment in Latin American coffee plantations. Since 1990, coffee cultivation has diminished in Africa and expanded in Asia, with the largest markets in Vietnam and Indonesia where most of the new production is done in an intensive style.

On the positive side, there has been a return to both traditional and new methods of growing shade-tolerant coffee varieties. Shade-grown coffee can often earn a premium as a more environmentally sustainable alternative to mainstream sun-grown coffee. And in response to the environmental impacts of coffee production, a range of eco-certifications have been established. Rainforest Alliance, the Smithsonian Migratory Center, Fair Trade, Utz and Starbucks café practices are among several that encourage sound environmental practices, as well a host of local arrangements between farmers and buyers.

Certification has grown significantly since the beginning of the 2000s, driven by consumers' concerns over the sustainability of the agro-food business, and by global buyers' commitments to purchasing more from certified suppliers. Certification is usually accompanied by the adoption of voluntary standards and codes of behaviour. It provides a set of principles for the certified suppliers, and a process for implementing and monitoring those standards. The Netherlands is the highest importer of certified coffee and in 2012, it accounted for 40% of all global production.[18] Large transnational buyers in the coffee industry such as Starbucks, Costa and Nespresso have developed their own in-house socio-environmental standards and related certification schemes, which are open to scrutiny.

A hefty body of research has assessed the impact of certification on the environmental conditions of farmers and small farms, but as with Fair Trade investigations, the studies remain relatively inconclusive.[19] In general, the weight of evidence is on the side of positive environmental impact. Several studies show that farms have increased their adoption of environmentally friendly management practices, and that organic certification improves coffee growers' environmental performance by reducing chemical input use.[20] While in-house certifications may improve how farmers deal with environmental issues, social issues are less straightforward to address. Farmers with in-house certifications tend to be more diligent environmentally, partly because of the tangible benefits its produces. For instance, re-use of sewage water may result in lower water costs, while measures such as recycling can improve the farm's waste management and provide direct benefits for the farm.

With the demand for coffee expected to increase by 25% over the next five years, propelled by the beverages gaining popularity in heavily populated Asian countries, it is anticipated that it could be difficult for suppliers to meet with the increasing global demand for coffee.

The global north: Environmental impact

Meanwhile in affluent countries, coffee consumption is on the rise. Alongside the environmental impact of coffee agriculture, other pollutants via international transportation networks which ship and truck coffee and its associated products around the world are adding to the planet's carbon footprint. Coffee waste products contribute to the sum damage, with one of the biggest offenders being the cardboard 'recyclable' cups that many cafés use, especially for take-away coffee. The practice of selling coffee in disposable paper and plastic cups, according to one UK study, contributes to around 2.5 billion cups being thrown away in Britain every year, or 5,000 a minute. Worse still, while many disposable cups are promoted as recyclable, they are not. A plastic coating made of polyethylene which provides water-proofing makes it difficult for the cup to be recycled because it is not easily separated from the cardboard. A growing awareness of the environmental impact of disposable cups has driven the production of reusable or 'keep' cups, with an increasing range on the market, but their uptake is slow. Many cafés today, including the large chain store cafés, offer discounts for customers with reusable cups. In Britain, steps are afoot to deal with the problem and politicians are calling for a 'latte levy' of 25 pence to discourage disposable cup use. Britain's high rate of disposable coffee cups which are thrown away, is no doubt similarly replicated in countries across the world.[21]

Coffee itself yields a waste product in spent coffee grounds, amounting to around six million tonnes going into landfill each year. As a plant product, it is able to be recycled and in recent years, scientists are discovering several useful applications for spent coffee grounds apart from compost. Potential applications range from biofuels to health products, to fertilizer for farms for the garden. Properly composted coffee grounds offer a cheap alternative to agro-industrial fertilizers, potentially helping urban communities become greener and more sustainable. An Australian company has begun processing coffee grounds on a commercial scale, turning them into nutrient-rich fertilizers or soil conditioners in convenient pellets for use in the garden. In Britain, a company has created a bio-fuel which blends oil extracted from coffee waste with diesel, and will be trialling the fuel in London buses. The start-up Bio-Bean has partnered with Shell and Argent Energy and has produced 6,000 litres of coffee oil for the pilot project with London's transport authority. It is enough to help power the equivalent of one city bus for a year.[22]

Other sustainable initiatives exist, such as the use of coffee beans for their antioxidant and neuroprotective properties. However, this and other uses are in the early stages of development awaiting further research and venture capital investment.

Changing urban lifestyles are driving the growth of the food and beverage industries, underpinning the rise of café culture across the globe. Coffee's worldwide consumption has been increasing steadily, but the Asia-Pacific is the fastest-growing market, with coffee consumption growing at a rate of 5% per year since 2000. Although Japan is by far the largest coffee market in the region, the populous countries of China and India are leading the uptake. Starbucks' push into China has paved the way for other coffee entrepreneurs who have followed in their wake, and Asia's growing consumer base of middle-class young professionals are fuelling the demand.

Specialty coffee continues to challenge and redefine both the café and the coffee industries' traditional business models. The specialty café can be a laboratory of artisan production and experimentation, with new styles of coffee formulations appearing regularly. While major corporations such as Starbucks continue to dominate the sector, specialty coffee's impact is significant. It has proved influential among several coffee chains, some of whom are adopting artisanal approaches, such as sourcing origin beans and introducing a wider range of coffee styles. Concomitantly, a growing cohort of discerning coffee drinkers, driven by changing consumer tastes and marketing, continue to support the dedication to the artisanal product.

One of the world's most traded agricultural commodities, coffee is a major source of revenue for many countries in the global south. But in coffee-producing nations, there are farmers who still exist on subsistence wages, with a trickle-down effect on agricultural workers. To some extent, there is greater awareness today of the problems in the coffee industry through the work of NGOs, government bodies and research which continues to shine a light on international trade that disadvantaged farmers and was brought to light by Mexican coffee farmers as early as the 1980s.

As worldwide consumption continues to grow, history shows us that coffee drinking has not been affected by the vagaries of financial downturns. Rather, it's more likely that coffee's future will be influenced by what collective measures are taken on climate change, environmental forethought and action. The World Health Organization regard climate change as a significant threat to the future health of the planet's population. Maintaining population health is dependent on life-supporting 'services' of the biosphere, on supplies of uncontaminated food and water, freedom from excess infectious disease and organic pollutants, and the physical safety conferred by climatic stability. Yet the evidence is that we are currently altering Earth's biophysical and ecological systems at the planetary scale.

Notes

1 Sinclair, John. 2017. "The last London." *London Review of Books* Volume, 39 Issue 7, March 30, pp. 7–11. https://www.lrb.co.uk/v39/n07/iain-sinclair/the-last-london. Ret. 25.3.17.
2 *International Coffee Organization*. 2017. Trade statistics. https://icocoffeeorg.tumblr.com/post/83000404043/global-coffee-consumption-has-increased-by-25. Ret. 16.4.17.
3 Lyons, James. 2005. "Think Seattle, act globally." *Cultural Studies* Volume 19, Issue 1, pp. 14–34 (p. 29).
4 Samper, Luis and Quiñones-Ruiz, Xiomara F. 2017. "Towards a balanced sustainability vision for the coffee industry." *Resources (Basel)* (2079–9276), Volume 6, Issue 2, p. 17.
5 Fairtrade Foundation. 2012. *Fairtrade and Coffee. Commodity Briefing*, May. http://www.fairtrade.net/fileadmin/user_upload/content/2009/resources/2012_Fairtrade_and_coffee_Briefing.pdf. Ret. 3.11.17.
6 *International Coffee Organization*, 2017. Trade statistics. http://www.ico.org/trade_statistics.asp Ret. 25.3.17.
7 Helmore, Edward. 2017. "Blue Bottle Coffee sells to Nestlé: So has it sold out?" *The Guardian*. https://www.theguardian.com/business/2017/sep/16/blue-bottle-coffee-nestle, September 16. Ret. 25.9.17.
8 Waters, Cara 2017. "Bold business podcast: Turning specialty coffee into a $50 million business at Veneziano Coffee." *Sydney Morning Herald*. http://www.smh.com.au/small-business/bold-businesses-podcast-turning-specialty-coffee-into-a-50-million-business-at-veneziano-coffee-20170925-gyo37y.html, September 27. Ret. 25.9.17. Pendergrast, Mark. 2010. *Uncommon Grounds: The History of Coffee and How It Transformed Our World*. New York: Basic Books, p. xvii.
9 Samper, Luis and Xiomara F. Quiñones-Ruiz. 2017. Ibid.
10 Summers, Chris. 2014. "How Vietnam became a coffee giant." *BBC News*. http://www.bbc.com/news/magazine-25811724, January 25. Ret.31.3.17.
11 Samper, Luis and Quiñones-Ruiz, Xiomara F. 2017. Ibid.
12 Valkila, Joni. 2014. "Do fair trade pricing policies reduce inequalities in coffee production and trade?" *Development Policy Review* Volume 32, Issue 4, pp. 475–493. Zeller, Manfred and Beuchelt, Tina May. 2011. "Profits and poverty: Certification's Troubled link for Nicaragua's organic and fairtrade coffee producers." *Ecological Economics* Volume 70, Issue 7, pp. 1316–1324.
13 Sylla, Ndongo Samba. 2014. (Translated by David Clément Leye.) *The Fair Trade Scandal: Marketing Poverty to Benefit the Rich*. London: Pluto Press.
14 Helena Holmes, quoted in Gooding, Sarah. 2015. "Grounds for complaint: Female baristas fail to change café culture." *The Guardian*. https://www.theguardian.com/lifeandstyle/australia-food-blog/2015/aug/19/grounds-for-complaint-female-baristas-struggle-to-change-cafe-culture, August 19. Ret. 17.11.17.
15 Tumbler post. http://68.media.tumblr.com/ce1afa626674c59d25be3686cde7b373/tumblr_inline_o7z1sim5Rn1scwanp_500.png. Ret. 17.11.17.
16 Moat, J., Williams, J., Baena, S., Wilkinson, T., Gole, T.W., Challa, Z.K., Demissew, S. and Davis, A.P. 2017. "Resilience potential of the Ethiopian coffee sector under climate change." *Nature Plants* Volume 3, Issue 7, pp. 1–14.

17 Jha, Shalene, Bacon, Christopher M.; Philpott, Stacy M., Méndez, V. Ernesto, Läderach, Peter and Rice, Robert A. 2014. "Shade coffee: Update on a disappearing refuge for biodiversity." *BioScience* Volume 64, Issue 5, pp. 416–428.

18 Guiliana, Elisa, Ciravegna, Luciano,Vezzilli, Andrea and Killan, Bernard. 2017. "Decoupling standards from practice: The impact of in-house certifications on coffee farms' environmental and social conduct." *World Development* Volume 96, August, pp. 294–314.

19 Guiliana et al. 2017. Ibid.

20 Blackman, Allen and Naranjo, Maria O. 2012. "Does eco-certification have environmental benefits? Organic coffee in Costa Rica." *Ecological Economics* Volume 83, November, pp. 58–66. Guiliana et al. 2017. Ibid. Jha et al. 2014. Ibid.

21 Harrabin, Roger. 2018. "Latte levy of 25pc urged by politicians in bid to cut cup waste." *BBC News*. http://www.bbc.com/news/business-42564948, January 5. Ret. 15.2.18.

22 BBC News. 2017. "London Buses to be fueled by Coffee." https://www.bbc.com/news/uk-england-london-42044852, November 19. Ret. 3.12.17.

4

THE EXPORTED CAFÉ

Australia

> The late AA Gill, acerbic British food critic, once wrote that Australians were 'the great new coffee bores of the world'.
>
> *Pat Nourse*[1]

The enthusiastic adoption of café culture in Australia has provisioned its city streets and malls with a staggering amount of places to eat and drink – traditional-style cafés, independent and third-wave cafés, funky cafés, café bookshops, café delis and, to a lesser extent, chain store coffeehouses because Australians resoundingly prefer independent cafés. Australia has been described as the world's 'coffee capital'[2] and its coffee shop culture has been exported across the globe from New York to London to Singapore, inserting its signature flat white on coffee menus.

This part of the story begins in Australia, a country perhaps better known for its robust beer-drinking culture. Yet the Australian café experience has become an interesting global export phenomenon and the country can lay claim to a few coffee achievements. For coffee connoisseurs, Australia is synonymous with specialty coffee and cafés, with their unique combination of artisan coffee and fresh, simple food. Australia claims to be the originator of the 'flat white' style of coffee, which first appeared in cafés in the 1980s, although this is a fact contested by New Zealand. Australian baristas have earned an international reputation for their skills, and a national penchant for travel has driven baristas, roasters and coffee entrepreneurs to other countries, where they've exported their ideas and expertise. In cities across the world, Australians have established coffee businesses, some of which are highly successful multi-million-dollar concerns. In New York, the renowned Bluestone Lane, Two Hands and Toby's Estate, opened in the early 2000s, are among a growing number of Australian-owned cafés. Among the several in London are the eponymously named Flat White and

Lantana, while other Australian coffee specialists can be found in Paris, Mumbai and Shanghai.

In another world first, Australia is the only country where US coffee giant Starbucks failed. In 2000, Starbucks began to roll out eighty-four cafés across the country and, by 2008, sixty-one had closed. By the time the company made its entry into the market, Australia already had a discerning and well-established coffee culture. Patrons were loyal to their local cafés and Starbucks coffee was considered too bland, too milky and too expensive. Starbucks' mission, 'to uplift the lives of our customers and become part of the local community', didn't wash with Australian consumers and they drank their coffee elsewhere. Ninety-five per cent of Australia's 14,000 cafés are independently owned and an Australian culture of resistance to international conglomerates and a spirit of independence may also account for Starbucks' demise.[3] Now recognizing the appeal of Australian-style specialty coffee, Starbucks and McDonald's introduced the flat white to their menus in 2016, boosting sales for Starbucks in the first quarter after the arrival of the flat white.

The growth of the café industry in Australian cities has been monumental. Australia is a highly urbanized country, with over 70% of its population living in cities, consolidating the nexus between cafés, urbanism and regeneration. Taking off in the latter decade of the 20th century during the period of urban regeneration across Australian cities, cafés began to dot the cityscape, alongside other urban amenities such as bars, restaurants and niche shops. Embedded in the urban fabric, cafés are now an intrinsic feature of urban life.

Colonial relations: The arrival of coffee in Australia

The history of the café and its coffee house origins in Constantinople and its journey to London and Europe in the 17th century are well documented,[4] but less has been written about how coffee and café culture made its way to other parts of the world. Coffee arrived in Australia later than in Europe, and Australia's establishment as a British colonial outpost in the 18th century embeds its place in the network of the coffee industry's neo-colonial relations. It wasn't until the First Fleet landed in Sydney in 1788 that coffee first appeared amongst the stocks of other plants. It is assumed that coffee was picked up along with cocoa beans, fig trees, bananas, sugar cane and a host of other goods when the First Fleet was stocking up in Rio de Janeiro in 1787.

The first recorded growth of the type of coffee in use today in Australia was in 1832 in Kangaroo Point, an inner-city riverside area in sub-tropical Brisbane, which is now a medium-sized city of nearly two million inhabitants. By the late 1880s coffee was growing along the east coast of Australia's warmer regions, in plantations in Northern New South Wales and across the tablelands of North Queensland to Cooktown, as demand for the bean had grown. Government botanists planted coffee, coconuts and other crops during their explorations throughout the state of Queensland. This period of coffee cultivation was very successful and garnered international recognition, winning awards in Paris and Rome. The industry grew to a level where around fifty to sixty growers were producing 40% of Australia's coffee supply. Unfortunately for the farmers and coffee lovers, success was short-lived. Coffee production went into serious decline during the Great Depression in the 1920s, and by 1926 the industry had all but vanished. The high costs associated with labour and transportation across such a large continent were no competition for cheaper imported coffee. The inability to compete with the lower prices of other countries is still a problem for Australian coffee farmers today.

Australia's Indigenous population, who had inhabited the continent for at least 70,000 years before British colonization, made great use of a wide range of edible native wild flora. They ground and brewed the seeds and leaves of numerous wild plants to create beverages, some of which the early British settlers used as coffee substitutes. British explorer Captain Cook recorded that the Aborigines drank an infusion of the leaves from the Leptospermum tree of which there are around eighty varieties. The plant now goes by the name of Ti Tree, and drinking its leaves was a practice that the British adopted and regarded as a type of tea. Chicory was popular as a coffee substitute, a blue flowered herb which still grows in many parts of the country; it is related to the dandelion and catsear. It was often mixed with all sorts of other ingredients such as parsnips, rye and carrot.

The new colonialists frequently set up home in remote and isolated places and had to improvise to reproduce the goods and products they would have had easy access to in their British homelands. On rural properties, the coffee was made from 'parsnips roasted to blackness and put through a grinder'.[5] The quality of the beverage no doubt cast a pall on coffee. Early settlers in bush camps would nail their coffee-grinders to the trees near their tents and huts.

The Mackenzie bean, a common creeper with pink flowers and pods like broad beans, grew alongside riverbanks and was also found to be an excellent substitute for coffee. Seeds from the lotus and kurrajong plants were also coffee substitutes, the latter an important Aboriginal food. Tim Low, in his book *Bush Tucker*, discusses the lengths to which early explorers went in their efforts to find coffee substitutes. These sometimes included risky experimentation:

> That most eccentric of Australian explorers Ludwig Leichardt, was one of the first to dabble with native coffees...on his second expedition, Mackenzie bean coffee was tried again, with disastrous results. Expedition botanist Daniel Bunce, claimed that 'one dose of this beverage was sufficient, as it created violent vomiting and diarrhoea'.[6]

Low details a long list of native plants which were used as coffee substitutes, and whose flavours must bear some resemblance to coffee, most likely having robust and bitter qualities. While two native plants go by the title of coffee bushes – Leuceana leucocephala and Breynia oblongifolia – there is no evidence that they were produced as a beverage before colonization. Another native coffee bush,

Coffea Brasii, was 'discovered' as late as 2011 by botanists in the far north regions of Australia, around the Cape York Peninsula, where it is believed to have made its way from New Guinea. For the early colonialists the drink of the day was, of course, tea, which is still widely consumed by Australians today.

The closest records of coffee-like plants being used by Aborigines is the wattle-seed, a common food source for the Indigenous population before colonization. Hailing from the ubiquitous Acacia plant, when ground and roasted it is described as having a 'delicious nutty coffee aroma'. The Aborigines used it to make flours and for flavouring, but it is free of stimulant properties.[7] The current popularity of novel and naturally sourced foods has driven several enterprising companies to produce and market 'bush tucker', Australian native food sourced through foraging in natural environments. Wattle-seed is sold as a substitute for caffeine-free coffee. It's promoted among foody communities as 'a beautiful and exquisite blend that tastes a little nutty and smells a little like chocolate'.[8] Somewhat ironically, caffeinated coffee does grow wild today in Australian rainforests, but it is of the imported variety and is considered a threat to natural habitats, listed as a 'priority weed'.

It wasn't until the mid-19th century that coffee became more desirable. Gradually appearing in Australia's major cities throughout the 19th century, some cafés were located in department stores and restaurants. In Sydney's café-restaurants, café au lait and café noir might be served until midnight.[9] These establishments, modelled on European cuisine culture, were considered bohemian places to visit. Although coffee still failed to make much of a dint in the tea-drinking habits of the nation, it is noteworthy that its early introduction began in Melbourne, where its fate is closely aligned with the fortunes of the city. Melbourne today is widely renowned as the coffee capital of Australia, a reputation that has travelled well beyond national borders.

The 19th-century coffee palace

The economic boom of the mid-19th century began with the 'gold rush'. The discovery of gold in fields outside Melbourne, Victoria and some areas of New South Wales attracted thousands of labourers, diggers and other fortune hunters to the fields and subsequently into the cities close by. People flocked to the gold fields mainly from Britain, but also from China, America, Germany and Poland. A manufacturing and construction boom followed the gold rush, occurring in the burgeoning cities, most notably in Sydney and Melbourne.

The influx of people to cities coincided with a significant increase in alcohol consumption. Public disorder became more visible on city streets, and drunkenness and anti-social behaviour were, for some, too common. It sparked something of a moral panic around safety and urban disorder. Back in the colony's motherland, similar concerns had been expressed in British cities a century earlier. The new factories and subsequent metropolitan development had produced an influx of agricultural workers looking for work in rapidly growing London.

The emergence of urban public space where people from all walks of life mingled for the first time caused a disquiet which cut across class and gender lines. As historians have written, much of this unrest was to do with the new mingling of social classes in the public spaces of the emerging metropolis, and the associated problems that rapid urbanization had produced.[10]

In Australia, lobby groups began to campaign against the dangers of alcohol, harnessing the momentum of the world-wide Temperance movement. Established in Scotland in the early 19th century, the Temperance movement gained traction in the United States and England, promoting abstinence from alcohol with the replacement of other drinks, such as coffee. The movement also campaigned for greater alcohol regulation and, in some instances, prohibition of alcohol sales altogether. In Australia it was promoted largely by Christian organizations concerned with upholding family values and discouraging drunkenness. Temperance lobbyists successfully advocated for the six o'clock closing of pubs and 'dry suburbs' where no public houses should be built. Coffee's growing appeal occurred during the country's first economic boom, and was, in part, fuelled by a growing public concern about the over-consumption of alcohol.

One of the upshots of the movement in Australia, was the establishment of Temperance hotels or 'coffee palaces' as they became known. The hotels began to appear in Australia's major cities during the 1880s, as well as throughout towns around the gold field areas in Victoria. The same phenomenon was occurring in Britain's cities, where the popular gin palaces were being converted to coffee palaces, promoting educative activities through the supply of newspapers and journals for working men. In Australia, coffee palace companies were established by leaders of the Temperance movement, often wealthy landowners who had built their fortune during the construction boom period. They built architecturally grand, multi-storey, multi-purpose buildings with elaborate rooms for drinking coffee and tea and assorted food. No alcohol was served, their point of differentiation from regular hotels. Coffee palaces, built during the first period of economic prosperity in Australia's colonial history, adopted an elaborate High Victorian architectural style, with rich ornamentation and intricate detail. The Federal, opened in Melbourne in 1888, was designed in the French Renaissance style with an extravagantly carved façade, and lavish interiors with chess, billiard, reading, writing and smoking rooms, six lifts and an ice-making plant. Their moniker of 'palace' was not an overstatement.[11] As hotels, coffee palaces were also built to accommodate people travelling from interstate to visit the international exhibitions held in Sydney and Melbourne in the late 19th century. By 1888 there were more than fifty coffee palaces in Melbourne. They were well patronized and were an important part of the city's social life, catering to a wide range of people, including families.

It is perhaps no coincidence that Melbourne, known today as Australia's premier city for café culture, was home to the majority of the early coffee palaces. Some still exist today, now repurposed into regular hotels. One of the better known, the Grand Coffee Palace, is the contemporary Windsor Hotel which, while initially built as a hotel, was later purchased by the Grand Coffee Palace Co. Ltd and converted into a Temperance establishment. The opening of the hotel became the topic of folklore when the hotel's managing director James Munro, struck a match in a symbolic gesture and burnt the hotel's liquor licence. The coffee palaces were found in every capital city, as well as regional areas such as Geelong and Broken Hill and locales as remote as Maria Island on the east coast of Tasmania. They were institutions that were associated with family values that discouraged drunkenness, and were most popular in seaside resorts such as Barwon Heads in Victoria, where they catered to families.

While the Temperance movement lasted well over 100 years, the life of coffee palaces was relatively short-lived. Nevertheless, coffee palaces were very much part of Australia's cultural landscape. A financial crash in Britain in 1891

FIGURE 4.1 19th-century coffee palace, Melbourne, Australia.

meant that banks withdrew their funds in Australia, resulting in a major crash of the construction and banking sectors. Many coffee palace owners, some of whom lost money through land speculation, became bankrupt. Others eventually resorted to applying for liquor licenses and the palaces became the hotels we have today. There was one exception to the coffee palace's demise in Australia. On the west coast of Australia, another gold rush occurred, and coffee palaces had a resurgence which resulted in the establishment of twenty coffee palaces in Perth by 1904.[12]

The rise and decline of the coffee palace in Australia was firmly embedded in the economic fortunes of the 19th-century metropolis. Coffee palaces were built on the crest of an economic boom and land speculation, an activity which is still the major force defining Australian cities today. Although their development was based on a moral imperative to regulate or prohibit the drinking of alcohol, developers of the period saw an opportunity and seized it for the prosperity it promised. After the demise of the coffee palaces, it didn't take long for Australians to abandon coffee drinking and, by 1928, the country had become per capita the world's leading tea-drinking nation.[13]

At the beginning of World War II, Australia was second only to Britain in its tea consumption, and keeping up an adequate tea supply was a challenge for the government.[14] It took another twenty years and major cultural change for the return of coffee to gain a firm foothold in Australia. In this second period of the country's café history, the association with urban development continued, brought about this time by a new wave of European immigrants and another manufacturing boom after World War II.

The second-wave café

> Australians have followed the Italians in making espresso and the French in sitting around in cafés.[15]

It was Italian and Greek immigrants arriving post-war who brought coffee back to Australia in the mid-20th century, with the arrival of the espresso machine and the origins of the café culture we know today. Their presence also signalled the acquisition of broader cultural tastes for the predominantly Anglo-Australians, particularly in the slow switch from tea to coffee as the preferred beverage.

However, the familiar narrative of European migrants' bringing coffee culture to Australia, overlooks the contribution that America played in the Australian coffee story. Prior to the arrival of the espresso machine and post-war European immigration, coffee had re-emerged during the war period with the presence of American servicemen who were stationed in Australian cities for World War II during the 1940s. The American influence in Australia was significant: approximately 250,000 servicemen were stationed in the country, and they came from a coffee-drinking culture. For Americans, coffee was as important as tea was to Australians. American coffee imports constituted the largest share of the world total, and mostly came from Brazil. Supplying the daily ration of coffee to American servicemen became an issue for the Australian government because Australia had insufficient roasting capacity to supply the coffee. To resolve the problem, three roasting machines were shipped to Australia to help meet this new demand.[16] American serviceman quickly became known for their friendliness and generosity and, as Michael Symonds observes in his *Gastronomic History of Australia*:

> when an American got on a friendly footing with an Australian family he was usually found in the kitchen, teaching the Mrs how to make coffee, or washing the dishes.[17]

American servicemen caused something of a stir among the local male population. They were better paid, with smarter uniforms and, more importantly, had winning ways among Australian women. The slogan 'over sexed, over paid and over here' became synonymous with the liaisons that resulted during this period between Australian women and American servicemen. These liaisons resulted in around 15,000 marriages at the end of the war.

Coffee's re-emergence in Australia coincided with the lifting of government controls on coffee importation and was pushed along by the growing influence of American culture and food. By the end of the war, Australian coffee consumption had increased by 500 grams per person per annum. Moreover, the influx of non-British migration and a growing engagement with consumerism contributed to significant shifts occurring with Australian cultural tastes and cultural identity.

The introduction of instant coffee is another interesting twist to the Australian coffee story and was instrumental in coffee's growing popularity. Instant coffee arrived at a time when the American lifestyle had great appeal and the price of tea was increasing. It was relatively cheap and easy to make compared to ground coffee beans.

The Swiss company synonymous with instant coffee, Nescafé, trialled its product on the Australian public during 1939–1940. Nestlé's creation of the new coffee product was in response to the oversupply of coffee from Brazil, brought about by the Wall Street crash in 1929 and the subsequent collapse of coffee prices. In America, Brazil's coffee surplus was immortalized in popular crooner Frank Sinatra's 1946 Coffee Song, written by Hilliard and Dick, with the well-known refrain, 'They've got an awful lot of coffee in Brazil'.

Nestlé was approached by government officials as a company known for its research and innovation, to see whether they could come up with a product that used the coffee bean. It took several years before a solution was found by a chemist, Max Morgenthaler, and Nescafé instant coffee was eventually launched in 1938. By 1940 it was being sold in thirty countries worldwide. In Australia, Nescafé was promoted as a convenient and easy-to-drink coffee. 'It only takes a jiffy to make' was the catchphrase of its advertising jingle. The product captured the imagination of a growing consumer market seeking products that made everyday life more convenient, particularly for women.

With the rising appeal of American culture in Australia, Nescafé came to represent post-war American glamour and modernity. Australia wasn't a hard market to break into; Nescafé already had strong brand recognition via its other products such as condensed milk and baby foods. Along with the endorsement of American servicemen, the coffee's take-up was swift. The arrival of instant coffee to Australia no doubt helped to boost coffee's popularity and the café as a place in which to drink it. In the absence of cafés however, coffee was consumed at home and at work, which later produced another Australian invention. In 1964 the café-bar was invented by a cigarette vending machine company to dispense instant coffee power, milk powder and sugar.[18]Coffee vending machines soon became commonplace, distributed throughout workplaces across the country.

Immigration's influence

Italian and Greek immigrants brought coffee to the country on a broad scale, arriving largely post-World War II, when the Australian government introduced an immigration scheme to assist in Australia's defence and development. Settling in inner cities across the country, immigrants established a range of small businesses, including cafés. The Australian Government had originally targeted migrants from Britain but, by 1949, it was clear that numbers were still insufficient for the country to grow and prosper, and the government was forced to recruit people from other parts of Europe. This was a potential problem for an insular and largely Anglo-Australia which had, in 1901, introduced a restrictive immigration policy, the Immigration Restriction Act, also known as the 'White Australia Policy'. The legislation was specifically designed to limit non-British migration to Australia and allowed for the deportation of 'undesirable' people who had settled in any Australian colony prior to federation. The policy was partly a response to Anglo-centric anti-migration sentiments, which were expressed during the gold rush period and thereafter, due to the influx of migrants from the Asia-Pacific region.

After World War II the policy was relaxed and eventually abandoned. By 1953, migrants from southern Europe outnumbered British immigrants, who were seeking a better future for themselves and their families fleeing a war-ravaged Europe. Concerned that Australians would resent their arrival, the government set about reassuring the local population, letting them know that the reason for southern European migration was that workers were needed for 'labour on rugged projects ... work which is not generally acceptable to Australians or British workers'.[19] Migrants soon found work in a post-war booming manufacturing industry and the government-supported Snowy River Hydroelectric scheme.

European immigrants established homes mainly in inner-city suburbs, across Sydney and Melbourne and to a lesser extent in other capital cities, as well as numerous large country towns. Rents and property were cheap because the vast majority of Australians lived in the suburbs, where a house and garden was considered the most desirable way to live. Across inner cities, immigrants established networks of businesses, clubs and services which catered for their interests, and distinct cultural precincts arose in areas such as Carlton, Melbourne and Leichardt, Sydney. In these inner-city locations, Italians and Greeks opened continental-style cafés, which provided a social and cultural hub for their predominantly European patrons. It was the large-scale importation of the Italian-made espresso coffee machines during the 1950s that heralded the transformation of coffee culture.

Although the first commercial espresso machine had been imported and installed in Melbourne's Café Florentino in 1928, the earlier models lacked the large-scale and milk-frothing capacities of the later models. Changes occurred with the arrival of a more sophisticated espresso machine from Italy in 1948, the machine we are familiar with today. Espresso coffee was made milkier with the creation of frothy milk for a cappuccino. It enabled the crema (the brownish foam that forms on top of espresso coffee) to be produced using water with a lever-driven piston rather than steam. Its innovation over earlier models was its greater water pressure, which flowed through a more tightly packed puck of coffee. This method also improved the flavour of the beans. The company who developed the machine, Gaggia, promoted the milky foam as 'Crema Caffe Naturale' or natural coffee cream. Disputes over who was the first person to import the machine to Australia have been longstanding, but it is commonly agreed that 1954 was the year that the first Gaggia espresso machines appeared in Melbourne cafés. Peter Bancroft had installed one in his Cafe Il Capuccino in St Kilda, a bayside suburb, and it wasn't long before other café entrepreneurs purchased the Gaggia espresso machines, among them the Universita Cafe in Lygon Street and Pellegrini's in Bourke Street in Melbourne. Gino di Santo was also active in Sydney, bringing espresso machines to the big department store's cafés, such as David Jones and Mark Foys in 1955.

Imported espresso machines soon dominated the market, but it wasn't long before a challenge came from a team of Sydney-based entrepreneurs and manufacturers. The Australian company Bo-Ema, capitalizing on the espresso revolution, produced their first machine in 1956. And while Italian machines were being manufactured under licence in Melbourne, the Bo-Emas were the first wholly Australian-made machines. Soon installed in Sydney cafés, including the well-known American Coffee Lounge in Wynyard, the company still designs and manufactures espresso machines today.

With the introduction of espresso machines, coffee was quickly adopted, and more cafés appeared across Australian cities.

Older-style tearooms were transformed into coffee lounges during the 1950s and espresso bars in Melbourne and Sydney began to appear, modelled on an Italian style. The early café designs were based on traditional Italian cafés, including features such as tessellated floor tiles, marble benchtops and drop lighting, evoking a European culture and ambience. They quickly gained popularity, mainly among the country's migrant population. The famous Pelligrini's Espresso Bar, still operating today, and the Legend Cafe opened in 1954 and 1956 respectively in Melbourne. In Sydney, Bar Coluzzi was established in 1957, followed by the Lincoln Coffee Lounge and Cafe in Rowe Street and Repin's in Pitt Street. The profusion of cafés in Sydney's inner-city areas where immigrants settled prompted Arnold Haskell, writing in *Waltzing Matilda*, to declare that Sydney now had a 'Cafe Society'. He remarked, somewhat flamboyantly, that 'King's Cross has been taken straight out of Paris and dumped into Sydney'.[20]The style of coffee that people were drinking was transported direct from Europe and, in spite of the espresso machines' association with cappuccinos and frothy milk, cappuccinos were rare and it was mainly espresso coffee that was sold. The ubiquitous flat white was non-existent then, let alone the plethora of varieties we consume today.

Largely patronized by European immigrants, some cafés and espresso bars aroused suspicion among sections of a conservative, post-war, predominantly Anglophone population. The concern that illegal activities and gambling might be taking place echoed an unease by authorities about café patrons which is centuries old. Examples of this are littered throughout the café's history, from its origins in the Middle East when various imams viewed the coffeehouse as places where political activity such as conspiracy and insurrection occurred. Such was the concern that eventually cafés were banned for Muslims in the period between 1512 and 1524. Subsequent monarchs and leaders throughout history have banned cafés – from early cafés in Istanbul to cafés in 17th-century London, where monarchs feared that sedition was being plotted. In Australia, this suspicion was short-lived as more locals acquired the taste for coffee.

Towards the late 1950s and into the 1960s the café's interior departed from its European template and began to adapt to new trends in interior design. This period coincided with a rise in local manufacturing and a greater awareness of design, with the establishment of several professional design organizations, including the Design Council of Australia in 1958. Coffee lounges and cafés came to epitomize a new, modern culture influenced by developments in the United States and Europe. Sleek chrome counter edges, cosy booths and chequerboard linoleum floors showcased new materials, manufacturing and design innovations. As a prominent and essential part of the café, espresso machines were also highly designed. Chromed finishes with futuristic rounded edges in the 1950s gave way to more functional, streamlined and harder lines in the 1960s.

While Italian and Greek immigrants might have been responsible for bringing espresso coffee to Australia, both arrived from different cultures and each, therefore, has left their unique cultural imprints on the café's development. Greek immigrants transported a different style of café culture which began with their arrival in Australia during the 1920s as a result of the 1919–1922 Greco-Turkish War. The conflict, linked to the partitioning of the Ottoman Empire and the World War I, resulted in the genocide of millions of Greek nationals. During the interwar period, the number of Greeks migrating to Australia increased substantially. Greece's coffee-drinking traditions came directly from the Ottoman Empire, of which it had been a part for hundreds of years. Originally known as Turkish coffee, it was later renamed Greek coffee when Greece gained independence from Turkey. It's made by boiling coffee grounds which are sugared to produce a rich, thick brew, and is drunk without milk.

In Alexakis and Janiszewski's book, *Greek Cafés and Milk Bars in Australia* (2016), the authors claim that the Greek café and milk bar became the 'Trojan Horse' for the Americanization of eating and social habits from the beginning of the 20th century in Australia. Greeks opened cafés throughout Australian cities and country towns and they played a key role in transporting, adapting and popularizing American food and drink culture to what was at the time a monocultural Australian palette. Greek migrants, drawing on their diasporas in the United States, introduced food such as hamburgers, chips, milkshakes and sodas and continued to serve espresso coffee. Their influence didn't stop at food and beverages and many Greek cafés were models of architectural style, transporting a 'streamline moderne' Art Deco type of architecture where customers sat in booths listening to the latest popular music on the jukebox.

In some places, Greek cafés acquired a certain cachet and were often the only places to socialize during the evenings because they remained open for long hours. They became important social places for gathering in cities, suburbs and towns and provided a more socially inclusive alternative to the traditional male-dominated pub. Joan Margaritis waitressed in Greek cafés in Queensland during the early 1970s and considers that 'you felt at home in a Greek café', that 'they were the focal point…where people used to meet…"I'll meet you at the Greeks", was a popular saying'. The cafés were selling the American dream, with names like the California, Hollywood, Monterey and the Niagara – connoting that life could perhaps be more exotic. The importation of American food rather than their own traditional Greek cuisine was strategic and prudent of Greek immigrants. In a period of racial and cultural Anglo exclusivity during the years of the White Australia policy, it was a safer option.[21]

Australian's initial reserve about European migrants and later Asian migrants settling in Australia has been challenged by the significant contribution migrants have made to the cultural life and the economy of the country. During the mid-20th-century period of mass immigration, the establishment of small businesses by Greek, Italian and Hungarian migrants was an attractive source of employment, providing regular income, maintenance of the family unit, and potential social and economic mobility, particularly for future generations. They also provided independence from union restrictions on foreign labour and required only limited formal education and knowledge of English. Later, during the 1970s and post-Vietnam war, it was the Vietnamese who became the new small business operators, introducing Australia to Asian cuisine. While Italian and Greek-owned cafés were more numerous in Australian cities, throughout country regions in Australia, Greek cafés provided one of the very few eating and social places of country towns.

FIGURE 4.2 Astoria Café, Newcastle, Australia, circa 1940. Photo credit: © National Project Archives, Macquarie University.

21st-century café culture

> We recently opened a cafe with a closed theme, that's its name, the Closed Cafe. It's playful, experimental...it's *confusing!* Every single bean is grown individually and then positively affirmed from a young age—you're great!—and then brought together in Tibetan singing bowls.
>
> *'The Bondi Hipsters', aka Christiaan Van Vuuren and Nick Boshier*[22]

Australia might be a world leader in specialty coffee, where artisan skills and connoisseurship are paramount, but such dedication to the connoisseurship of the bean can sit awkwardly with a national distrust of success, and a population quick to sniff out any whiff of pretension. Satire is an effective strategy which can lay bare a nation's cultural vulnerabilities, and the connoisseurship of coffee culture is sometimes the target of satirists such as comedic duo the Bondi Hipsters, quoted above, who poke fun at Australian contemporary culture. The signature coffee for a skit in which they have opened their Closed Café ('we don't want anyone to belong or feel part of a tribe') is the Frackacino. According to the Hipsters, the coffee is based on the controversial fracking process, 'not only devastating to planet earth but a unique way of filtering coffee...a process that filters the coffee mixture down into the dirt and filters up through the aquifer, contaminating it and producing a great cup of coffee'.

Café culture took a couple of decades to reach the artisan-inspired focus it is known for today. Throughout the 1970s, 1980s and early 1990s, urban café culture continued its slow growth in Australian cities. Urban revitalization from the mid-1990s was the first sign of major changes occurring in cities. It was heralded by the implementation of the Building Better Cities Program 1992, a federal Labor government initiative which spawned a series of urban renewal and infrastructure programs in cities across the country. Town planning regulations during urban renewal periods of the 1990s mandated for mixed-use development to activate streets, encouraging the establishment of commercial urban amenities such as cafés and restaurants. Throughout the next decade, the intensification of urban development produced an explosion of amenities – of cafés, bars and restaurants throughout Australia's inner-city areas. In Brisbane, the removal of the ban on outdoor eating spawned an instant culture of outdoor cafés and restaurants. For a city with a subtropical climate, being able to eat and drink outside was a long overdue boon and it became an instant success.

Melbourne has a reputation as the coffee capital of Australia, but a vibrant, independent café culture exists in Sydney, Brisbane and all the country's cities. Sprawling beyond inner cities, café culture is making its mark across suburban and regional locations. Metropolitan cafés can be found much like cafés the world over, in converted industrial and commercial buildings and in former domestic dwellings such as terrace row houses and timber houses, which line the high streets of inner cities. Improvised spaces extend to café carts wedged between buildings, garden sheds and converted petrol stations. While some cafés come and go, they mostly seem to stay. And across inner city areas cafés are always busy.

During the mid-1990s, a series of developments in coffee gradually saw a more complex product evolve, with a focus on the provenance and terroir of the bean, artisanal methods and a range of brewing techniques. In the café itself, the experience was something the urban population gravitated to, and filled a need that entrepreneurs were quick to seize. A new breed of café entrepreneurs, drawing on the traditions of Italian and Greek immigrants, experimented with espresso coffee – from roasting to brewing – producing the variety and types of brews available today. Whether this occurred in tandem with other coffee entrepreneurs in other countries is hard to say but, somewhere along the way, the flat white became synonymous with Australian coffee. A flat white differs from the traditional latte or cappuccino in that it is usually made up of a double ristretto and lightly textured milk. There's less foam than in a latte. A ristretto is a short shot of espresso coffee, made with the normal amount of ground coffee but extracted with about half the amount of water, giving it a rich flavour.

The arrival of specialty coffee was supported by a population with a strong preference for independent cafés. Against this backdrop, Starbucks didn't stand a chance and the company could not have done much research before they launched over eighty cafés in 2001. If the company had been familiar with Australian tastes and habits they might have predicted how locals would view Starbucks coffee, as distinct from Australian specialty coffee as chalk and cheese. Moreover, as a community hub, the café is more likely to attract local customers who know the staff and feel a loyalty to support their local businesses.

FIGURE 4.3 Busy café in Carlton, Melbourne, Australia. Photo credit: © Chrissie Trabucco.

Australian coffee importers and roasters have established successful businesses and several export internationally while remaining based in the country. Brisbane-based Merlo Coffee and Di Bella Coffee, both with Italian origins, are market leaders with Merlo an early arrival on the Australian specialty coffee scene over twenty-five years ago. Melbourne-based Grinders, also with Italian origins, have been operating in various forms since 1965. Sydney company Campos and Melbourne's Seven Seeds are two other companies who emerged early on in the specialty coffee scene, and many more too numerous to mention.

The first Australian specialty coffee roasteries were established in the early 1990s and the Australian Specialty Coffee Association (ASCA) was founded in 2001. Café owners have collaborated to promote specialty coffee to consumers

FIGURE 4.4 Café extension in improvised space, inner city Brisbane, Australia. Photo credit: © Tricia King.

FIGURE 4.5 Café in inner city Brisbane, Australia, adapted from vernacular housing. Photo credit: © Tricia King.

in Australia, to try new methods of roasting and ensure the distribution of information. There are a plethora of national and international competitions to challenge and improve competitors' roasting techniques, latte art and barista skills. Australians have performed well, and in the World Barista Championships in 2015 Sasa Setic won overall, helping to cement the reputation of the coffee professional's expertise. The gold standard of barista skills, the competition began in 2000 and an Australian has made it to the final rounds of nearly every World Barista Competition since 2008. The first Melbourne International Coffee Expo, a coffee-dedicated trade show, was held in 2012 and Australia continues to host world coffee events.

Australian baristas have garnered an international reputation and are sought after for their expertise. Their rise in the pantheon of global baristas has been swift, as has the growth of the specialty coffee movement, occurring over a short period of time. For instance, in the 2001 Australian Census, the term barista was not even listed as a profession. Things changed in the next five-year census and by 2006, 8,000 baristas were registered. But by the following 2011 census the number had exploded to 22,000.

Australian coffee skills are exported in the form of coffee education, which has become something of an import export industry. Several national companies that offer barista and Q grading training market to potential café entrepreneurs throughout Asian countries. Australian training standards are highly regarded internationally, and students earn valued international certificates of accreditation. Some barista training schools target international university students, encouraging them to learn English while they learn their barista skills. Successful coffee professionals also hire their expertise as coffee consultants.

Exporting Australian café culture

Since the beginning of the 21st century, Australian café culture has flourished both domestically and internationally. Australia has exported its café culture to cities across the world, located in what were, or are, emerging areas of gentrification. When Australian cafés first appeared in Brooklyn, New York or Soho, London, these areas were the more affordable parts of the city, on the cusp of gentrification. A crop of Melbourne café entrepreneurs who established café businesses in New York from the early 2000s have given their cafés Australian-inspired names, in a nod to their home town. Bluestone Lane is named after the paving stones in Melbourne laneways; Flinders Lane and Little Collins are streets in Melbourne. Some flout their Australian origin with the moniker The Thirsty Koala and the Northern Territory. Nicholas Stone's Bluestone Collective has become a chain, with fourteen locations across New York and others in Philadelphia and San Francisco. Such are Australian cafés' reputations that a café in Sausalito, San Francisco, sported a sign on its window saying 'We make coffee as good as Australians'. In London, Peter Hall opened Flat White in 2005, and a host of other cafés have since followed, including Kaffeine and Workshop Cafe Company, both winning European awards. Australian café culture has made it to the heart of 19th-century café culture in Paris, and across the cities of Barcelona and Beijing.

It would be an exaggeration to claim that Australian cafés are present in vast numbers in global cities, but it's something of a curiosity that the style of café has been transported in the numbers it has. Various reasons are offered for this successful export in the last decade. Among these are that, on the local front, cafés have proved to be financially rewarding and have provided the model for a potentially lucrative export industry. But this couldn't occur if many Australians didn't have the ability to earn and accumulate money, especially when compared with people from many other countries. It provides an adventurous entrepreneur with more capital and freedom to establish businesses abroad. Australians are keen travellers and, in 2016, 38% of the country's 24-million population left on a short-term basis. Five per cent of the country's population is expatriated in other countries, the majority in Europe.

But perhaps the café's success has more to do with the type of coffee and café styles being exported. There's a common view among the foodie community that it's not simply Australian coffee that's responsible for the export success story, but rather the total café experience. The influence of Australian café styles includes the type of food sold, table service and high-quality coffee for dine in or take away, something far less common in other parts of the world.[23] In Europe and the United States, espresso bars serving pastries or all-day cafés without the artisanship of Australian coffee are the norm. Australian café food, by contrast, is characterized by its versatility and freshness, so the items that appear on a breakfast menu might also suffice for a light lunch. Eggs cooked any way and avocado on toast are ubiquitous; bircher muesli and array of freshly made gourmet sandwiches are everyday items on café menus. The change in eating patterns, food and beverages requires adaption for the traditional cultures in which the Australian café has been exported. Assisted by global flows of products, foods and beverages in a closely connected world, the flat white and avocado on toast have found their way onto menus in cafés across the globe. In Paris, once the café capital of the world, several Australian-style cafés have made their mark, replacing the traditional breakfast of croissant and tartine or yoghurt and fruits with foods such as eggs and avocado. Honor, Hardware Societe and Holybelly and Fondation Café serve Australian coffee and food and are part or fully owned by Australians.

For Australia, as a post-colonial and multicultural nation, tradition is less of an encumbrance than it is for countries whose cuisine and culture has developed and survived over long periods of time. The country's relatively short period of British colonization and its amalgam of ethnicities have provided Australia with freedom and licence to experiment with aspects of culture that might be considered sacrosanct elsewhere. Its multicultural population – 180 nationalities – has endowed the country with a myriad of culinary and aesthetic experiences from which to draw upon. Australian experimentation and innovation with food culture has been vigorous since the early 1990s, where the imaginative synthesis of Asian, European and Middle Eastern traditions produced food that has garnered international recognition. The espresso, cold press and French press are styles of coffee that have long traditions, but they have also provided the basis for experimentation and innovation.

Home-grown coffee

Australia imports most of its coffee from coffee-producing nations, including from its near neighbour Indonesia. Currently at about 90,000 tonnes a year,

FIGURE 4.6 Food board in Australian café. Photo credit: © Tricia King.

FIGURE 4.7 Fresh food typical of Australian cafés. Photo credit: © Tricia King.

coffee imports have been growing steadily each year since the beginning of the century, with only a slight decline in 2017.[24] While it's almost completely dependent on imports, Australia does, however, produce its own coffee, but only the higher-quality Arabica bean that's used in the specialty or roast and ground market. Coffee grows in the subtropical regions of northern New South Wales and North Queensland, where the climate is best suited to this bean.

In recent years Australian-grown coffee has continued to gain recognition as the consumption of coffee has increased and the distinctive qualities of Australian coffee have become more broadly recognized and appreciated. It is 10–15% lower in caffeine than most imported coffee and is noted for its sweetness and medium body. The lower rate of caffeine has been attributed to the fact that the bean is grown in a comparatively stress-free environment without serious pests or disease. However, its quality in comparison to coffee from coffee-producing nations is a subject of debate among connoisseurs. While some specialty cafés stock Australian coffee, there are others who regard it as inferior, principally because it is argued that the best coffee is found grown in equatorial regions at high altitude.[25]

As noted earlier in the chapter, Australian-grown coffee went into decline during the 1920s and it took another sixty years before production picked up again in the mid 1980s. The invention of mechanical harvesting, which made labour cheaper as well as the high quality of Arabica coffee produced from the earlier plantings, created a renewed vigour in the Australian coffee industry. One of the largest among the current crop of coffee farms is the award-winning Skybury Estate in the Atherton Tablelands in north Queensland, established in 1987. Skybury exports approximately 60% of its coffee to Europe, Japan and the United States due to the fragmentation of local markets. Coffee production almost doubled in a five-year period from 1998 to 2003 in plantations in North Queensland. Among coffee farms in northern New South Wales in the same period, production increased fivefold from 20 tonnes to 100 tonnes.[26] While coffee production is still a developing industry in Australia, with an estimated fifty commercial coffee growers producing coffee on a total of 300–350 hectares, it is more likely that coffee consumption rather than coffee production will keep rising. Australia produces such a small amount and price can be prohibitive, making it hard to compete on the larger world stage.

While coffee consumption in Australia is rising, there is also a concern among some in the independent specialty café community that the economics underpinning the café are under pressure. Mounting operating costs and a limit on what Australians will pay for coffee means that healthy margins are diminishing. Several well-established cafés have recently closed in Melbourne and several café owners I spoke with wondered whether the country had reached 'peak' café. Although Australians, in the main, place a premium on artisan coffee and have replaced tea with coffee as their favoured drink, they are not high consumers of the brew in comparison to many other countries. Australia ranks only forty-second in the world at three kilograms per year per capita. None the less, if the relationship between café culture and urban growth remains, it's unlikely that coffee consumption will decrease.

Australia's rapidly expanding population is occurring in its cities, with the highest growth in the country's two largest cities of Melbourne and Sydney, whose populations hover around five million. Melbourne has experienced massive growth of one million people in a ten-year period, and Sydney's expansion is not far behind. Population increase has well outstripped that of government forecasts. And despite a public discourse which hovers between a quiet acceptance of immigration to more vocal and vociferous objections, successive governments have continued to support relatively high levels of immigration. Governments of all persuasions recognize the value of immigration for the health of the country's economy.

A contributing factor to the growth in Australian cities is an historical retreat from suburban living; people are flocking to amenity-dense urban and inner-urban locations. Urban historian Graeme Davison famously wrote that 'Australia was born urban and quickly grew suburban'.[27] Since 18th-century colonization, Australians have been deeply wedded to suburban living, inheriting the British aspiration for a house and garden. As a retreat from the city, the suburbs were regarded as the most desirable way to live, particularly for families. But that's all changing now, and even families – something unheard of until recently – have taken to apartment living in unanticipated numbers. As a consequence, many urban and inner-urban areas are undergoing revitalization and intense re-development. The new high-rise apartments and regenerated urban precincts might, at times, be controversial for their height, scale, design and lack of planning controls, but they all share the popular amenity that café culture provides. Among the environs, new inhabitants flock to their cafés to gather and meet, drink their daily brew and to be somewhere that's not-quite-home or not-quite-work. Influenced by immigration, urban regeneration and the ideals of cosmopolitanism, Australians have begun to embrace urban life, perhaps for the first time since white settlement.

Notes

1 Nourse, Pat. 2017. "Why Australian coffee is the best in the word and where to drink it." *Aussie Cuisine.* https://aussiecuisine.com.au/2017/07/why-australian-coffee-is-the-best-in-the-world-and-where-to-drink-it/, July 20. Ret. 21.5.18.
2 Payal, MGM 2016: "MICE 2016: 3 days of specialty coffee heaven in Australia." *Perfect Daily Grind.* https://www.perfectdailygrind.com/2016/05/mice-2016-3-days-specialty-coffee-heaven-australia/, May 6. Ret. 10.9.17.
3 "Cafes and coffee shops – Australia market research report." *Ibis World.* https://www.ibisworld.com.au/industry-trends/market-research-reports/accommodation-food-services/cafes-coffee-shops.html, January 2018. Ret. 29.06.18.
4 Ellis, Markman. 2004. *The Coffee House: A Cultural History.* London: Weidenfeld and Nicolson.Hattox, Ralph. 1985. *Coffee and Coffeehouses: The Origins of a Social Beverage in the Medieval Near East.* Seattle, WA: University of Washington Press.
5 Khamis, Susie. 2009. "'It only takes a jiffy to make': Nestlé, Australia and the convenience of instant coffee." *Food, Culture and Society: An International Journal of Multidisciplinary Research*, Volume 12, Issue 2, pp. 217–233 (p. 5).
6 Low, Tim. 1989. *Bush Tucker: Australia's Wild Food Harvest.* Sydney: Angus and Robertson Publishers, p. 27.
7 *Taste Australia.* http://tasteaustralia.biz/bushfood/wattleseed/. Ret.13.7.17.
8 *Food and Beverage Industry News.* https://foodmag.com.au/Wattle-seed-latte-a-bush-tucker-alternative-to-coffee. Ret. 24.7.17.
9 Symonds, Michael. 2007. *One Continuous Picnic: A Gastronomic History of Australia.* Melbourne: Melbourne University Publishing, p. 132.
10 Wilson, Elizabeth. 1991. *The Sphinx in the City:* Urban Life, the Control of Disorder, and Women. Oakland, CA: University of California Press.
11 Noyce, Diana Christine. 2012. "Coffee palaces in Australia: A pub with no beer." *M/C Media Culture Journal* online, Volume 15, Issue 2.
12 Noyce, Diana Christine. 2012. Ibid.
13 Khamis, Susie. 2009. Ibid.
14 Adams, Jillian Elaine. 2012. "Marketing Tea against a Turning Tide: Coffee and the Tea Council of Australia 1963–1974." *M/C Media Culture Journal* online, Volume 15, Issue 2.
15 Symonds, Michael. 2007. Ibid., p. 324.

16 Adams, Jillian Elaine. 2012. Ibid.
17 Symonds, Michael. 2007. Ibid., p. 165.
18 Symonds, Michael. 2007. Ibid., p. 224.
19 Grieve Black, Robert 2012 *The Story of Australia*. Self-published. ISBN: 9781105578298, p. 81.
20 Symonds, Michael. 2007. Ibid., p. 261.
21 Alexakis, Effy and Janiszewski, Leonard. 2016. *Greek Cafés and Milk Bars of Australia*. Sydney: Halstead Press.
22 Van Vuuren, Christiaan and Boshier, Nick. 2016. http://www.dailymail.co.uk/video/tvshowbiz/video-1146492/The-Bondi-Hipsters-introduce-The-Closed-Caf.html.
23 Hassard, Cam. 2017. "Third Wave Coffee and how Australia is paving the way." *The Upsider*. http://theupsider.com.au/third-wave-coffee-and-how-australia-is-paving-the-way/1766. Ret. 10.9.17.
24 Australia Green Coffee Imports by Year. 2018. *Indexmundi*. https://www.indexmundi.com/agriculture/?country=au&commodity=green-coffee&graph=imports.
25 AgriFutures Australia. 2018. "Coffee." *AgriFutures*. https://www.agrifutures.com.au/farm-diversity/coffee/, May 24. Ret. 18.7.18.
26 AgriFutures Australia. 2018. Ibid.
27 Davison, Graeme. 1994. "The past and future of the Australian suburb." In *Suburban Dreaming: An Interdisciplinary Approach to Australian Cities*. Ed. L. Johnson. Geelong, Victoria: Deakin University Press, p. 98.

5

CAFÉS IN ASIA

Japan

> A commodity with a long and complex chronicle of consumption and production, coffee is a perennially global product par excellence.
>
> *James Lyons*[1]

Introduction

Café culture is a truly global phenomenon, and perhaps some of its most interesting manifestations are to be found across Asian cities, where local and hybrid cultures have produced distinctive café experiences. Third-wave-style café culture is growing at a phenomenal rate in Asian cities, where populations are higher and more youthful than cities in the global north. While people of all ages frequent cafés, the cafés I visited in Asian cities tended to be patronized by a predominantly youthful clientele. In cities such as Bangkok, Seoul, Hanoi, Mumbai, Delhi, Taipei and many others, a thriving café culture animates the metropolitan landscape. Better known for their tea-drinking cultures, Asian countries' coffee culture is on the ascendency, and it's not just consumption based. The 2016 World Barista Championship in Dublin – the industry's gold standard competition for baristas – was won by Berg Wu from Taiwan; in 2014 it was won by Hidenoru Izaki from Japan. This competition has been hosted by a different city each year since it began in 2000 in Monte Carlo, Monaco, and in 2017 for the first time was hosted by an Asian city, Seoul in South Korea. Café culture is by no means limited to these Asian cities, and this chapter begins its exploration of Asian café culture in the world's most densely populated city of 37 million inhabitants, Tokyo in Japan.

Like the café's historical ascendency in cities across the world, Japan's café history is closely linked to its metropolitan development. Shaped by colonial exchange, Western modernity, local entrepreneurship and gender relations, Japanese café culture is culturally rich and varied. From temples of connoisseurship to tiny holes in the wall, the café in Japan provides a window into the country's unique culture.

Global/local

The café, like many industries, is embedded in a global network of transnational economic and cultural flows. One of the major criticisms of globalization is the ways in which it impacts on local cultures – the argument being that what is unique about a place and its local culture is diminished in service to global capital, producing an homogenized consumer culture (sometimes referred to as the McDonaldization of the world). Although the tentacles of globalization are evident in cities everywhere, it would be a crude assessment to say that local cultures have been obliterated. It is true that the third-wave style of cafés I visited in several Asian cities displayed all the hallmarks of a standardized, global café culture: dedication to coffee roasting and brewing, an emphasis on origin beans, an armoury of coffee-making equipment and the ubiquitous minimalist café aesthetic. Nonetheless, a distinctive local presence invariably announced its robust existence upon entering the café. The vernacular stamp appears in a variety of ways – in the accommodation of local foods, such as in the type of coffee – macha lattes for instance and the types of Japanese-inspired pastries – to the interiors whose elements, even in third-wave cafés, incorporate local aesthetic details. Not all cafés in Asian cities are third-wave either; as we shall see, this is especially the case in Japan, which has had a strong coffee-drinking culture for over a century.

National histories and traditions are embedded in a country's food and drink cultures, declaring their distinction. None of this is easily eradicated. Other aspects of culture prevent the complete subservience to globalism, however intangible this may seem on first appearance. Face-to-face interaction and in-situ cultural absorption produce intangible but real feelings that are unique to a place. This is especially the case in the food industries, and in the act of drinking coffee, where sensory experience is paramount. Our 'sensorium' is harnessed in the café - the taste of the coffee, its smell, the sounds of the café and coffee machines, and the sights we see are all products of the local culture. As David Howes points out, the senses are imbued with cultural meaning and social values, which are not necessarily articulated through language, but practised and experienced.[2]

Japan: Direct origins

The broad appeal of contemporary café culture in Asian countries might be well known now through internet communication and travel, but coffee had found its way into parts of Asia well before the 21st century. The Asian part of the coffee story begins in Japan, because contrary to the cultural stereotype of Japan as a nation of ritual tea-drinkers, Japan had a well-established, sophisticated coffee culture for over 100 years, long before specialty coffee appeared in the West. Such was Japan's enthusiasm for coffee that, in 1907, the world's first coffeehouse chain store, Paulista, was created by a Japanese entrepreneur who had links to the Brazilian coffee industry.[3]

The popular Hario V60, an inverted, cone-shaped funnel which slowly extracts coffee through a filter, was invented in Tokyo by a company that first produced this style of coffee maker in 1949. The pour-over is the preferred method of coffee making in Japan and the Hario V60 is used among coffee connoisseurs around the world in combination with a Hario kettle, whose long, elegant gooseneck spout allows water to be spiralled from a height. The country is the third biggest importer of coffee after the United States and Germany, and in a recent development, according to the All Japan Coffee Association, Japanese consume twice as much coffee as green tea.

Among coffee aficionados, Japan is the country credited with setting the high benchmark for specialty coffee worldwide. In fact, Merry White in her book *Coffee Life in Japan* argues that Japan is where specialty coffee first began. Japanese coffee makers are known for their extraordinary attention to detail and the care taken at each stage of the process: from bean selection to the level of roast and grind, and the technique of the maker. An important element that defines coffee culture in Japan is *kodawari,* a Japanese term which refers to the desire and goal for perfection, dedication to work, perfecting the skill, attention to details and fastidiousness. *Kodawari* can apply to many areas of endeavour and is embodied in the person or master, and therefore the product they create. The attention and care taken to try and perfect a cup of coffee can seem almost religious or sacred from a Western perspective. Today the term has been somewhat corrupted, and *kodawari* is now used as a commodity for marketing purposes, liberally applied to a diverse range of products, from *kodawari* restaurants to *kodawari* yoga studios.

In Japan, coffee first arrived on Dutch and Portuguese boats operating in Dejima, Nagasaki prefecture during the Edo period (1603–1868) in the 16th century. The Japanese word for coffee is *kouhii* (コーヒー) and originates from the Dutch word *koffie.* It was first traded in 1724 and was used for medicinal purposes – to strengthen the appetite, cure headaches and 'women's diseases' and stop diarrhoea.[4] International trade was limited during the Edo period and coffee was initially only available to a select strata of society – Imperial governors,

FIGURE 5.1 Coffee brewing in Tokyo, Japan café. Photo credit: © Emma Felton.

merchants and translators. It was regarded as bitter and rather unpleasant, and due to this and its limited distribution, was not widely consumed.

Coffee took off when Japan opened up to Western trade for the first time in 200 years during the Meji period at the end of the 19th century. The café, or *kissaten* as it later became known, was introduced during this time. From the outset, coffeehouses (as they were known) were linked to modernity, Western influences and urbanization. And like today's global café, its rapid take-up and popularity was essentially an urban phenomenon.[5] The first coffeehouse in Japan appeared at a time of rapid political, social and urban change, which was resonant of its establishment in other parts of the world.

During the 19th century Edo became Tokyo and the concentration of state power was a stabilizer. The first coffeehouse, named Kahiichakan, appeared here in 1888 and was opened by Tei Ei-kei, who had studied at Yale University in America, where he acquired the taste for coffee. On his way home, he travelled to London and although the coffeehouses were on the wane, due to the influx of tea as the colonies harvest was in surplus, he enjoyed London's coffeehouses as places of conversation and information. The story goes that he wanted to do "something for the younger generation by opening a coffeehouse, which would be a space to share knowledge, a social salon where ordinary people, students and youth could gather".[6] His two-storey coffeehouse in Tokyo was inspired by the Western traditions he encountered in London and America and as common for the era, catered for masculine tastes and interests. It offered reasonably priced coffee with newspapers, leather chairs, pool tables, desks, stationery, baths and even rooms where patrons could nap. Unfortunately, Tei Ei-kei was not a savvy business person and the café was closed only five years after it opened. Such is the reverence for coffee in Japan that a brick monument topped by a large white coffee cup was erected on the site of the country's first coffeehouse in front of the Sanyo building in Ueno, Tokyo.

With the establishment of the Meji period (1868–1912), the coffeehouse really began to gain a foothold in Japanese urban life. This was a period of radical change in Japan's history and the beginning of Modern Japan. The Meiji government promoted widespread Westernization, importing Western advisers with expertise in fields such as education, science, industry and mining. Such was the enthusiasm for all things Western, that during this period the Japanese adopted Western clothing and hairstyles.[7] Urbanization grew, and many rural workers moved to the city in search of work. Coffeehouses became popular very quickly and were established around transport nodes and the newly established railway stations. Coffeehouses acquired cachet as a symbol of Western modernity and attributes of the newly introduced Western lifestyle. As Grinshpun notes:

> They served as entry points for foreign products, and shaped new local fashions and trends resonating with the wider international context. To some Japanese commentators of the era, the cafés ranked in significance with the establishment of the Diet.[8]

Although the Japanese café began as a 'Western' concept and a symbol of the modern, it soon became 'Japanese modern'. In other words, it assumed its own identity and distinction, in a departure from European café culture.

Perhaps better known for its teahouses, known as the *chaya*, the Japanese coffeehouse bears little resemblance to its teahouses. Apart from the differences in beverages – no green tea or dango was served in the coffeehouse —there were considerable differences between the social functions of the traditional teahouse and the coffeehouse.[9] The teahouse was a highly ritualized space and a gathering place for social engagement, usually among people who were very familiar with each other. By contrast, the coffeehouse offered a more open and fluid site, more able to be put to individual use. Newspapers and tobacco were provided, and the furnishings were modern – Western table sets and bars. Coffeehouses appeared in Japan around the same time as transport hubs developed and were dotted around the new entertainment and communication centres of cities. From the beginning, they became associated with a spirit of cosmopolitanism rather than tradition as in the tea house. As Merry White observes, they provided a place where 'identities were not confined by older social codes'.[10] Indeed, for an urban dweller living in a densely populated city such as Tokyo, one of the contemporary café's primary assets is that it offers privacy *as well as* social communion. Crowded living conditions and the intensity of familial and social obligations can mean that privacy is hard to come by and there are few places to be private in public. For a short period of time, the café sanctions a reprieve from social and domestic duties.

Direct trade: Brazilian connections

Another contributing factor to the development of Japan's unique coffee culture is that the country imported coffee directly from Brazil, not via Europe as had occurred in other countries such as China and Australia. How this came to happen is a curious story, beginning with one of the more egregious features of colonialism. Towards the end of the 19th century, Brazilian coffee farmers were low on agricultural labour. Coffee plantations were worked largely by African slaves, and Brazil was in the throes of abolition, being the last country to abolish African slavery in 1888. The Indigenous Indian workers were also no longer a robust source of labour, many having succumbed to diseases of the time. To keep its thriving and profitable coffee industry afloat, Brazil established an agreement to recruit workers from Japan and Europe. The Brazilian government designated Japan as a key partner in the development of the coffee industry and the two countries signed a treaty permitting Japanese migration to Brazil to bolster trade between the two nations. Between 1908 and 1924, about 35,000 Japanese arrived in Brazil ready to work on coffee farms. Today, Brazil remains the largest exporter of unroasted and instant coffee to Japan.

Merry White tells the intriguing story of Mizuno Ryu, a dynamic Japanese entrepreneur, who had walked across the Andes to reach Brazil where he organized the first and subsequent recruitment of Japanese labour to the coffee plantations. He became the founder of the world's first coffeehouse chain, Paulista previously mentioned, which was based in Tokyo and Osaka and eventually grew to about fifty coffeehouses. In Brazil, many Japanese workers overcame extremely harsh circumstances, and at the end of their tenure, a steady flow of Japanese farmers decided to stay in the country and bought land with which to farm coffee and rice. By 1932, there were 6,000 Japanese-owned coffee plantations in Brazil, who according to White, brought 'zeal and entrepreneurial modernisation to the coffee industry'. Thus, the coffee relationship between Japan and Brazil became well and truly cemented and proved mutually beneficial to both countries. The saying 'a coffee a day' became commonplace in Japan and demand for coffee grew throughout the 1920s.

The beginning of the twentieth century strengthened the relationship between coffee and modernity.[11] During the Taisho period (1912–1926), coffeehouses began to diversify and morph into several distinct types, with different purposes. Although brief, the Taisho period was known for its openness, political and social ferment and new ideas in design, art and personal style. Coffeehouses were an increasingly visible part of urban life and offered an accessible space that expressed modernity in several ways. The ordinary neighbourhood *kissaten* developed from its original coffeehouse, to a space for quiet relaxation. As women began to enter the public sphere, their appearance in coffeehouses became more commonplace. Essentially places for middle-class customers, women occupied important roles in the coffeehouse, both as clients and as service-givers. The coffeehouse provided a new occupation in the waitress. Typically from a working-class background, the café waitress enjoyed greater personal freedoms than her middle-class sisters because of her working capacity.

But the coffeehouse waitress was something of a controversial figure, in part due to her lineage from the Japanese pre-modern teahouse. Waitresses were employed to 'feminize' what had previously been a masculine space. Waitresses – called *jokyu* – were hired to attract men, and to 'perform' in roles for whom names were provided. Their roles were adapted from the earlier teahouse with its entertaining women, and during the 1920s the café waitress's role became eroticized, where certain types of cafes resembled cabarets rather than coffeehouses. In these places alcohol as well as coffee was served and, with the performing waitress, promised added sexual frisson for the male customer. Women's performance skills focused on being flirtatious, a somewhat perilous negotiation, treading a tightrope between emotional and sexual entanglement, and falling prey to the concept of the fallen woman. In these cabaret type café venues the *jokyū* became the working-class personification of the 'Modern Girl' (Moga), and something of a construct in Japan's modern transformation. Thus it was that this style of café became associated with eroticism, and could be seen as a place that was morally questionable.[12] Indeed the coffeehouse's association with Westernization and the growing popularity of the *jokyu* provided the justification for increasing restrictions in the late 1930s. As late as 1939, the enduring attraction to the coffeehouse was criticized as a demoralizing aspect of modernity.[13]

Western-style jazz was introduced to cafés in the 1930s, enabled by the new recording technologies. Known as jazz *kissa,* these cafés still exist today, as does the *utagoe* café, which emerged post World War II. The *utagoe* was a precursor to the karaoke bars, where a musician might be playing and singing, sometimes along with customers. Other cafés appeared with a different musical focus. The *ongakua kissa* simply played live or recorded music with no fixed genre. Towards the end of the 1920s, some cafés were shut down because of their questionable activities, but many others continued to thrive, especially in Osaka. By 1930 there were 18,000 cafés in Japan. Certain *kissatens* became associated with scholars, writers and artists who engaged in debate and discussion, much as they were in Europe at the same time. As a growing feature of urban life and urbanization, cafés continued their connection with Western modernity.

Cafés disappeared briefly during World War II, when bans on imported products and coffee occurred. However, they were soon opened again once the war was over and quickly became popular. As food was in short supply and there was no requirement to serve food in Japanese cafés, opening one presented a straightforward business prospect; it was simple and economical to serve coffee exclusively. After World War II, another coffee entrepreneur emerged to make his enduring mark on Japan's coffee scene. In 1951, Tadeo Ueshima, known as the 'father of coffee in Japan', established the Ueshima Coffee Company Ltd (UCC). Ueshima was an importer of Western goods and came across coffee through his import networks. The company initially imported and roasted beans, but later expanded with cafés, the first in Kobe in an underground arcade. In 1969 the company developed the unique canned coffee product which became successful in the further adoption of coffee among the Japanese. The advertising slogan aimed at the ordinary person used to promote coffee was 'civilized folk like coffee'. Vending machines selling hot and cold beverages were introduced into Japan in 1973, and canned coffee consumed this way was very popular. The demand for coffee grew throughout the 1960s and 1970s and to secure a stable supply of beans, the company established a coffee estate in Jamaica, the well-known Blue Mountain Coffee in the 1980s. The company remains one of the largest coffee producers in the world today, with bases in twenty countries throughout Europe, Asia and the Americas.

During the 1960s and 1970s, throughout the period of social upheaval which occurred largely in the West, some cafés in Japan became the site for political discussions and politically oriented groups, including feminists, as well as experimental musicians and the artistic avant-garde. According to White, unlike their Western counterparts, Japanese cafés were not sites of resistance; rather, they were places that allowed for the exchange of ideas without disrupting the social order. The kissaten's popularity continued to grow and during the 1970s, many small, independent cafés appeared in Tokyo's fashionable districts such as Shinjuku and Ginza, as well as the popular student area of Kanda. The cafés adapted over time and changed in response to the changing urban life, offering their patrons spaces as diverse as their clientele. The 1980s witnessed a coffee shop boom, as coffee shops competed among

FIGURE 5.2 The first canned coffee drink developed by Ueshima Coffee Company. Photo credit: © Ueshima Coffee Company.

themselves, offering their patrons not only different styles of coffee, but also various gimmicks, styles of atmosphere and décor.[14] However, the impact of globalization from the 1980s presented a challenge for these quaint local cafés. Concentrated around populous train station precincts, they faced rising rents through the increase in land values. This combined with the introduction of the chain store café with their lower coffee prices due to economies of scale meant many of the cafés were forced out of business.

Contemporary Tokyo cafés

There is no shortage of cafés in Tokyo and some reminders of the crop of quaint, independent cafés that flourished during the 1970s and 80s remain, several can still be seen dotted around Ginza and other areas. In Tokyo, specialty coffee shops are scattered around the city, with many located around the peripheral areas of Shibuya. Although hardly non-commercial, Shibuya is known as the centre of Tokyo's youth and fashion culture, its hip vibe and Love Hotels. The tiny but now famous kissaten, Cafe de L'Ambre in Ginza, appears on many coffee and foodie blogs and would be on any self-respecting coffee connoisseur's itinerary. It came to fame for the unique manner in which the coffee has been aged and roasted by the same person, Sekiguchi Ichiro, since 1948. Ichiro stores and ages the beans, so you could be drinking coffee brewed from 1973 Brazilian beans blended with beans from a later era. The story goes that ageing the beans was something Ichiro discovered by accident, when he realized he'd left beans stored for longer than intended, but then he began to blend them with younger beans and found the combinations improved the coffee. Ichiro is about 102 years old and according to the café's website still fronts up to the café three times a week to roast the beans. Needless to say, he has become something of a legend in the coffee world.

On the day we visited, Ichiro could be glimpsed in a small room, adjacent to the narrow entrance corridor, settled at his roaster. I was struck by the way Cafe l'Ambre oozes the sense of another, earlier era; the café's tiny interior space is a sensory experience of dark timber, potent coffee aroma and intimacy. From the café's front door, we walked down a long narrow corridor to arrive at the tiny jewel box of the interior. Sitting at one of the café's four tables, it is easy to conjure up ideas about old Tokyo, another time, another place. Bar chairs place the customer in immediate proximity to the barista and café staff, inviting conversation or at least, acknowledgement and perhaps remarks about the coffee. There is a discernible atmosphere of reverence, something I noticed was not uncommon amongst Japanese specialty cafés and their baristas. The coffee is brewed in a pot and served without milk, presumably so you can savour the full, unencumbered flavour of the bean. If you must have milk with your coffee, it comes in a tiny jug on the side. There is no food, this is strictly coffee pure, and to our delight we discover that it is indeed very smooth and flavoursome coffee.

Cafe l'Ambre's history, ambience and coffee, create its authentic aura, and its narrative of the aged Ichuro and his aged beans cements its place in the pantheon of coffee connoisseurship. Narratives of places or products activate our imaginations, enhancing or embellishing our experience in a variety of ways. Narrative is increasingly used in branding of consumer products, based on the premise that consumers derive meaning from stories which enables them to self-fashion their lifestyle and identities through consumption and cultural practices. In Japan, the Western association with coffee is still evident, for example in Starbucks marketing, which has used an array of Western celebrities such as Brad Pitt to promote their products, and celebrates Western events such as Christmas and Valentine's Day.

Another specialty café on the connoisseur's list is Fuglen, the renowned Norwegian roasters and café established in 1963, which has played a key role in developing the internationally acclaimed Oslo standard. Fuglen opened its only other café outside Oslo in 2012. It's located in Shibuya, Tokyo, which is the home of many specialty or third-wave cafés. Apart from the distinctive

FIGURE 5.3 Coffee at Café de L'Ambre served without milk. Photo credit: © Emma Felton.

FIGURE 5.4 Café de L'Ambre Tokyo. Photo credit: © Emma Felton.

mild-flavoured coffee, Fuglen's interiors are homey, mid-century Scandinavian. Comfortable lounge chairs arranged in intimate manner give the visitor the feeling of walking into someone's home. Both the café in Oslo and Tokyo have a secondary business, selling Scandinavian furniture and objects, which adorn their interiors. Tucked away in the Yoyogi Park area of Shibuya, Fuglen's Tokyo premises attracts a large youthful crowd and, on the day we visited, was staffed by female baristas.

Among the non-specialty cafés we visited were several Japanese owned chain-store cafés such as Excelsior and Doutor and Ginza Renoir, which all serve quality coffee with simple Western-style food. Sandwiches, croissants and other pastries are offered at reasonable prices. These cafés were usually busy during the times we were there. Offering a relaxed and casual ambience, some of the signage is in English, and along with the Western food, the experience felt somewhat international, though with an attention to detail that is not always evident elsewhere. Excelsior, slightly more upmarket than its sibling Doutor, offers a wider selection of food such as pasta and hot sandwiches with a greater variety of breads such as focaccia, ciabatta and pannini, which speaks to the café's European origins. Sets are also offered, which include a combination of food and drinks including soft drinks and salads, perhaps less European inspired.

The Ginza Renoir is a more luxurious experience; we sat in velvet bucket chairs eating daintily cut sandwiches among the mainly middle-aged, female, smartly-attired clientele. The Renoir serves specialty, carefully prepared drip coffee and is slightly more expensive than Excelsior and Doutor, but the quality is certainly discernible. Tea is also served and so is cake, but there are no cookies or scones on the menu. If you stay a long time, extra tea is served free of charge.

The chain was established in 1964, and most of its cafés were opened in the 1960s and 1970s located around Tokyo. The 1960's era décor remains, in a style known as Taisho-roman, which is inspired by 19th-century European Romanticism – carpets, velvet and marble – indices of Western luxury. Smoking is popular in cafés, but the Ginza Renoir has introduced non-smoking seats.

A culture for novelty

The practice of *kodawari*, although focused on perfection, does not exclude experimentation and novelty. In the 19th century, Japanese coffeehouses were already promoting novelty and community, a feature that remains a staple part of many Japanese cafés today. Because the café is a somewhat ambiguous and adaptable space, especially in comparison to the tea house, the conditions for experimentation are more readily created. The novelty of Japanese cafés is in ample evidence today – Google 'novelty cafés' and Japan is the first country that appears, the internet offering up multitudinous list of the better-known types of novelty cafés; maid cafés, butler cafés, monster cafés, vampire cafés, Alice in Wonderland cafés and a lot more. Such willingness to bend and play with the genre comes from a lineage where novelty has long been a part of the culture.

Combing the streets of Tokyo, we visited cat cafés and a vampire café, and we stumbled across the curiously named Bondi Cafe, Yoyogi Beach Park in Shibuya. Being Australians, we felt compelled to enter. Inside the café brimmed with surfing paraphernalia, television screens of surfers riding waves, and painted surfboard fins decorated the walls. Its interior is constructed with timber deck flooring and natural timber walls, the café aiming for a beach shack ambience. Outside the café's deck, lounge chairs draped with towels looked out across the road at the large, verdant Yoyogi Park. It was a cool February winter afternoon, so the sunbaking or relaxing opportunity wasn't enticing. On the way back to our hotel, we passed other themed cafés – animae and monster. In department stores I spotted coffee jigsaw puzzles.

A visit to an Owl and Parrot café in Asakusa, Tokyo, is a startling experience for the unwary; the moniker 'café' a misnomer. Trekking across the city to investigate, I wondered how an owl and parrot theme might be interpreted. We entered the café down a steep flight of stairs, into a basement area where we found ourselves in a small foyer. Here we learnt that we were required to purchase plastic ponchos with hoods, before entering into the café's main space, which was concealed behind a large door. On entering, it was not surprising (by this stage), but still somewhat alarming to see that the space was more aviary than café. Behind the door, the 'café' room was bursting with parrots of all hues and varieties, flapping around unrestrained, but no sight of coffee. Toucans, lorikeets and numerous other species of birds flapped around our heads, with one occasionally alighting on my plastic poncho. We spotted a kookaburra and could only speculate how it washed ashore in Tokyo. With no coffee in sight, and somewhat disturbed by the presence of so many birds in a small underground space, we made a hasty retreat. Outside behind the foyer, we noticed the owls (of the parrot and owl café) perched on rods, guardians to the aviary. We had neglected to read TripAdvisor reviews before we set out, where animal sympathisers advised people not to support the café.

Perhaps more well-known themed cafés are the Japanese maid cafés which cater for a predominantly male clientele. They have their precedent in the earlier sekuhara cafés. These sprung up during the 1980s, apparently in response to anti-sexual harassment laws in the workplace, which were established after

FIGURE 5.5 Novelty coffee jigsaw puzzle. Photo credit: © Emma Felton.

the rise of social movements and second-wave feminism. Some sections of the population took exception to the laws, which were regarded as an affront to cultural traditions, and the sekuhara cafés were a way of reinserting certain cultural mores. In reaction to the prohibition placed on predominantly male behaviour, the female café staff wore low-cut clothing and they enticed the male clientele to ogle and touch them. Mirrored floors provided the opportunity for customers to gaze at women's reflections and in a further snub at the new legislation, the cafés declared in their advertising that 'what you can no longer do at the office, you can do here'.[15]

Maid cafés are still around today and a variation on the theme was recently introduced in Tokyo, with the Soineya or Cuddles Cafés. Soineya translates to 'co-sleeping' and is aimed at single men who can enjoy a platonic relationship with one of the café's girls. This could mean cuddling, napping together or laying in her arms for twenty minutes or up to ten hours. Soineyas are referred to as cafés but, as the main aim is to sleep or snooze, it is doubtful that coffee is served there.

Beside the crop of independent cafés, there are several Japanese café chains which are well regarded and well patronized. Doutor and Excelsior were established in the 1980s and have 1,300 cafés across Japan, recently expanding into Taiwan, Malaysia and Singapore. Toriba Hiromichi, who established the chain, was inspired after visiting Paris and enjoying what French cafés offered: coffee with a quick, easy breakfast in a roll or croissant, which people would purchase on their way to work. This seemed a great idea for the busy Japanese businessperson, and quickly became very popular. The brand's more upmarket offshoot Excelsior cafés all have dedicated smoking rooms because many Japanese people enjoy smoking with their coffee. As its founder noted in response to the invasion of Starbucks in Japan:

> Starbucks is a good concept, but Japanese people want to eat proper food and smoke. Plus, by having the shops a bit brighter, people think of Excelsior as a great place to go on a date. It doesn't look so seedy.[16]

Another local chain, Komeda Kohikan, has been around since 1959, and Moriva was established in 2015 and is part of the Zensho food retailing giant. Its Fair Trade, specialty coffee approach sets it apart from other chains. The Ginza Renoir, along with other Renoirs which first appeared in 1964, adopts a luxurious model, befitting of its first location in the exclusive shopping strip of Ginza in Tokyo. Its cosy velvet chairs, marble table tops and cut sandwiches speak to an aspirational Western modernity, which may appeal to older patrons rather than a younger generation immersed in global culture.

It is not possible to talk about coffee culture almost anywhere without mentioning the conquest of Starbucks and its global dominance. Japan is Starbucks' fourth biggest market and opened its first café in Japan in 1996. At the time of writing in 2018, the company had 1,039 cafés throughout the country. Part of its success is due to the concession the company makes to the local culture in which it is situated. The inclusion of items on its menus such as the Matcha green tea latte, and seasonal themes for beverages where seasonality has been part of Japanese tradition, has helped to integrate the brand into Japanese culture. However, its success is also predicated on its representation as a Western lifestyle brand. Starbucks commemorated its tenth anniversary in Japan with a special Anniversary Magazine. On its opening page a photograph of Tokyo's Shibuya district with the green Starbucks sign on one of the buildings declares: 'Without Starbucks, it's not Shibuya'. Starbucks' hegemony is further cemented in an article entitled 'The development of Japanese merchandise: Born between the global and the local', which describes Starbucks merchandise as combining a global set of values with local cultural roots.[17]

Foreign terms and slogans are commonly used in Japanese coffee business, written either in Roman letters or in *katakana*, a writing system assigned for borrowed words. This is the case for coffee-related vocabulary: words such as 'blend', 'drip', 'shot' and 'aroma', as well as the more specialised terminology referring to types of roasts, blends and coffee equipment. This helps Starbucks' modus operandi for global success and its promotion of aspirational Western lifestyles, with some concession to local values. Despite being an integral part of urban Japanese life, the foreign influence remains part of Japanese coffee culture.

An intense localism and the pursuit of *kodawari* may well have elevated Japanese coffee-making to a status that is aspired to by many coffee professionals around the world. Japan's unique coffee history with its direct relationship to Brazil, its links to Western modernity and a cultural thirst for novelty instils its café culture with a multitude of diverse and interesting cafés. What café culture in Japan shares with café culture elsewhere is its relationship with urban and social development. Like cafés around the world, it provides a vital social space for urban citizens, a space in which to manage increasingly complex and busy lives.

Notes

1 Lyons, James. 2005. "Think Seattle, act globally." *Cultural Studies* Volume 19, Issue 1, pp. 14–34. p. 29.
2 Howes, David. 2005. *Empire of the Senses: the sensual culture reader.* Oxford. Berg.
3 White, Merry. 2012. *Coffee Life in Japan.* Berkeley, CA: University of California Press.
4 White, Merry. 2012. Ibid., p. 108.
5 White, Merry. 2012. Ibid., p. 14.
6 White, Merry. 2012. Ibid., p. 21.
7 Wikipedia. *History of Japan.* Ret. 19.9.18.
8 Grinshpun, Helena. 2014. "Deconstructing a global commodity: Coffee, culture, and consumption in Japan." *Journal of Consumer Culture* Volume 14, Issue 3, p. 348.
9 White, Merry. 2012. Ibid., p. 15.
10 White, Merry. 2012. Ibid., p. 17.
11 Grinshpun, Helena. 2014. "Deconstructing a global commodity: Coffee, culture, and consumption in Japan." *Journal of Consumer Culture* Volume 14, Issue 3, p. 348.
12 White, Merry. 2012. Ibid., p. 46.

13 Silverberg Miriam. 2006 *Erotic Grotesque Nonsense: The Mass Culture of Japanese Modern Times*. Berkeley: University of California Press.
14 Grinshpun, Helena. 2014. "Deconstructing a global commodity: Coffee, culture, and consumption in Japan." *Journal of Consumer Culture* Volume 14, Issue 3, p. 349.
15 White, Merry. 2012. Ibid., p. 79.
16 Lewis, Leo. 2003. Coffee kings and the end of the Starbucks effect. http://www.japaninc.com/article.php?articleID=1218. Ret. 13.5.17.
17 Grinshpun, Helena. 2014. "Deconstructing a global commodity: Coffee, culture, and consumption in Japan." *Journal of Consumer Culture* Volume 14, Issue 3, p. 343.

6

CAFÉ CULTURE IN MAINLAND CHINA AND HONG KONG

> There is a Chinese saying that, if you dislike someone, just persuade him or her to open a coffee shop.
>
> *Jing Wang*[1]

In contrast to Japan, China's coffee culture is a nascent one, with the exception of Hong Kong, where the British colonial occupation has left its indelible trace on the local food and drink culture. As with Hong Kong, Singapore's coffee culture, which is very briefly touched on in this chapter, is also a unique amalgam of local and colonial influences.

It is only recently that cafés have begun to appear across Mainland China's major cities where they are a distinctly urban phenomenon; there is little evidence of cafés in rural areas. While third-wave-style cafés are a very recent addition to the country, international coffee shop chains made their entry into Chinese cities over two decades ago. Even more are entering the market now, seizing the opportunities that China's scale of population and rising middle class promises. Tea is still by far the most popular drink in China, but the signs for coffee entrepreneurs must be encouraging – since 2004, coffee consumption has kept growing at 16% per year, with some estimates as high as 22%. This outstrips all other countries' dedication to the bean. Major global players such as Starbucks, British hospitality company Costa and several Asian companies mainly from South Korea are investing heavily in China's coffee future.[2] The prevalence of Starbucks is often cited as evidence that China is embracing coffee and, although the company is expanding and has 600 cafés in Shanghai alone, it over-expanded earlier and had to close down stores. In 2017 the café chain began rolling out around one café a day and is planning to double the number in Chinese cities by 2021, to reach 5,000.[3] Starbucks is banking on China mirroring Japan's coffee surge that occurred from 1963–1973 but, as we have seen in the previous chapter, Japan is a unique story and comparisons may not bear up.

The urbanization of China

On my first trip to Shanghai in 2009, I combed the streets looking for a café that looked as if it might sell a reasonable cup of coffee. After trawling a circuit of the streets around my hotel in Xuhui, the closest I came to a café was a franchise donut shop that sold coffee on the side. Certainly Starbucks had a presence in the city then, but being Australian and used to strong coffee, and holding the view that Starbucks sold only unappealing milky coffee, I didn't enter. I returned to Shanghai in 2017 and stayed at the same hotel in the same area, only to discover that the streets had been transformed (as indeed had the hotel) by the presence of cafés of all descriptions. Among the several I visited, the coffee was of the specialty coffee standard. And as in cafes in the global north, the staff and clientele were mainly young, disporting the current fashion styles of middle-class youth across the globe. Globalization was evident, but in one sense this is nothing new, the history of coffee is a story of global trade and culture.

Asian cities are among the most rapidly growing in the world, and China is at the vanguard of metropolitan growth. The urbanization of China beginning in the late 1970s, is the most remarkable social and economic transformation of any country in the 20th century. China's cities have radically changed the culture and daily lives of hundreds of millions of people, and they continue to grow at a staggering pace into the 21st century. It takes a leap of the imagination to consider what life was like in China less than fifty years ago. Predominantly an agricultural society, most of its population eked out a living as impoverished rural or factory workers. Today, over half of its people are living in cities, and over a third are middle class and are participating in consumer culture, with access to countless products and services.

China was catapulted into urbanization by the economic reforms and 'Open Door' policy initiated by Deng Xiaoping in 1978, and its land reform launched in 1987. Today, over 750 million people live in cities and the country is home to nine out of the world's top ten mega-cities. A mega-city is defined as having a population of over ten million and China alone has fifteen. Hong Kong, one of the world's most important financial centres located on a very small land mass, though not a mega-city, is a densely populated urban conglomerate of 7.3 million. By contrast, the sovereign-city state of Singapore and an important financial and transport hub is a small land mass, with a population of just over five million.

Just as cafés established in the last decade or so have sprung up in gentrifying districts of cities in the global north, this is often the case in many Asian cities. Attracted by the lower rents than those in central commercial districts, cafés appear in Shanghai, Beijing, Hong Kong, Tokyo and Singapore and other Asian cities across a range of locations inside but also outside the central business districts. In Singapore, for instance, a café culture can be found in the increasingly gentrified Tiong Bahru, a location on the periphery of the CBD, established for public housing in the 1930s. Tiong Bahru's international modernist-style housing blocks, with ample green space, pedestrian access and pleasant streetscape, have attracted local and foreign inhabitants as well as the inevitable tide of developers and the amenity that follows.

All the coffee in China

If coffee culture in Japan shook off its aspirations to Western modernity and made it its own, China's adoption has taken a different trajectory. Its relationship to modernity is more visibly expressed in urban café life, but not without the complex negotiations with its own cultural traditions. After the United States and Canada, China is the country with the most cafés, more due to its large population, however, than to a preference for coffee.

As the birthplace of tea, China's rich tea tradition has dominated for over 5,000 years. Coffee is a recent arrival, dating back to the mid-19th century when the country opened up to foreign trade, but its presence was short lived. Western missionaries and businessmen brought coffee to treaty ports, among them Shanghai. Coffee first appeared in restaurants and cafés at the beginning of the 20th century, but was limited to consumption by foreign politicians, military personnel and local cultural elites. During the 1920s and 1930s, cafés could be found in colonial Shanghai, which was then known as the 'Paris of the East' for its adoption of Western styles. While cafés symbolized the country's industrialization and Westernization – an attachment that lingers today – they were generally regarded with suspicion because they served 'foreign food and drink'.[4]

The reappearance of coffee shops in Shanghai today, albeit of a different style than those in the early 20th century, is tied to the redevelopment of the metropolis itself. China scholar Jeffrey Wasserstrom comments that the current explosion of coffee shops in Shanghai represents 'both a novelty and a resumption of an old cosmopolitan trajectory that was interrupted for a time'.[5] More recently, Shanghai's influence on the global stage was further boosted as an international city when it hosted the World Expo in 2010, which was well received and attended. Along with the Beijing Olympics, the Expo was symbolic of the economic and political rise of China in the 21st century. In other Chinese cities whose history bears less of a cosmopolitan influence, the café's appearance is relatively new.

During the Communist period and reign of Mao Zedong from 1949 to 1970, there were no cafés in Chinese cities. It wasn't until 1988, after the economic reforms of the Den Xiaoping era, that coffee reappeared when the Swiss-based behemoth Nestlé Company carved its way into China. Establishing a centre and crops in Yu'nan province, the company cultivated, produced and distributed instant coffee throughout the country. Nestlé adopted a shrewd approach in introducing coffee to a tea-drinking nation. It marketed the instant coffee in a way that appealed to the Chinese tradition of gift giving; Nescafe was promoted as a gift to give to friends and family. In this way, the company leveraged Chinese cultural tradition with a desire for foreign products. Coffee had once again become a symbol of desirable Western modernity, something to be acquired and admired. This time it took a foothold, but its ascent was slow and inconsistent.

21st-century metropolitan ascendency

Now in the first decades of the 21st century, with the advent of chain store coffee shops such as Starbucks and the growth among independent cafés, café culture's uptake seems more assured. Since the reappearance of coffee in the late 1990s, its popularity continues to grow, despite the relatively high cost of a cup of coffee in China. At approximately (AUD) $6 for a latte, the price is high in relation to local wages, where the average wage in Shanghai is (AUD) $1,200 a month. This makes café culture a lifestyle activity for the middle and upper-middle classes. According to estimates, about a third of China's overall population is middle class and growing.[6] It is predicted that by 2022 over 550 million people will be considered middle class.

There's no doubt that the café's recent appeal in China is prompted by many of the same changes occurring in cities everywhere. China's cultural economy is booming, and is most evident in its cities. The cultural and creative industries, as in Europe and Australia, have been a vigorous force for urban regeneration in China. Driven by government policy and entrepreneurial activity, there are myriad programs, subsidies and creative platforms fuelling their growth. Shanghai, China's historically modern city, is one of the key sites for creative industry development where the repurposing of former factory or large-scale industrial sites into creative parks or creative clusters has been a significant driver of urban regeneration. Cultural precincts such as M50 and Bridge 8 in Shanghai and 789 in Beijing, attract a network of cafés clustered around the sites, and are heavily patronized by national and international visitors. Promoted as 'art precincts' and 'art streets', they draw thousands of tourists a day to their boutique design shops, galleries and hospitality industries. The impact of the creative industries as a policy framework, might be somewhat contentious, but their imprint on China's main cities is indisputable, not just in the large arts precincts, but in the smaller design shops and galleries scattered throughout the city's streets in gentrifying areas.[7] Like cities in the West, a growing food and drink culture is fundamental to these art spaces; they are mutually dependent, symbiotically sustaining each other's growth.

Another compelling reason for the café's appeal might be attributed to the density of Chinese cities where the majority of residents reside in high-rise apartment buildings. A demand for hybrid spaces – not work and not home – means the café has quickly gained traction, particularly among the middle-class youth. Prior to the growth of cafés during the 1990s, it was common for young people to meet and study in international fast food outlets such as KFC and McDonald's. Both venues have spacious environments for groups to gather and are well lit, which is important for studying. Unlike many university dormitories, the stores have the added bonus of being air-conditioned in summer and heated in winter. However, students sitting at tables for long periods of time working created an issue for management and frequently staff tacitly encouraged people to leave.

The importance of hybrid spaces such as the café to meet, work and hang out is evident in densely populated cities, but in China, the café's appeal according to Jeng Wang, is also underpinned by the needs of the so-called 'lonely generation'.[8] These are the children of the one-child policy that was implemented by Mao Zedong in 1979 in an attempt to curb China's rapidly ballooning population growth. With both parents working full-time, this generation grew up in single children households and they are now in their 20s and 30s and are the main patrons of China's burgeoning café culture. They are often stereotyped in the media as spoilt, self-centred and obsessed with consumption. Yet this generation lives with a paradox, on the one hand they are part of a global culture which emphasizes individuality, but the cultural tradition of community remains strong in China. For a generation raised without siblings, community can acquire greater significance. Part of the café's appeal is that it caters to the making and selling of lifestyle experience in which community is promoted symbolically. Starbucks was the global behemoth that led the adoption of café culture in China, and a large part of its marketing and attraction is the ways in which the brand promotes the creation of community. For the 'lonely generation' there remains a tension between collectivism and individualism. Many of this generation are university educated, have travelled or studied abroad and have been exposed to a range of foreign cultures through books, movies and music. Wang observes:

> With this interesting tension between individualism and collectivism, the atmosphere provided by cafes has fostered a series of curious temporary communities built on cultural and culinary tastes.[9]

For this generation, the traditional teahouse is not an attractive alternative as a place for community. Teahouses were originally seen as places for cultural elites and intellectuals. Moreover, similarly to tea drinking traditions in the West, it is more commonplace to make and drink tea at home where it can be enjoyed among friends and family. But recently new teahouses have emerged in Chinese cities which are targeting a younger generation, utilizing similar styles to the contemporary café and offering more affordable prices and a greater range of products.

China – first phase: Starbucks and Costa

The Starbucks story and its rapid growth is often quoted as an example of China's rapacious uptake of coffee culture, but there's a certain amount of hyperbole attached to this claim. While coffee consumption is on the rise and is certainly evident in China's main cities, it is confined to a relatively small population of the urban middle class. With China's massive population of 1.3 billion and the increase of the urban middle class, Starbucks, like many foreign companies, sees China as an opportunity for growth. Recognizing the Chinese preference for Western brands, Starbucks opened its first store in Beijing in 1999. There are currently about 2,500 Starbucks in China, with plans to double the amount by 2030. Starbucks is credited with introducing contemporary café culture to China and, from its inception, was promoted as a Western lifestyle brand. The first store was opened in Mainland China in Beijing's China World Trade Centre and targeted mainly white-collar workers and foreigners. Starbuck's symbolic value as modern, Western and therefore desirable makes it a potent symbol of the 'new' China, and the cafés are a common feature of upscale shopping malls and gentrified neighbourhoods.[10]

The cafés, comfortably fitted out with lounge chairs and reading material and whose staff are trained to be friendly, were one of the first hybrid places for a younger generation to gather in China's burgeoning cities. Everyday life was changing rapidly and, as in other densely populated cities, places for gathering or being alone provide a valuable reprieve from the obligations of social responsibility. As is the case in Japan, Starbucks' adaptation to local tastes, with the addition of products specifically aimed at the Asian market, such as the green tea latte – matcha latte – and red bean scones helped to bolster its popularity.

Starbucks' entry into China was assisted with the partnership of Taiwanese company Presidential, a business which had helped to introduce 7-Eleven stores into the Philippines and which was seen to understand Asian markets and tastes.[11] Further expansion in China is occurring with the recent establishment of Starbucks Reserve, a sector of the company which is aimed at the specialty coffee aficionado. The coffee company is taking advantage of the desire for artisan and hand-crafted products and has launched fifty-five Reserve cafés in the major cities of Beijing, Shanghai, Guangzhou and Chengdu since 2015. Its coffee is marketed on its website as "rare, limited, small batch roast coffees". Again, it has made specific changes to accommodate the local market. Its stores are larger than those in other countries, so that meetings and dining are more easily facilitated among larger populations and a culture with a greater focus on the collective and group gatherings. In 2016, Starbucks CEO Howard Schultz announced that the company would offer housing allowances for some full-time baristas and supervisors, something rare in the hospitality industry. But in China the move follows an expectation, established by Chinese industrial companies' practice of providing accommodation for their staff, mainly when moving from rural areas to cities for work.[12]

Despite its popularity, Starbucks has come under fire by Chinese media for their high prices. In general, Western companies enjoy considerably cheaper overheads when doing business in China, which local media think should be reflected in the price of the product or service, i.e. a cup of coffee. Yet, for consumers, a high price is generally considered a sign of quality in China. Starbucks and Costa understand this and take advantage of local attitudes towards Western brands.[13]

Consumption is a complex and symbolic process, and even more so when it has been recently introduced full-scale to a collective culture like China. Brands such as Starbucks build semiotic meaning and value for products or services. Meaning is conveyed primarily through visual communication, using imagery and advertising. Values such as status are encoded into brands through a range of marketing tactics and consumers deploy these to craft their identity and lifestyles preferences. For a rapidly modernizing China, many Western high-end brands have significant cachet, their acquisition signals Asian modernity and knowledge to peers and colleagues.

In the creation of a social identity, Starbucks' predominantly middle-class patrons, like the patrons of the independent or specialty café, fuse collectivism with individualism. The capacity to negotiate across cultures is a large part of the brand's appeal. In a 2013 study of Starbucks' customers, many interview respondents referred to the status of modernity that the brand generates when they participate in café life. The most common expression of Starbucks' value was that it provides a 'cultural bridge' which allows its patrons to experience another way of life, straddling the local and the global, as this forty-three-year-old male expressed:

> When I was young, China did not 'open door' to the Western brands and goods in 1970s. All the people at that time wore the blue uniform. I am not free to choose the foreign goods. Interestingly, I get information about the outside world from my uncle who has been to foreign countries for business. He told me that foreigners like sitting in the coffee shops and reading newspaper. I think this kind of experience is enjoyable but is quite far away. I hope that one day I can enjoy the coffee in a foreign coffee shop in my city. Now, Starbucks is coming. My dream comes true...I feel that I will become international when I am sitting in the Starbucks, partly because many foreigners are chatting in the Starbucks. Sometimes I imagine I am sitting in the foreign countries.[14]

This sentiment may be less about Starbucks as a brand and would apply to other foreign coffee brands, and indeed to the independent third-wave café sector itself. Numerous coffee chains from other countries are realizing the potential and forging inroads into Chinese cities. Costa Coffee, a British company, has a strong presence with hundreds of cafés, as do Gloria Jeans and Coffee Bean & Tea Leaf, both American multinational companies. The Japanese-owned Manabe and several South Korean brands have cultivated a growing and loyal following in China. Caffe Bene has 700 stores and other South Korean competitors are entering an increasingly crowded field – Zoo Coffee, Maan Coffee and Tous Les Jours.

The café environment of the Korean brands is quite distinct from Western foreign brands. Eschewing the homey or third-wave cool, their interiors tend to be flamboyant by comparison, with features such as internal trees (Maan Café), life-size model animals – zebras, pandas and giraffes (Zoo Coffee) – and other novelty items included in the decor. South Korean culture is eagerly consumed in China and Korean pop music and television dramas are very popular. Exploiting this following, Caffe Bene employs South Korean television star Kim Soo-Hyun to appear at marketing events. For Chinese youth, visiting a Korean café is one step closer to the somewhat intriguing culture. There are a growing number of Chinese coffee chains as well, such as Pacific Coffee or Xingbake Coffee, but it is Nestlé that maintains the largest foreign foothold in China as the coffee to drink at home. This is due mainly to its instant coffee and the brands Nespresso and Dolce Gusto.

Alternative business models

Cafés can be robust businesses in their own right, but they also exist as ancillaries of other businesses, co-located in another industry such as a bookshop or cinema. China is no exception, and cafés can be found in bookshops, department stores, hotels, airports, railway stations, and hospitals – places where people are spending time either waiting or involved in another endeavour. Co-located cafés can add value to the core business and provide an additional service for the consumer.

China has a unique example of one café chain whose allied business is not physically co-located. The highly popular Line Friends Cafe in Shanghai was established from a Japanese-Korean social media company, where it began life as a subsidiary of a social messenger app. It is the physical manifestation of a digital phenomenon. The Line Friends Corporation is built around Line Friends characters, originally just a sticker for the social messenger app. The characters became very popular with the promotion tagline 'cute Asian no 1 Characters'

FIGURE 6.1 Line Friends Cafe Shanghai. Photo credit: © Emma Felton.

and the company sells related Line Character merchandise. Although the app itself is banned in China, the company has several cafés throughout the country as well as across Asia and the United States. In the Shanghai Line Friends Cafe, life-sized, anthropomorphized bears and rabbits, mainly all head with cute faces and some adorned with bows and polka dots, are scattered throughout the multi-storied themed café. Hugely popular, the café was packed on the day we visited, with a polyglot of people – predominantly young Asians, friends and families – lining up to take photos with the cast of Line Characters. On the opening day in 2015, people lined up for three hours to be part of the experience. The café, straddling six floors, is divided into a series of small themed spaces and rooms. For example, 'Ye old library room' whose walls are adorned with bookshelves, where a Line Character sits reading illuminated by an art deco light next to an old-style radio, signalling a Shanghai of yesteryear. Other rooms are decorated in candy stripes, with similarly dressed Line Characters.

Although not a part of traditional culture, the novelty factor is popular in China, as it is in Japan. Café menus and interiors on the whole show bolder experimentation than cafés in the global north, and their designs often reflect an interesting hybrid of traditional, current and futuristic cultural aesthetics.

Technology's impact

Technology and social media have become vital to a café's success and this is especially the case in China. Chinese people are big users of social media, and the internet has been accessible in the country since the late 1990s. The influence of social media apps is fundamental to building and maintaining café patronage and the three most popular apps are WeChat, a hybrid messenger, e-commerce, Facebook and Instagram-style app; QQ, with similar functions; and Weibo, often called the Twitter of apps. WeChat, the most widely subscribed of China's social media apps, has about 500 million Chinese-based active subscribers. The multi-dimensional apps which enable a range of functions work something like this: they allow friends to message each other (to let them know which café they are at), upload photos and music, and order as well as pay for products via the app. This makes ordering in some hospitality venues impossible unless you have the right app, as China is rapidly moving towards a cashless society. Most café menus are available on apps such as WeChat or Sina Weibo.

Facebook, Instagram and Google are all unavailable in China. Despite this, it is possible to find some cafés with Facebook homepages, presumably posted once outside the country. Cafés attract large followings on social media via the sharing of photos and tags of the café experience, and Starbucks is no exception. It has acquired the somewhat paternal moniker of 'Papa Star' on Sina Weibo. Starbucks has increased its growth in China by partnering with the Hong Kong-based multinational technology company, Tencent Holdings, in 2017, which runs WeChat and is a larger company than Facebook. Starbucks is using the partnership with the tech giant to leverage its business by drawing on the gift-giving tradition of

Chinese culture. WeChat now has an in-app feature which enables gift cards and purchases for Starbucks.

Apart from promoting cafés and showing your friends where you are, social media can be essential in tracking down some of the cafés dotted through the streets of Shanghai and Hong Kong's fringe urban areas. In China as elsewhere, third-wave cafés are more often located in secondary streets and areas, keeping to low rents and relying on social media and word-of-mouth reputation. Nestled among the historical layers of the city's built form, on our exploration of cafés in Shanghai, we found buildings inconspicuously tucked away behind other buildings, or down alleyways with little signage or indication of commercial activity, making it hard to find without apps and digital maps. Some cafés don't have signs on the door, as is the case with Cafe on Air in Shanghai. This café won Time Out's Café of the Year in 2015 and is accessed via a small laneway behind a building. Without a name on the closed door, we were only able to identify it as a café when we glanced through the window and saw an espresso machine and people drinking coffee. If, as the Starbucks patron quoted earlier stated, people go to Western-style cafés partly to be seen, then the only way this can happen is in obscurely located and signed cafés such as On Air is through photographs customers upload onto social media.

As I discuss in detail in Chapter Eight, the technology industry itself has transformed everyday life across the world. China has invested heavily in technology and is rapidly outstripping the United States and Europe in research and development. Professions that didn't exist two decades ago are now flourishing because of technology and providing employment in the areas of graphic design, web-based writing, photography and a host of other work that can be done partially via the internet. With a strong creative industries workforce, China employs many freelancers across the sectors. The café is a convenient workspace for people who aren't attached to a dedicated work place.

Home-grown exports

With the growth of coffee consumption in China, so too has its production increased. Although China imports most of its coffee from plantations around the world, as with other recently adopted beverages, such as wine and grape growing, China grows its own coffee. Most of the country's coffee is grown in the Arabica producing region of Yunnan province in southern China, where it was first introduced by a French missionary in 1892. Yunnan borders on Vietnam, Laos and Myanmar and almost half the coffee produced in Yunnan comes from the extremely mountainous Pu'er Province, an area traditionally associated with tea production. The region, which is larger than the country of Ecuador and known globally for its fermented teas, is fast becoming the coffee-producing capital of China.

It is only since 2008 that coffee has been grown on a large scale as a commodity. In the past five years, the production volume has increased steadily by around 60,000 tons per year. Coffee is frequently grown alongside tea and is proving more profitable than other crops in the coffee-growing regions such as sugarcane. Such is coffee's escalating popularity that demand has outstripped supply. But like many other parts of China, Yunnan has suffered from droughts in recent years, making water scarce for the water-intensive coffee bush. Much of the coffee grown in Yunnan is sun grown, which requires more fertilizers and water than shade-grown coffee.

The majority of the coffee produced in Yunnan is exported as green beans to European markets and the United States, with only around 30% consumed domestically. Starbucks and another American-based company Coex and London-based Volcafe have established trade with coffee suppliers in Yunnan.[15]

On the ground in Shanghai

In my second visit to Shanghai in 2017, some eight years after my first encounter with the megalopolis of 24.5 million, independent cafés are everywhere, particularly in the inner and middle core areas which tend to be relatively affluent and middle class – Xuhui, Luwan, Huang-pu, Jing-an and in Tianzifang. The latter precinct, grew organically as an arts precinct, was established by the artist Chen Yifei who took over two abandoned factories in 1998. Known as Lane 210 it is now something of a tourist mecca, an enclave brimming with cafés, bars, design studios, craft shops and galleries. Its traditional Chinese architecture – a housing style known as Shikumen, developed in the 1920s and 1930s – features engraved stone door frames and house solid wooden doors. These houses are still intact among the laneways and are now the galleries, cafés and boutiques that draw large crowds. A multitude of third-wave coffee-style shops nestles among a network of tiny laneways. Several of these have the ubiquitous minimalist third-wave style interiors, but with local adaptions to the theme. Dedication to the bean is evident. In one café, I observed a barista perfecting the art of brewing filtered coffee over the duration of about forty minutes. With meticulous attention to the height from which he poured the water and the precise place where it fell, he carefully calibrated the water's flow with a repetition of circular movements. When the water hit the coffee, he tasted the coffee and after each tasting he altered the variables incrementally.

I came across Taste café, and while distinctly third-wave looking at a quick glance, once inside local differences were evident. This included an eclectic collection of objects such as ceramic bow ties, tools, cast-iron scissors and assorted homewares displayed in glass cases and along the walls. These are for sale, as the café began life as a store, and now includes an art exhibition space upstairs. This combination of arts space, exhibition space and café is not uncommon among cafés in China's cities. Taste's owners are Japanese and Chinese–Canadian designers, and owner Yukata originally trained as a fashion designer, then trained as a barista before opening up his café. This is no ancillary business café added to a core existing business, here the connoisseurship of coffee appears to be as important as the products sold.

In these popular and tourist populated parts of the city, competition is fierce, and there are plenty of eye-popping cafés of varied themes. Zoo cafés, cute bear cafés and cat cafés are not unique to China, but appear more numerous perhaps due to the sheer density of urban amenity. Some make bold design statements. One such example is Fumi Café, located in a quiet street in the Xuhui district and designed by an Italian designer based in Shanghai. The overall look is modern and clean with sleek metal benches and chairs. The space has elegant details,

FIGURE 6.2 Items sold in Chinese café. Photo credit: © Xin Xin Wen.

including a whitewashed wall adorned with silver Bialetti Moka percolator pots, behind which is cleverly concealed illumination. A striking black wave assemblage is suspended from the ceiling and the interior shouts cool and hip. The coffee and food are highly customized, offering a range of 'Fumi Signatures', coffee-inspired drinks such as Matcha Matcha, Matcha Mocha and Snowy White Mocha. You can purchase tasting sets of three coffees: a piccolo, espresso and a filter coffee and the price is dependent on bean origin.

Such attention to high-end design and connoisseurship distinguishes Chinese independent cafés from chain store cafés. While the décor and dedication to coffee artisanship generate a sense of the local and the authentic, café culture's global presence underpins this experience. The transnational flow of commodities and experience has accelerated exponentially with technology and mobility. On the day I visited Fumi, it was filled with young, mainly female customers who were mostly attentive to their mobile phones and devices. Lots of photographs were being taken. On a brisk winter afternoon, people spilled out onto the street, or sat at the window bench looking out onto the street and to passers-by, perhaps hoping to be seen. The café appeared to be one of the most popular places in the area for young Shanghainese, located in a street among traditional Shikumen architecture, now repurposed to house countless design shops, boutiques, cafés and restaurants in this burgeoning middle-class neighbourhood.

China's historically distinctive traditions of imperialism, colonialism, communism and modernity provide many complex layers to the country's current evolution and way of life. Its transition to a rapidly urbanized, consumer-focused society is nothing short of astounding. And while the café in China might signal Western modernity, a place to be seen, it is clearly fulfilling a more fundamental need.

FIGURE 6.3 Fumi Café wall decorated with percolators, Shanghai. Photo credit: © Emma Felton.

Hong Kong

It would be an oversight in a summary of China to exclude Hong Kong, where a robust specialty coffee culture with its own distinctive characteristics exists. Between 2008 and 2018, Hong Kong's net coffee imports have increased by 40%.

Hong Kong's history of cosmopolitan food and drink culture sets its coffee scene apart from Mainland China. It too has experienced the accelerated growth of third-wave coffee shops, and Hong Kong baristas are winning awards on the international stage. Its specialty coffee business is more mature than Mainland China's, and coffee shops continue to appear all over the city's several islands, particularly in the rapidly gentrifying areas of Sheung Wan, Kennedy Town and Tai Kok Tsui. Part of that explosion in coffee culture is to do with the foreign exchange of young university students, who had experienced coffee culture in other countries while studying overseas, and were inspired to emulate the Western café experience.

Situated on a series of densely populated small islands just south of the China mainland, Hong Kong's colonial history gives its coffee culture a unique hybrid twist. A British colony for 200 years from 1841 to 1997, Hong Kong was returned to China in 1997, although it retains its own independent, administrative system – 'one country, two systems' – which enables it to preserve its function as a world financial centre. It's a cosmopolitan city with seven million inhabitants and the world's third densest population per square metre. It is home to a population of

FIGURE 6.4 The Coffee Academics cafe and coffee trainers, Hong Kong. Photo credit: © Daniel Schefler.

FIGURE 6.5 Kopitiam, traditional cafe Hong Kong circa 1950s. Photo credit: ©Victor Cheok.

mainly Chinese and includes many foreign expatriates working for international corporations and other organizations. Like Australia, Britain has left its colonial footprint on the country's food and drink cultures, and tea has long been the preferred beverage.

Hong Kong was a busy trading port during colonization, and powdered coffee arrived along with other canned and preserved food stuffs from Britain and other European countries via international traders in the 19th century. By the 1930s, coffee shops were prevalent and patronized largely by the colonial population and some of the local South East Asian Chinese community. The latter group barely drank anything else except for coffee and had acquired their taste for the drink in Indonesia, from where they fled in the 1950s due to anti-Chinese turmoil and political upheaval. Having grown up in a coffee-producing country, where the drink was an everyday commodity for even the poorest members of society, they sought a reliable supply in Hong Kong. Numerous small 'Toko Indonesia" shops opened in Hong Kong, all supplying high-quality coffee at reasonable prices, as well as other familiar Indonesian foods. Coffee was usually roasted on the premises, often with an addition of butter or margarine to aid caramelization, and then ground when required to ensure freshness.

During this period of its colonial history, Hong Kong became known for its unique dining culture, of which the *cha chaan teng* or the tea restaurant was the most popular. It offered Western-inspired food to a local population and coffee was typically served at the end of the meal. For the next few decades, this was the main way coffee was consumed in Hong Kong but, with increasing globalization, along came the next influence from Japan in the 1980s and 1990s.

Japanese coffee houses such as UCC set up shop, while Pokka Cafe modelled on the Japanese style of café was established in 1989. Following on the heels of coffee's growing popularity were international coffee chains Starbucks and McDonald's. Hong Kong has produced its own specialty coffee chains, and one of the first was launched by a local businesswoman, Jennifer Liu, and now goes by the name of Coffee Academics. Within five years it was one of the Hong Kong's largest coffee chains.

On the ground in Hong Kong

In 2017 I was back in Hong Kong, after a six-year absence. Staying on the fringes of Central to the west, in the lively Sheung Wan area, there is little sign of its colonial past, the local culture appears to be thriving. As we explore the neighbourhood, winding our way through the narrow streets among the bustling crowds, Chinese food stores and grocery shops, every now and then a third-wave café catches our attention. The third-wave style cafés, with their cool minimalist look, can look incongruous among the busy streets, amidst the plethora of brightly coloured Chinese signage and shops with their foodstuffs spilling out onto the footpath in large plastic bags. The well-known Cupping Room cafe, one of four in Hong Kong, is tucked around a corner from one of Sheung Wan's main streets, in slightly calmer environs. It's so full that its patrons – locals and Caucasians – are hanging about outside drinking coffee and chatting on the footpath. Offering flat whites and the usual array of specialty coffees, it also sells all-day breakfast café-style food. It has an award-winning barista, no doubt a drawcard, and has been around since 2014. Specialty cafés have taken off rapidly since then, though it might be easy to miss other recent players on the scene due to their compact size and low-key shopfronts. Barista Jam, Brew Bros Cafe and Amber Cafe are among the many coffee shops that have opened in the area since 2015. Competition is strong, and cafés vie for distinction. The local taste for sweet beverages (tea with condensed milk for instance), is met with Amber Cafe's pineapple-infused cold press, developed by the café's award-winning barista. Other café operators in Sheung Wan talk about the rising costs involved in maintaining a profitable business as the area becomes gentrified. For some, their rents have risen by 15% in two years, and they are concerned the rise will continue to 30% or 50%.

As we made our way up the endless flights of steps towards the mid-levels, away from the crowded streets, I have two important assets to help me locate some of Hong Kong's more obscurely located cafés. One is a Mandarin-speaking companion, and the other is the app Open Rice. My companion was taking me to Lof 10 (Love Often), a café which received good reviews on the app and, although hard to find, we eventually spotted it tucked away inconspicuously in a laneway amongst several nondescript buildings. The café imports its beans from Los Angeles's Blue Bottle roastery and its coffee looks serious. The café décor and coffee signals third-wave minimalism, but in Hong Kong fusion style, its menu reflects a mix of contemporary China and old colonial Hong Kong. Green Tea Lattes, Rose Latte, Satay Angus Beef Noodles, Marshmallow Toast and Peanut Butter and Milk Toast are menu items among the more conventional café offerings of lattes and espressos. On the day we visited, a handful of patrons sat around a communal table and at a bench, if alone, attentive to their mobile devices. Next to us sat two young local women, who had also found their way to the café courtesy of Open Rice's recommendation. As we sat chatting to them, they told us they chose the café because they liked the sound of the food and they wanted somewhere to catch up with each other. On the way down the hill, using a different route, we discover more third-wave style cafés, mostly well patronized.

The mélange of cultures that has peppered Hong Kong's history has had a significant impact on its food and drink culture and it is well known for its interesting diversity of fusion food. This hybridity provides a unique take on what might ordinarily be humble café food, and where the British colonial diet is sometimes evident in an amalgam of expressions. For instance, cafés offer tea sets (coffee or tea) which include items such as 'marshmallow on white toast', or peanut butter and chocolate sauce on whole-wheat toast. Coffee and milk tea are sometimes mixed together, creating a drink called Yuan Yang (in Cantonese, Jin Jyun), which is 70% of coffee and 30% milk tea.

A growing concern

While Hong Kong has maintained a level of café culture since colonization, the type of specialty cafés discussed throughout this book first began to appear in districts on the periphery of the main commercial areas of Kowloon and Central from about 2010. They are scattered throughout Sheung Wan; Lan Kwai Fong; Mongkok; Sai Kung, a beachside area; and further out in the New Territories. Sheung Wan, situated in the north west of Hong Kong Island close to Central, is an area where the traditional Chinese culture has not given over to the Western commercialism. The district is on the fringe of renewal and, at the time of writing, a few boutique hotels and specialty cafés had begun to make their mark, creating the typical setting for third-wave café culture. The neighbouring Lan Kwai Fong, long known for its cosmopolitan diversity, nightlife and fine cuisine, is another example of a place where hybrid identities fuse through lifestyle consumption practices such as fine dining, cafés, night-clubbing and bar life.

The globalization of café culture has ensured the growth of third-wave cafés in Hong Kong and Mainland China in a short period of time. These cafés are by no means confined to China and Japan, and appear in many Asian cities from Seoul and Bangkok to Hanoi and Kuala Lumper. As with cafés in other global cities, they are readily identifiable by their demonstrations of connoisseurship, as well as the ubiquitous interior design template. With their minimalist aesthetics, Hong Kong cafés are more closely aligned with cafés in Western cities, rather than those in Mainland China where individual design expression is more common. Hong Kong's history of cosmopolitan food and drink, which saw the introduction of café culture during its colonial period, has fuelled the enthusiastic adoption of the contemporary café. Its baristas are growing in stature each year. Since 2014, Hong Kong baristas have been represented in the World Barista Championships finals or semi-final rounds. Kapo Chiu, Owner of Cupping Room Coffee Roasters, placed second in the World Barista Championship in 2014 and third in 2017. Lok Chan of Craft Coffee Taster also became the World Cup Tasters Champion in 2017. High urban populations, dense apartment-style living, rising middle classes and a taste for Western lifestyles are all factors that suggest that contemporary café culture in Mainland China and Hong Kong will keep on its upward trajectory.

Notes

1 Wang, Jeng. 2012. "The coffee/cafe scape in Chinese cities." *MC Online Journal of Media and Culture* Vol 15, Issue 2. (Since cafes provide spaces where one can spend a relatively long period of time for little financial outlay, owners have to increase prices to cover expenses.)
2 *Bloomberg News*. 2017. "Chinese millennials swap tea for coffee as Starbucks pushes east." *Bloomberg.com*. https://www.bloomberg.com/news/articles/2017-08-08/china-millennials-swap-tea-for-coffee-as-starbucks-pushes-east, August 8. Ret. 4.8.17.
3 Meyer, Zlati. 2017. "Starbuck's CEO gets off to start on decent earnings." *USA Today*. https://www.usatoday.com/story/money/business/2017/04/27/starbucks/100990396/, April 27. Ret. 4.8.17.
4 Wang, Jeng. 2012. Ibid.
5 Cited in Cunningham, Maura Elizabeth. 2010. "China's coffee culture." *Forbes*. https://www.forbes.com/2010/04/28/starbucks-china-consumers-markets-economy-coffee.html#3a6d872d3a0e, April 28. Ret. 18.8.17.
6 Smith Maguire, Jennifer and Hu, Dan. 2013. "Not a simple coffee shop: Local, global and glocal dimensions of the consumption of Starbucks in China." *Social Identities* Volume 19, Issue 5, pp. 1350–4630.
7 Keane, Michael. 2007. *Created in China: the Great New Leap Forward*. London: Routledge.
8 Wang, Jeng. 2012. Ibid
9 Wang, Jeng. 2012. Ibid.
10 Smith Maguire, Jennifer and Hu, Dan, 2013. Ibid., p. 60.
11 Wasserstrom, Jeffrey 2007. "Sipping Starbucks from Bloomington, Indiana to Shanghai, China." *World Hum*. http://www.worldhum.com/features/speakers-corner/sipping_starbucks_from_bloomington_indiana_to_shanghai_20080128/, January 30.

12 Gonzales, Angel. 2016. "Starbucks to help pay for China workers housing." *The Seattle Times*. https://www.seattletimes.com/business/retail/starbucks-to-help-pay-for-china-workers-housing/, July 11. Ret. 30.6.18.

13 Duggan, Jennifer. 2015. "Spilling the beans on China's growing coffee culture." *The Guardian*. https://www.theguardian.com/sustainable-business/2015/may/18/spilling-the-beans-chinas-growing-coffee-culture, May 18. Ret. 4.6.18.

14 Smith Maguire, Jennifer and Hu, Dan. 2013. Ibid., p. 678.

15 Cohen, Luc 2014. "Starbucks scoops up coffee beans from China for blends in Asia, sales." *Business News*. https://www.reuters.com/article/us-coffee-china-starbucks/starbucks-scoops-up-coffee-beans-from-china-for-blends-asia-sales-idUSKCN-0J32CX20141119, November 19. Ret. 30.6.18.

7

AMBIENCE, ATMOSPHERE AND DESIGN

> Cafes are vitally about atmosphere and kindled memories.
>
> *Iain Sinclair*[1]

> It needs to look good, but it doesn't have to be the perfume box.
>
> *Ralf Ruller*[2]

It's not just about the coffee...

Gemütlichkeit. Hygge. Gezellig. Many cultures have a word that captures that sense of when the ambience of a place is just right. In German, the word *gemütlichkeit* is used to convey a range of affect – a sense of good feeling, cheer and conviviality. The Danish and Dutch words have similar meanings. Each word has its own cultural nuance, but the three northern European words can be broadly translated into English as a sense of comfort and social and emotional well-being. They have a domestic connotation. Whether the hospitality space is a café, restaurant or bar, its ambience is vital to the overall experience of the place.

For some coffee aficionados, all that matters at the café is that the coffee tastes good. But for the majority of us, the enjoyment of the coffee is intrinsically entwined with the ambience or atmosphere of the experience itself: what it looks like, where it is, how the staff treat us and how it feels. The total coffee experience is regarded as critical in traditional Japanese cafés, where the role of the coffee master is to ensure the ambience is right, along with the coffee and service: 'The quality of coffee, the ambience and service, everything is in the hands of the master, whose authority is secondary to his affectionate obligation to his clientele.'[3] This includes attention to every aspect of the experience, including the café's interior. Contemporary coffee maestros might agree, but each has their own view on how this is achieved, and what is prioritized.

Ralf Ruller of Berlin's The Barn Café and Roastery is alert to the nuances of ambience, particularly after encountering negative publicity for banning strollers at his café in Berlin's gentrifying area of Prenzlaur Berg. Ruller is unrepentant about this move and thinks that people should be allowed to enjoy their coffee without being disturbed or distracted by other loud intrusions. For that reason, there is no music played in his cafés; Ruller wants his customers to really focus on the taste and sensation of the coffee itself. Specialty coffee connoisseurs with their artisanal hands-on sensibility are attentive to the whole café experience, despite their main dedication to the coffee.

When applied to the café, the concept of *gemütlichkeit* might conjure up associations of early European coffeehouses, whose convivial atmosphere attracted customers principally for the sociability and conversation. Eighteenth-century representations of the coffeehouse typically show a throng of people gathered around tables and benches engrossed in lively, animated conversation. Or *gemütlichkeit* is gleaned in the elaborately decorated 17th-century Ottoman coffeehouses, whose wealthy merchant customers disported themselves on luxurious cushions in spaces adorned with internal water features, decorative walls and windows. So popular was this mise en scène, replicated in lithographs, that when coffee was first introduced from Turkey to France in the 17th century, the enthusiasm for all things Oriental escalated. It wasn't just the exotic and luxurious interiors that were sought after; some café patrons were after a truly immersive experience. Wolfgang Shivelbusch describes how court society during the Rococo period loved to dress up in Oriental style 'a la Turque' and would don turbans and caftans when visiting the popular coffeehouses. They'd drape themselves over cushions and on rugs, in rooms decorated with Chinese porcelain rooms, drinking coffee and chatting.[4]

Many elements work together to create the type of ambience and feel of the contemporary café. A visit to the café is a sensory experience, created through the combination of drinking and eating, visual features and the assortment of personal interactions that occur. Lighting, furniture, colour, music and other elements all trigger a repertoire of imaginative and emotional responses. The senses are activated, in particular the senses of smell and taste, both powerful triggers of memory and feeling. This is what Ian Sinclair alludes to in the forefront quote when he says that cafés are about atmosphere and memories. Immersed in an embodied experience, you might be conjuring up an assortment of ideas and connections – consciously or unconsciously – to community, identity, authenticity or simply sensual enjoyment.

Kojima Kenji, who is manager and head roaster of the café Fuglen in Tokyo, recognizes that service and ambience are an intrinsic part of what makes the coffee taste good. The café is the sister location of Fuglen in Oslo, Norway, and its interior of mid-century Scandinavian furnishings and dark timber reflects its Scandinavian origins. The café is so homey it has the feel of walking into someone's lounge room. Kenji observes:

> If you get bad service, then the coffee suddenly tastes bad. You also have to think about the atmosphere of the cafe. Music, glassware, all of these things influence the taste of the coffee. The human mind is really strange, and it will perceive taste differently depending on the experience about it.[5]

Kenji's reflection underscores too how the café can play an important role in the attachment of place, a concept discussed in detail in Chapter Two. It refers to the special bond that we develop with places, environments or settings so that a place or space acquires meaning for us. Although the experience of place is unique to each person and is related to personal history, the attachment we feel to somewhere is in essence a set of feelings. It is shaped by knowledge, beliefs and social relationships about a particular place or space, and has a bearing on the types of attachments we form.[6]

Interpersonal relationships with staff and customers affect our experience, and the expectation of staff in the service industries is that they are friendly and welcoming, irrespective of how they actually feel towards the customers. This 'labour of aesthetics' is fundamental to the service industries for cultivating an experience that helps to generate satisfaction, enjoyment and customer loyalty.[7] Starbucks is well known for training its baristas to convey qualities such as friendliness through small talk, hospitality by being welcoming, and recognition through remembering customers' drinks. Many independent café owners use the same techniques, cognizant of the importance of social connection to make their customers feel at ease and welcomed.

Renee and her husband own a café in Brisbane and Renee tells how her husband Mikey, who is the main barista in the café, remembers his regular customers' coffee so that when he's able he'll make it before they've even ordered it:

> depending on how busy it is, he'll see a car pull up and he'll know *exactly* who it is, *exactly* what they're having and he'll make it for them and have it sitting on the counter by the time they get out of their car. Which they love…

The behaviour and performance of café staff contribute to the space's ambience, determining whether it is welcoming, casual, efficient or offhand. A café's reputation can hinge on the attitude of staff. As well as generating a sense of belonging that Mikey strives to achieve, the entertainment impulse may also be part of a hospitality servicescape.

In some cafés, the antics of the staff perform the work of the spectacle, without the props of a themed café. An Australian researcher, Emma, enjoys the theatrical performance of the baristas at her regular workplace café, and felt compelled to share a particular encounter on Facebook:

> My favourite part of the day at work is getting my morning coffee from Danny and Dan at z9. Those two complement each other so well! Danny with his skater boy anything goes attitude and Dan with his ambient utterances and slow, long-limbed movements. Their banter sounds like the bitonal ping pong of a table tennis match. They stand a bit higher than us because the container that houses their coffee shop must be a bit elevated. It's like they are on a stage and listening to their conversation I often feel like I am watching a show and often chuckle to myself. There's always something interesting being said in that container. Like yesterday, when I was waiting for my double macchiato and a man came up and asked Dan why he has an American accent. Dan explained that he was born in Canada, then looked the person in the eye and (solemnly? or faux solemnly?) spoke the lyrics of the Judith Durham song:
>
> > We are one, but we are many,
> > And from all the lands on earth we come.
> > We'll share a dream and sing with one voice,
> > I am, you are, we are Australian
>
> ...pointing to his chest, the man, and palms upturned at 'I', 'you' and 'we'. Then continued on with his work, quietly.

If your barista isn't exuberant and extrovert, other forms of human interaction with café staff help to produce distinctive ambiences. One of our interviewees, Frank, an architect, observed that when he travelled in different countries, the cafés he visited in various cities had different ways of serving the cup of coffee. In Germany, in Berlin's cafés, you order and pay at the counter, provide your name, and then find a table to sit while your coffee is being brewed. When the coffee's ready, your name is called out and you fetch it from the counter, where barista and customer acknowledge each other. Frank said that for him, hearing his name called out among a crowd of strangers helped to make him feel part of the group and create an aura of intimacy and familiarity in the café space: 'It makes you feel like you're a friend, because you hear your name being called out among a group of strangers.' This was no doubt something he was more conscious of as a foreigner to a country in which his native language differed.

Atmosphere and interiors

Writers have tried to put into words what is exactly meant by the concept of atmosphere, ambience or aura. The expression 'atmosphere', like ambience, is common in discussions of aesthetics, but it can also have a political dimension. As applied to spaces, people or nature, atmosphere is a feeling that's attributed to either the environment or persons experiencing them. Atmosphere is something we experience when we walk into a room or space – for example, we feel immediately whether it is cosy, sterile or something else. Although atmosphere might be considered something that is 'indeterminate and difficult to express', because it's relational between humans and the combination of environmental elements, it is nonetheless significant. When we talk about atmospheres in a vague sense, it doesn't mean that the feeling or expression of them is vague.[8] Atmospheres might be spatially blurred, but they are powerful expressions of feeling and spatial bearers of mood. In the café, atmosphere is generated by a 'sensory aesthetics', which include the design elements, staff and customer behaviour, all playing a unique role in the customer's emotional response to the physical environment.[9]

Sociologist Michel Maffesoli sees sensuous, social engagement as a central appeal of cafés and bars, in the ways it is manifest through social interaction, drink, food and the ambience of the venue. He uses the term aura to describe a 'complex movement of an atmosphere emitted by places and activities giving them a unique odour and colouring'.[10] Auras can be generated in specific places, by 'networks of convivial cells', the sociality of being-together.

Representations of 18th century animated coffee houses are something of a contrast to today's cafés, where customers tend to be more sedate, talking quietly amongst themselves often in pairs rather than large groups. At least half of the café patrons today are women, whose presence generates a sensibility that is altogether different from that of the all-masculine environment of the earlier coffee houses. Another difference is the introduction of technological devices into the café, adding an entirely different dimension to the café's atmosphere as many customers communicate silently via their mobile phones and laptops. But atmosphere is not static, nor are places fixed; rather, they're fluid and may shift – perhaps subtly – if components within the space are changed. The interactions and behaviour of employees and customers are the most mutable elements, while the extrovert performance of a barista generates a spectacle and concomitant response, the atmosphere is returned to status quo a little while later.

Part of the café's sensory aesthetics is sound, which of all of our senses, unless loud and obtrusive, is the least registered consciously. As we move around the city, the background hum and flow of urban living is registered almost subliminally. Traffic, footsteps, voices, doors closing and horns all meld into a background soundscape. So it is in the café, where we're exposed to a certain quiet rumble in the background: the gargle of the espresso machine, the quiet chatter of voices and usually some innocuous music (but not always), perhaps a roaster, but nothing that jars or disturbs the customer's equilibrium. Sound has to be carefully managed in the café, so that the environment remains welcoming and easy. Customers share a tacit understanding about this – it's a behaviour learnt through the process of acculturation that when in public or the hybrid spaces of the city, we respect each other's privacy. It is rare to see someone listening to music or watching video content without wearing headphones. It is equally rare despite the many conversations occurring in the café, that people talk loudly.

The spatial arrangement of elements inside interior spaces not only affect how people use that space but also determine comfort and well-being. For instance, in the café, differences in layout and proximity of tables and chairs impact on customers' comfort levels, something that may be driven by idiosyncratic or cultural norms. In Australia, many cafés have large central communal tables, with smaller tables scattered around the interior and outside space. Communal tables were also common in the Asian cities I visited – in Hong Kong, Shanghai and Singapore. Thrust in closer proximity to strangers, this arrangement enables the opportunity for spontaneous encounters and conversations with people we don't know. I wouldn't typically choose to sit at a large communal table but, in several cafés I visited in Tokyo and Hong Kong, this was the only option. Interestingly, the close interpersonal proximity with strangers did in fact produce social interaction, which I wouldn't have otherwise engaged in.

People's comfort levels of interpersonal distance vary and are influenced by culture and our own subjectivities. The amount of interpersonal distance between people helps us to regulate intimacy in social situations by controlling sensory exposure. Some cultures prefer greater interpersonal distance than others. In a cross-cultural study of nearly 9,000 participants across forty-two countries, which measured levels of comfort at interpersonal distance, it found that social distance towards strangers was predicated by a country's average temperature, age and gender. Perhaps it is no surprise that people in colder climates, and women, preferred greater distance towards strangers. Countries in northern Europe were among those whose preference was for the greatest interpersonal distance.[11] Indeed, this appears to be the case in Germany, where one café proprietor told me that he couldn't put the tables too close together as people would only sit at them if there was nowhere else to sit. This was also borne out in observations of cafés in Berlin, where in general the distance between tables was quite generous. Despite the prevalence of communal tables in Australian cafés, amongst the people I spoke with, the majority of whom were women, most people preferred single tables, though a small number of people were prepared to sit at communal tables if there was sufficient space.

The idea that urban hybrid places such as the café function as a sanctuary, a place of retreat away from family and work obligations or simply a refuge from our complex lives in the 21st-century city has historical origins in the 18th-century city when the concept of home became paramount. From this time, the importance of interior spaces acquired greater significance and the interior's role in providing sanctuary was particularly pronounced with the advent of the Industrial Revolution. Richard Sennett in *The Conscience of the Eye*[12] traces the historical significance of place as refuge, a concept which gathered greater weight during this period. With the momentous shift from a predominantly agricultural society to an increasingly urbanized one, the newly created public world of the cities and streets was often harsh, crime-ridden and above all, confusingly complex. Much of this was to do with the mix of social classes, who had previously lived in greater geographical segregation. Interior spaces provided a sanctuary from the public life of crowded and dirty city streets; the vision of a warm, cosy interior where people could enjoy close social interaction was important to the sense of retreat and protection.

From the 19th century, interior spaces and the ways in which they were decorated became associated with bourgeois domesticity, which emphasized a newly articulated and widespread desire for privacy and comfort.[13] The historical arrival of decorative interiors for a growing middle class was made possible by the bourgeois distinction between dwelling and work. It was also the point at which the feminine became associated with interior, domestic space. That the desires for comfort and sanctuary are transported to the hybrid spaces of the city, its bars and eating houses, is not hard to imagine. In Britain and other European countries, cafés and bars adopted many of the design features of domestic comfort and ease – warmly glowing wall lamps, wallpaper, tapestry and other rich fabric upholstery, comfortable chairs and tables.

In many contemporary cafés, most notably among the specialty variety, the sense of cosiness created by the lush interior elements of early coffeehouses is clearly absent and frequently gives way to stark, minimalist spaces. Yet perhaps the modern cafés' pared-back, simple aesthetic, which is undemanding and easy on the eye, might well have the same impact as a cosy environment, its plain spaces providing a quiet contrast to the noise and complexity of the urban environment outside the café's doors.

While cafés in 19th-century England were enclosed interior places, no doubt because of the cold climate and streets which were unclean and spread infection, many European cafés opened onto the street and came to dominate the footpaths. Their terraces full of outward-looking tables and chairs were striking features of 19th-century cities. According to historian Philipe Aries, industrialization brought with it increasing social control and regulation, and the café was one of the few places where people, including families, managed to escape this type of surveillance – despite state attempts to intervene. He attributes the café's lively and well-patronized ambience largely to this factor.[14]

At certain periods throughout the café's history, café styles have been at the forefront of design trends. Utilizing new materials and new design features, some styles became influential and later adapted into the kitchens of domestic interiors. The 1950s espresso bar in Europe, America and Australia introduced a new, modernist aesthetic with contemporary furniture such as bar stools, novel wall lighting and chequerboard linoleum on the floor. The latest technology and materials such as plastic and aluminium were introduced in imaginative ways.[15] In Australian cafés at this time, the 'neo deco' style was popular in many cafés and milk bars, particularly those run by Greek owners. Based on the 1920s Art Deco style, the style's modernist aesthetic featured sleek, chrome-edged counter tops and bar stools, cosy seating booths and jukebox machines.[16]

Interior exemplars: Authenticity and simplicity

With the exception of the third-wave or specialty café's ubiquitous aesthetic, there is as wide a variety of café interiors as the combination of individual elements – and the designer's and owner's imagination – allows. Themed cafés provoke playfulness and fun, with some countries enjoying greater experimentation than others. Cat cafés, monster cafés, board game cafés, hammock cafés – there are even toilet cafés such as the Poop café in Toronto, Canada, replete with toilet chair seats and poo-shaped chocolate desserts. By contrast, the traditional European-style café with its iconic wicker chairs connects with a cultural history of cafés as a convivial gathering place for the exchange of ideas and sociality. Chain store cafés such as Starbucks use standardized, but homey, designs and branding to produce a sense of the familiar no matter where they are located. Contemporary café designs make an appeal to a new generation of café clientele.

Many cafés exist alongside allied businesses, such as those situated in bookshops, cinemas, car-washes or department stores, where their co-location influences the look and ambience of the space. Social enterprise cafés in Britain and the United States are sometimes recognizable by their temporary pop-up style. Other social enterprise cafés employing young homeless people, people in recovery from addiction or disabled people seek to maintain a conventional café aesthetic that doesn't draw attention to its purpose. Whatever the combination and assemblage of design elements, and the performance of the staff, all communicate meaning. Who does this space appeal to? How seriously is coffee treated here? Can I sit here and work on my laptop?

Specialty cafés: The template

The aesthetic 'template' of specialty cafés we see in cities around the world has been transmitted by technology and population mobility via the rapid global flow of products and people. Historically, cultural products have long been transported and adopted across the world, particularly during the 18th-century period of colonial expansion. The major difference is that today, technological innovation has accelerated the speed and pace at which designs are transmitted and adopted on a global scale. Social media apps such as Four Square are charged with promoting the homogenous, transnational design of many cafés and bars. Because of their universal global use, they help to produce 'a harmonization of tastes' and tend to promote hospitality places that all look similar.

Designed products communicate meaning via their visual signs in a process known as semiotics. We attach associations and connotations to visual signs, a practice that advertising relies upon. Products or services can convey characteristics such as distinction and culture; for example, the traditional European-style café, with iconic rattan chairs and dark timber tables sometimes cloaked in white linen, conjures up connotations of good taste, tradition, culture and civility. Those specialty cafés, with a minimalist, naturalistic aesthetic, convey a sense of the authentic. It is as if the environment, unadorned, is in service to the main game, which is the coffee.

Most specialty cafés begin their life on the fringe of the city centre, where rents are cheaper. As starter businesses, their budgets are usually modest and

FIGURE 7.1 Coffee Heroes, Berlin. Photo credit: © Emma Felton.

so the fit-outs tend to be too. Some features of the café may be constructed by the café owners themselves or their friends. And yet, walk into a café in Tokyo, Melbourne, Shanghai or Berlin and you will see the similar features, with small variations. The specialty café is usually identifiable by its design elements alone, before you even begin to browse the coffee menu. Simple blonde timber veneer tables and chairs or boxes, whitewashed, brick or plain tiled walls, Edison lights, unadorned counter tops perhaps in stainless steel, a blackboard menu and sometimes a selection of hanging plants, which might reinforce the natural artisanal ambience of the café. The baristas might be wearing leather aprons, with heavy brass clips. The coffee-making equipment, from the espresso machine to the pour-over coffee apparatus and aero press, are all part of the display of visual elements that signify what artisanal coffee makers and drinkers value: authenticity, ethical choices and artisanal approaches.

Where cafés have their own roasteries, the roasting machines are usually on display, rather than concealed behind walls, or hidden away as too industrial, noisy or messy. Their visibility helps to reinforce the connection with coffee's source – the bean – and underlines its authenticity. The roasting machine captures the senses' attention, via sight, sound and smell, adding more dimensions to the sensory experience of the café. The roaster or artisan is also on display, in a performance which demonstrates their artisan skills.

While the artisan style of interior has the appearance of a café that has been established economically and efficiently, it belies the carefully constructed assemblage of elements that together create meanings and associations. Simplicity and authenticity are hallmarks of specialty cafés, where the origin of the bean is known and where the roasting and brewing is conducted in an artisanal manner. Simplicity conveys a sense of honesty and 'emphasizes its distance from the complexities and manufactured quality of modern industrialised life'.[17] Nonetheless, the idea of simplicity can obscure a complex process which, in coffee production, it does. It may also conceal the complexity of the café business itself, in which the proprietor is juggling multiple competing demands.

The specialty café's aesthetic standardization has generated satirical reactions in Australia and probably elsewhere – and social media provides an outlet for disgruntled consumers. The Melbourne-based café blogger referred to in Chapter Three is a female Australian café owner. Having worked in the industry for several years, she became irritated by the precious attitude of some male baristas and responded by dedicating a review blog, where she is not reluctant to remark on aspects of café culture that annoy her. Here she's describing and deriding a café interior:

> Generic. That is the first word that comes to mind when I think of this place…[it] is your typical minimalist, lifeless, soulless cafe with dudes making the coffee and women polishing cutlery mindlessly, bored out of their brains…Let's start with the aesthetics: White walls, check. Hanging plants, check. Minimalist decor, check. This cafe is so tediously hipster that it has no individuality at all.[18]

Although the homogenous aesthetic clearly annoyed this blogger, some people might find it reassuring, in the same way that a chain store café signals the comfort of the familiar. The combination of elements indicates the known, and not only to what type of coffee experience you're about to find. It also suggests the types of people you might be mingling among, and perhaps who share similar lifestyle practices. Visual aesthetics are a powerful way to communicate meaning about who belongs in that space and who might not. If a significant part of the

FIGURE 7.2 The Barn cafe and roastery, Berlin: in-house roasters adds to cafe's ambience.

café experience is about generating community, then visual indices or signs are a useful short-hand expression of the type of community.

Aesthetic criticism is perennial, and this is not the first time that charges of design uniformity have been made against café interiors. In the 1950s, during a surge in popularity of the coffee bar in London and other British cities, similar accusations were made against their ubiquitous interior styles. Partly driven by a class consciousness that anyone could open a café, critiques of cafés and their interiors were also about a schism between the roles of the amateur and the professional. The satirical magazine *Punch* ran an article, 'Coffee-bar theory and practice', which was accompanied by a cartoon of a 'scientist' indicating that an interior with a rubber plant, bamboo and contemporary furniture equals a coffee bar. However, some professionals recognized that amateurs could make a good job of the café, and in a 1954 edition of the journal *Architectural Design*, a report stated that 'Many bars appear to be run by catering amateurs but making a professional job of this new type of establishment—and a good income'.[19]

Variations on a theme

Not all specialty-style cafés are, of course, exactly the same, and the simple design elements provide scope to adapt the theme. Variations on designs can be subtle or dramatic. Whether a newly created space or a converted warehouse or building, this is the canvas upon which the other elements are layered. In the many specialty-style cafés we visited, elements such as the introduction of colour, art and photography on the walls, designed counters, unconventional light fittings and other features helped to create a café's individuality. Although the cafés share similar design elements, each appeal to people in different ways – it's the sensory combination of the coffee's taste, the visual appeal and the interactions of others, sound and music that produces the total experience. Describing a specialty café in Sydney, Australia, in the industrial space of a converted hardware store, David acknowledges that some of the elements that create an ambience don't always work, but the whole experience is greater than its parts:

> I love the space – it's a converted Mitre 10 hardware store. I know that doesn't sound promising, but it has high ceilings, good acoustics, pleasing lighting, and an interesting mix of people. The seating isn't especially comfortable, but you can't have everything apparently.
>
> Coffee is really excellent (that's key for me), and I like the staff who know me and my preferences. The music tends to be terrible (80s death metal, or some such thing played a bit ironically), but played at a non-intrusive volume.

David's prepared to overlook the death metal music and the slightly uncomfortable chairs for the other aspects of the café and particularly the coffee that he enjoys. Scale is important in the space, the high ceilings of a converted industrial building. Chris, an Australian woman, also singles out scale when she tells of one of her favourite cafés in Melbourne, Australia, although in this instance it is the intimacy of the small space she enjoys:

> I love the location – the arched walkway is lovely, chilly in winter but then you can head inside to the tiny but convivial indoor area. I like it because it's of a scale and ambience that's comfortable for a lone visitor, as I am when I'm there. The location is also just a bit off the beaten track, so while it can be busy at lunchtimes it feels like it provides welcome respite from the city hubbub.

Chris identifies the importance of the café's location; its appeal as a sanctuary from the busy city streets, which is somewhat reminiscent of historical accounts of urban interior spaces as a refuge. Both David and Chris used affective language to describe their regular cafés; they 'love' the location or the space. When we feel a sense of belonging and attachment to a place, it's an embodied, affective experience. All our senses are engaged: memories, feelings and imagination work to maintain the sense of attachment.

There are many variations on the specialty café's interior. Eye-catching elements might be used, while still retaining elements of the specialty café aesthetic. Coffee bean sacks were the inspiration for the interior of The Don House Café in Pristina, Kosovo. The architects InArchh, created a dramatic play of timber and light, featuring a striking, organically shaped timber wall, timber light shades inspired from the coffee bean and dark timber tables to create a coffee mood in a stylish, coherent way.

When I visited China I saw many examples of imaginative and playful café interiors. At a quick glance, Shanghai's Fumi Café is identifiable as a specialty café with its simple clean interior, timber floors and whitewashed walls, but its detail reveals the carefully considered design effort that has gone into producing what transpires, once inside, to be a highly designed space. Bialetti Moka coffee pots of varying sizes are fixed onto a whitewashed brick wall, with concealed lights, producing a warm backlit glow (see Chapter Six for image). A sculptural ceiling is suspended over part of the café in a series of dark waves, which represent the coffee's fumes. Chrome chairs and sleek chrome bars add another dimension of light to the tiny 33-metre square space. The designer, Italian Alberto Cailoa, is one of the many international designers to set up a design studio in Shanghai.

FIGURE 7.3 Don Café House, Prishtina, Kosova. Photo credit: © Adthe Mulla. With kind permission from Innarch.

The café is clearly a big drawcard for young Shanghainese, where it is nestled in a quiet street in Xuhui, the former French Concession area of the city. Blogs and reviews attest to the café's popularity, several stating that it frequently gets too crowded and noisy.

One of Tokyo's oldest café's, Cafe l'Ambre, discussed in Chapter Five, oozes authenticity and its history, ambience and coffee support this sensibility. The café's associated narrative confirms its place in the pantheon of Japan's café history. Narratives of places or products can enhance our experience in a variety of ways and are increasingly used as a communication strategy, deployed in a variety of ways including branding and marketing. Company websites often feature a link that declares 'Our Story', with a narrative that creates a point of identity and difference in an ever-expanding field of products and services.

I visited a café in London whose narrative and distinction was artfully created by its name. Checking Google maps for a café in the Bermondsey area where I was visiting that afternoon, one caught my attention because of its name – Fuckoffee – a cheeky play on words, it had the desired effect and grabbed my attention. As well, the café had good reviews so I set out to find it. The café served specialty-style coffee and hearty, organic food, but its interior was an exercise in contrast to the minimalist interiors of many specialty cafés. *Gemütlichkeit* comes to mind: Fuckoffee was cosy, packed with soft, comfortable old furnishings where people lounged around chatting or were occupied with their laptops. Children, a rare sight in the specialty café, played quietly among the old lounge chairs. In a quirky twist on the café's name, its loyalty cards expanded upon the Fuckoffee theme, – each time you purchased a coffee a tick was made next to the following words: F★CK: it, me, you, off, them, this, coffee. While the café has

FIGURE 7.4 Fuckoffee café, London, busy interior. Photo credit: © Emma Felton.

FIGURE 7.5 Assembly Café, Melbourne, display features incorporated into design. Photo credit: © Patrick Hayes.

courted controversy and even legal action due to its name, its moniker remains intact and unabashed.

Aesthetics and appeal

The coffee chain Starbucks and others such as McDonald's are frequently criticized for their corporatization of the café, their global dominance and the impact of homogenized food and drink served in their spaces. As branded cafés, their aesthetics are standardized; visual and discursive devices are used to create meaning about the product and experience, and ultimately to generate brand loyalty.[20] The familiar green and white colouring of Starbucks, the earth-toned palettes and homey interiors are the same the world over. In practice, the independent coffee sector, with its focus on the artisanal and the hand crafted, exists in opposition to café chains such Starbucks, rejecting the corporate values it stands for. Yet both types of cafés – one a chain and the other independently owned, – use aesthetics in a coherent manner to communicate values about the type of experience the customer is likely to encounter. Somewhat ironically, the specialty café with its rather uniform aesthetic is almost as identifiable as a Starbucks anywhere in the world, using signifying, semiotic cues in a manner similar to the branded coffee shop. Starbucks promotes itself as an 'experiential brand', and its environment is carefully assembled to produce a pleasant, sociable 'third-place'. The same could be said of the independent café where, although the coffee is paramount, the emphasis is on the total experience.

Despite the ubiquity of the specialty café in cities across the world, not everyone finds them a welcoming experience. A study of chain store cafés in Britain found that cafés such as Costa and McDonald's attracted a greater number of ethnically diverse customers amongst the study's three sites, more so than other cafés in the area. In the United States, another study of 862 café patrons who attended three different types of cafés found that the chain store café had a 25% increase in 'minority' customers, that is black, Hispanic and Asian, over the other two cafés styles.[21] Similarly, for migrants from across European Union (EU) in Poland, chain store cafés and restaurants were recognized as familiar places of cultural recognition and comfort.[22]

In the British study, one of the sites in Hackney, London, was a rapidly gentrifying area and participants voiced concern at the changes occurring in their gentrifying neighbourhood. Part of this anxiety was expressed in the arrival of what one South Asian participant articulated as 'dinky little cafés' – or independent cafés – cropping up everywhere. Other participants also felt excluded from the new cafés and felt more at home in the 'corporate openness' of the franchised Costa café. As the researchers point out, the 'knowledge' about a café, its character and image all work as taste markers of class and social distinction, with the attendant tacit understanding of who belongs and who doesn't.[23]The independent café often represents a white, middle-class space in which ethnic minorities might feel excluded. Goffman's idea of 'civil inattention' is germane here to the comfort that people feel in a particular public space, whereby strangers who are in close proximity show they're aware of one another without imposing on them. It's the balance between enough and not too much social recognition being given, such as brief acknowledgement through eye contact, which enables a comfortable co-presence or 'light-touch' sociality.

The design and aesthetic industries: Another growth story

Food, drink and design, including cafés, bars and restaurants, are all part of what is known as the aesthetic industries. The aesthetic industries exist within an eco-system of supply and value chains, which typically have their genesis and fullest expression in the city. The growth of cities and urban regeneration have generated a rising demand for the flourishing design industries, which are related not only to the built environment, but also to a host of products and services.

Cafés and restaurants draw on a range of design professionals in the establishment phases of their business. Among these are architects, interior designers, web designers, graphic artists and industrial designers, whose skills are all evident in the servicescape. From the café's chairs and tables, cutlery and crockery, to the espresso machines and other technical apparatus and to the company website and aesthetic, most of these elements have been designed.

The highly specialized, artisanal approach to coffee making of third-wave cafés has spawned myriad equipment to meet the needs of the café industry and the home brewer specialist alike. Espresso machines are now commonplace in many homes and the home brewer can pay up to (US) $14,500 for a state-of-the-art van der Westen Speedster made in the Netherlands. The choice of espresso machine for a café owner is important to produce an efficient and good-quality cup of coffee. Machines today are sophisticated, incorporating features such as water softening functions and computer technology to customize and calibrate coffee. The design of the espresso machine has to be considered as it reflects a desired aesthetic of the café. There are vintage-style espresso machines, featuring timber and ceramic; sleek, chrome machines; and customized machines. AnZa Coffee, a US-based company, are currently crowd-sourcing their range of Modernist brutalist home espresso machines. The machine is cast in concrete and 'offers Brutalist overtures at once softened by white ceramic accents'.

New or revivified apparatuses allow the café professional to cultivate the perfect espresso or macchiato and meet the consumer demand for the best brew.

FIGURE 7.6 AnZa espresso machine. Photo credit: © AnZa Espresso.

Domestic coffee makers have been given a new lease of life and now are part of the third-wave café's armoury. The French Press has been reinvigorated. First appearing in 1921, it was popularized by the Swedish Bodum company during the 1970s and 1980s. In Australia it was known as 'The Plunger' but its use has since acquired greater levels of attention - to water temperature, timing and bean grind. The popular AeroPress is a recent arrival and was invented in 2005 by Alan Adler, an engineer, lecturer and inventor. The AeroPress uses a similar principle to the French Press, but with slightly different results, producing a coffee which is comparable in taste to an espresso. There is filtering equipment and Pour-Over Coffee kettles and drippers; the first of its kind was invented in 1941 under the name of Chemex by Peter Schlumbohm, an American-based German. Chemex, essentially a glass container in which water is poured over a quantity of coffee, is still manufactured today. The most ubiquitous of the pouring kettles seems to be the Hario V60, with its elegant gooseneck spouts, which give greater precision as pour-over brewing requires incremental pouring. All home brewing devices, they are also found in cafés alongside the espresso machines.

The design industries, as with the food and drink sector, have been on the ascendency since the late 20th century. A greater public awareness and appreciation of design has been fuelled by a range of innovative developments. Technology has created new design fields in the area of digital, web and graphic design, and revolutionized existing industries. Architecture's and industrial and interior design's traditional ways of working have been radically transformed by the introduction of design-based software, 3D printing and modelling, and virtual reality.

The promotion of the design industries was assisted by the governmental policy strategy of the creative industries framework, which first appeared in Britain in the late 1990s. It was quickly adopted by many city administrators in Western nations. The creative industries and their role in urban regeneration and urban amenities were discussed in greater depth in Chapter One. To briefly reiterate, this development – recognizing the value of the creative industries to national economies, the British government developed a strategy which reframed art and culture in an evolving and dynamic context. It situated the industries in the broader application of fields of employment, so that those working along all supply chains were recognized as part of the creative industries workforce.[24] The thriving design industries, especially in the digital sphere, continue to create new employment and business opportunities – some of which are evident in the café, particularly in the field of industrial design.

In Australian studies, the design and creative industries' growth is measured against traditional industries commonly believed to be high-income and high-employment such as mining and agriculture, only to reveal that employment in the creative industries outstripped them by two to one. Sector definitions of creative industries are important here; for example, software development and advertising are high employment sectors. Growth in the creative industries was twice that of other industries in a five-year period, from 2011 to 2016 than any other national industry.[25]

In China, rapid urbanization on such a momentous scale has meant a huge demand for architects and other related design disciplines. Initially, talent was drawn from a pool of international 'starchitects' for marquee projects, something of a sore point among local architects. Architects and designers from all over the world flocked to China, seeing the new growth opportunities. More recently, overseas education and a boost to local education have helped to produce a steady growth of local designers. An adventurous design culture has developed in Chinese cities, evident in its interior servicescapes such as cafés and restaurants. Observing the growth of the design industries over a number of years, China scholar Michael Keane notes that design has 'come of age' in China.[26] While China's rapid urbanization accounts for the massive uptake of the design industries, what might explain its exuberant and expressive manifestations? Anyone who has visited Chinese cities cannot fail to notice eye-catching buildings, spectacular public art and adventurous interior spaces. Imaginative and creative hospitality spaces are common in its main cities of Shanghai and Beijing, where seemingly generous budgets support a flair for the exceptional.

Perhaps China's unique approach to design is also to do with its history of aesthetics, where its contemporary designers, unlike their Western counterparts, are unburdened from the weight of a design history that informs and appraises their work. It is not possible to provide a detailed history of aesthetics in China, but for many centuries the primary concern was with beauty and the arts and their interrelationship with morality. The contemporary word for design – sheji – has only recently been introduced in China and, for many centuries, design was largely decorative.[27] The tradition of Confucian principles, which informs the lives of many Chinese, emphasizes obedience and harmony; in aesthetics this has been expressed in patterns of ritualized behaviour relating to the concept of Heaven. Moreover, under Mao Zedong (1949–1976) the term 'creativity' was deemed to be a bourgeois value and creativity in the arts was not encouraged. Today, the narrative is different. Most universities in China run art courses, and the continuing demand for urban infrastructure provides a canvas for imaginations, unleashed from traditions of the past. The influence of contemporary Chinese design spills over into neighbouring countries such as Korea and Japan, partly because of the country's capacity for large-scale manufacturing, with the export of products and pre-fabricated materials.[28]

Across the globe in Britain, the design industries are the ninth-largest employer and generated £71.1 billion in gross value added (GVA) in 2016. In a five-year period from 2009, the design industry grew by 27.9%. The story is similar in Australia, where the growth of architecture and interior and industrial design continues to transform the built environment through the acceleration of domestic and commercial buildings in a period of rapid urban intensification. Indeed, the design professions are incorporated into most of the world's industries, integrated throughout numerous layers of a business, often unnoticed to the untrained eye.

Expressions of design are everywhere, and the café is just a microcosm of the ubiquity of the design industries in everyday life. Design is something not always apparent to the casual observer, and we often take the designed environment for granted. The variety and typologies of designed products and services available today are unprecedented, and it is easy to forget that this abundance is a relatively recent phenomenon. As in the café, the design industries work within an eco-system that help to create the aesthetic, look, feel and ambience of a space. Aesthetics can go far in generating an experience, an aura of serenity or an atmosphere of cosiness, but there are other important elements at play – human interaction, sound, smell, taste and touch – all sensory registers that help to trigger our imaginations in a psychological relay, which creates the feeling that a place is right for us.

Notes

1 Sinclair, Iain. 2010. "Classic cafes." http://www.classiccafes.co.uk/Psy.html. Ret. 15.5.17.
2 Ralf Ruller in interview with the author, Berlin, September 2017.
3 White, Merry. 2012. *Coffee Life in Japan*. Berkeley, CA: University of California Press, p. 61.
4 Schivelbusch, Wolfgang. 1992. (Translated David Jacobsen). *Tastes:A Social History of Spices, Stimulants and Intoxicants*. New York: Random House.
5 Quoted in Teisser, Eric. 2016. "Tokyo coffee profiles: Kojima Kenji of Fuglen Coffee Roasters." *The Daily Coffee News*. http://dailycoffeenews.com/2016/04/07/tokyo-coffee-profile-kojima-kenji-of-fuglen-coffee-roasters/, April 7. Ret. 17.10.17.
6 Waxman, Lisa. 2006. "The coffee shop: Social and physical factors influencing place attachment." *Journal of Interior Design* Volume 31, Issue 3, pp. 35–53.
7 Witz, Anne, Warhurst, Chris and Nickson, Dennis. 2003. "The labour of aesthetics and the aesthetics of organization." *Organization* Volume 10, Issue 1, pp. 33–54.
8 Bohme, Gernot. 1993. "Atmosphere as the fundamental concept of the new aesthetics." *Thesis Eleven* Volume 36, pp. 113–126 (p. 113).
9 Cuthill, Vivienne et al. 2007. "Consuming Harrogate: Performing Betty's Café and Revolution Vodka Bar." *Space and Culture* Volume 10, Issue 1, pp. 64–76 (p. 63).
10 Maffesoli, Michel. 1996. *The Time of the Tribes*. London: Sage, p. 22.
11 Sorowkowska, A. 2017. "Preferred interpersonal distances: A global comparison." *Journal of Cross-Cultural Psychology* Volume 48, Issue 4, pp. 577–592.
12 Sennett, Richard. 1992. *The Conscience of the Eye: The Design and Social Life of Cities*. New York: W.W. Norton and Co.
13 Rice, Charles. 2007. *The Emergence of the Interior: Architecture, modernity, Domesticity*. London. Routledge.
14 Aries, Phillipe. 1977. "The family and the city." *Daedalus* Volume 106, Issue 2, The Family (Spring), pp. 227–235.
15 Ellis, Markman. 2004. *The Coffee House: A Cultural History*. London: Weidenfeld and Nicolson, p. 234.
16 Alexakis, Effy and Janiszewski, Leonard. 2016. *Greek Cafes and Milk Bars of Australia*. Sydney: Halstead Press.
17 Johnston, Josee and Baumann, Shyon. 2015. *Foodies: Democracy and Distinction in the Gourmet Foodscape* (second edition). New York: Routledge, p. 67.
18 Douche Dude Baristas blog. 2017. http://doucheydudebaristas.tumblr.com/Ret. 28.9.17.
19 Partington, Matthew. 2009. "The London coffee bar of the 1950s – teenage occupation of an amateur space?" *Occupation: Negotiations with Constructed Space*. Proceedings

of the Conference held at the University of Brighton, July 2–4, 2009. http://arts.brighton.ac.uk/__data/assets/pdf_file/0004/44842/33_Matthew-Partington_The-London-Coffee-Bar-of-the-1950s-.pdf. Ret. 15.4.18.

20 Bookman, Sonia. 2014. "Brands and urban life: Specialty coffee, consumers, and the co-creation of urban café sociality." *Space and Culture* Volume 17, Issue 1, pp. 85–99.

21 Jones, Hannah, Neal, Sarah, Mohan, Giles, Connell, Kieran, Cochrane, Allan and Bennett, Katy. 2015. "Urban multiculture and everyday encounters in semi-public, franchised cafe spaces." *The Sociological Review* Volume 63, pp. 644–661.

22 Piekut, A and Valentine, Gill. 2017. "Spaces of encounter and attitudes towards difference: A comparative study of two European Cities." *Social Science Research*, Volume 62, February, pp. 175–188.

23 Piekut, A. and Valentine, Gill. 2017. "Spaces of encounter and attitudes towards difference: A comparative study of two European cities." *Social Science Research* Volume 62, February, pp. 175–188.

24 Higgs, Peter and Cunningham, Stuart. 2008. "Creative industries mapping: Where have we come from and where are we going?" *Creative Industries Journal* Volume 1, Issue 1, pp. 7–30.

25 Digital Media Research Centre. 2017. *The Creative Economy in Australia.* Queensland University of Technology. Ret. 30.9.18.

26 Keane, Michael. 2013. *The Creative Industries in China: Art, Design and Media.* Cambridge. Polity Press.

27 Keane, Michael. 2013. Ibid.

28 Keane, Michael. 2013. Ibid.

8

WIRED AND WORKING

Technology, the café and work

> Networked digital information technology looms ever large in all of our lives. It shapes our perceptions, conditions the choices available to us, and remakes our experience of space and time.
>
> *Adam Greenfield*[1]

Last, but by no means the least, is technology, the greatest instrument of change since the turn of the century. In this final chapter, I look at how technology has shaped a new generation of café culture, and how it has completely transformed the experience of everyday urban life. Technological innovation is so rapid, so intense and so ubiquitous that even in the brief period of writing this book, major developments have occurred.

Technology has had a profound impact on all industries and subsequently on how people work. While the café is the site of this exploration, the digital practices that occur in its spaces are just a microcosm of changes that are happening across all domains of quotidian life. Since the beginning of the 21st century, monumental transformation and 'digital disruption' has occurred from innovations in technology such as Wi-Fi, cloud computing, Artificial Intelligence (AI), machine sentience and Augmented Reality (AR). We are at the very beginning of an era that will transform society as radically as, if not more than, the 18th-century Industrial Revolution, and which is now known as the Fourth Industrial Revolution. As with most emerging technologies, its impact is most acutely felt in the city.

Urbanism is being changed by networked technological infrastructure and, while many cities struggle to maintain physical infrastructure, they are probably well serviced by Wi-Fi and other technology networks.[2] Global Positioning Systems (GPS) and access to maps, transport routes, timetables and up-to-date localized information such as the whereabouts of the nearest restaurants, cafés, shops and services remove the serendipitous and unknown from the metropolitan experience. If you can't speak the language of the country you're in, Google will translate for you. 'Smart cities' and 'digital cities' have become terms *de jour* for urban administrators across the globe. But the terms have rapidly become redundant. All 21st-century cities are smart cities, each with varied technological capacities, using ICTs and the Internet of Things (IoT) to manage their urban infrastructure and engage more efficiently with their populations.

The volume of available data is growing exponentially, harvested from billions of mobile phones, sensors, payment systems and cameras. 'Big data' is enabled by recent innovations in cloud computing, which have significantly reduced the cost of data storage. Urban administrators have access to a vast array of information, and the expanding eco-system of sensors allows cities to track and respond quickly to such events as traffic congestion, air pollution, crime scenes, fires and so on. Civil analytics, the analysis of data, is typically focused on concerns around urban sustainability, economic efficiencies and communication between citizens and urban officials aimed at generating greater political participation. The virtual world is so seamlessly integrated into everyday life that virtual spaces are also considered to be 'places' in which citizens navigate effortlessly between the virtual and the material city.

Cafés and technology: From social to business

Cafés are primarily the sites of social interaction and communication, whose lineage of sociality dates back to their 16th-century urban origins. The spaces of the café, animated by human interaction and conversations of all descriptions, are thus infused with affect and emotion. They are intrinsically social, places 'where we can be excited by others, their opinions, their stories and more'.[3] And yet technology has introduced a completely new dimension to the café as a social space. One might think that the café is more immune from technology's influence than many other environments – it is after all a sensual and social space. Café culture is about an embodied and emplaced experience; we go to enjoy the taste of the coffee, soak up the ambience of the milieu, appreciate the conviviality of our friends or to be alone – all activities deeply rooted in the materiality of place.

But, because our lives are increasingly mediated by technology, the café experience today is markedly different from a pre-digital era. Technologically mediated spaces – that is, interpersonal communication delivered via mobile phones, tablets and other electronic devices – are the socio-cultural environments in which we live our daily lives, maintaining social relationships and forging new ones. Interpersonal communication is the dominant use of the internet and, as a consequence, social relations are being re-formed and shaped by technologies.[4] Globally, people spend an average of four hours a day online and the amount of time is growing annually. Much of this time is spent communicating with friends, colleagues and strangers using affordances such as email, Instagram, Twitter, Snapchat, WhatsApp, Facebook and a host of other social media apps.

So ubiquitous is the use of technology for communication that it is easy to forget that it is less than twenty-five years since the World Wide Web was created and transformed our daily lives. The wholesale take-up of the smartphone, which links to the affordances of the World Wide Web, is even shorter. Just over ten years old, its destiny was launched when Apple released the iPhone in 2007, followed by Android versions the following year. While some technical writers chart the smartphone's first appearance in 1996 with the arrival of Nokia's 9000 Communicator, the smartphone was not widely adopted until the introduction of the iPhone and subsequent 3G technology. The exception is Japan, where the company NT DoCoMo had launched an earlier version in 2001 and acquired 40 million subscribers.

The tiny pocket computer that is a phone for many of us has a processor which is more than 30,000 times faster than the computers that NASA used to put men on the moon in 1969. It has made communication, leisure, work and information available in an instant, collapsing distance and time in ways previously unimagined. The smartphone provides finger-tip access to a plethora of instant communication platforms: text, messaging, apps, visual apps and a bottomless well of information at our fingertips. Technology has revolutionized the experience of mobility and travel, making cities the most navigable and known they have ever been. New ontologies are being created at the intersection of people, place and technology.[5]

Take the café as an example. Here you could be drinking your coffee and chatting with a friend, but they might not be sitting beside you. In what is understood as 'co-presence', you could be engaged in conversation with a person located somewhere else in the city or perhaps on the other side of the world; their location for the technologically mediated conversation is irrelevant. 'Co-presence' or 'absence/presence' is a recent ontological phenomenon and it has become fundamental to new ways of being in the world.[6] It describes the experience of intense and intimate connectivity using internet-activated devices, through continuous communication with those absent, creating an active sense of the other's presence. In this scenario, our attention is shifted from the immediate physical place to the virtual but social and affective space of mediated communication technologies. Geographical distance is collapsed, and intimacy is aided through the real-time applications. Platforms such as Skype and Snapchat enable this sense of apprehending the person we're talking with and, conversely, that others are perceiving us, which is vital for empathic communication. Once the exclusive domain of face-to-face encounters, online communication technologies are also spaces of 'feelings and imaginations'.[7] It's still early days in technology's evolution and, already, our social and psychological experience is being changed in ways that are, as yet, little understood.

Another function of the café is its place as a locus of information. Historically cafés have always been sources of mediated information, initially through the availability of newspapers and journals in the early coffeehouses of London, Vienna and Paris. In Chapter One I discussed how several well-known newspapers began their life in the coffeehouse; people visited to catch up with the daily news, firstly through word of mouth and, more latterly, in print with the advent of newspapers. Today, the internet provides our main source of information via a multitude of platforms and apps. While many cafés still supply print newspapers, the number is declining as customers use their own devices such as smartphones and laptops to browse the news using Google or apps. This has an impact on the café's atmospherics. There is something more singular and solitary about reading online in a semi-public space, rather than reading a print newspaper. The café's ambience shifts subtly when the majority of its customers are absorbed on their digital devices: the sense of a collective activity such as reading a newspaper, and mutual recognition of the daily routines of the news, is lost or diminished. Reading a print newspaper is a visible activity, alerting everyone in that space to its purpose, in which others might also be engaged. Whereas reading online is a less visible and ambiguous practice, and so the mutual engagement is gone.

Technology has made an impact across every industry, in countless ways, and the café is no exception. Think first of how you might have tracked down a new café, perhaps through an app on your phone such as Beanhunter or via Google maps, or you may have read reviews on a review website. Even if you didn't use an app to find a café, if you're a specialty coffee aficionado, it's likely that you've read blogs and gleaned information about the coffee industry from crop to drop, where a specialty café sources its beans, and who the roasters are. You may be a regular listener to coffee podcasts, episodic series on digital files, such as *CoffeeAwesome* or *Cat and Clouds.* If you live in China, it's likely that you'll be paying for your coffee via an app, rather than cash or card, as China moves towards a cashless society. Wherever you are, it's possible that you or a friend has photographed your coffee and food and uploaded it to a photo-sharing platform such as Instagram and checked to see how many people have interacted with and 'liked' your photograph. In a 2017 technology audit, 39% of the world's population were using social media on a regular basis, with Filipinas and Brazilians the highest users on a daily basis.[8]

Café aficionados and foodies use blogs to share and keep up to date with information about developments and trends in the coffee industry. The internet and its abundant supply of information has encouraged a culture of sharing among special interest groups, including those in the specialty coffee movement. James Hoffman, one of the pioneers of the British coffee movement and a writer, has been writing a coffee blog since 2004. Hoffman says a lot of his learning about coffee came from blogs and internet writing back in the early 2000s, a period he refers to as 'open source coffee' when people freely shared information on the net.[9]

Social media plays a vital role in the creation of communities of interest. For a global specialty coffee community, many of whom are mobile international café workers blogs such as *jimseven*, *Sprudge*, *Daily Coffee News* and apps such as Instagram are important for people keen to learn about coffee and get to know one another across borders and continents. Although people who share information online might never meet, or meet eventually, a sense of the 'imagined community' is generated, based on the shared perception that one is part of the community (after Anderson 1983). Susie, a barista from Ireland who works in Berlin, discusses this aspect of social media in the context of 'imaginary communities':

> There is very much an imaginary community…that comes to fruition as well because you end up meeting these people at events and you already kind of know each other. So you'll follow someone on Instagram for two years and you may never have met them. You comment on all their stuff. *And then you meet them and it's like you've always sort of known each other.*

Susie alludes to that sense of absence/presence which, with the use of technology, creates a sense of knowing a person who we may not have met face-to-face. The online world is a place of feelings and, as such, can be a powerful vehicle for connection, particularly when there is a mutual interest and shared lifestyle. In my discussions with café specialty staff, many people referred to the support they felt from social media and online communities.

Tech business

Instagram is primarily an app for uploading photographs and, for coffee connoisseurs and those working in the industry, it's a Pandora's box of visually oriented coffee-related information. Find your topic via a hashtag: #latteart has over four million posts of patterns displayed on a cup of coffee's frothed milk and #coffee has over 75 million coffee-related photographs. It's not just coffee consumers who upload photographs; social media apps are used by café proprietors as a marketing strategy. The accessibility of data collection provides a host of information for business owners and the curious. In Sydney, Australia, the Grounds Cafe was the sixth most Instagrammed place in 2015. It's a large complex that includes a café, roastery, bakery and garden, and the café employs two full-time social media staff and a stylist. Much effort has been expended to produce the photogenic environment of the café. The Grounds is one example among many café entrepreneurs who use social media to promote their business. Chapter Six discussed how coffee retail giant Starbucks has used technology to grow its business through commercial partnerships with Chinese technology behemoth, Tencent Holdings. The app also enables Starbucks customers in China to make purchases in their stores. The cashless digital payment experience, in which consumers pay for their goods and services from their mobile devices, is one of the most popular payment methods in China. For a company whose initial strategy was based on the idea of the café as 'third place', Starbucks is now promoting cafés as the fourth-place experience, the digital place.[10]

For most industries, technology is utilized for replacing or reducing the tasks that were previously performed by people. There are software applications for retailers designed to provide seamless integration of sales and accounting, from the point-of-purchase to the final accounts balance, which is supposed to make tracking of profits and loss instant and efficient for business practices. In practice though, some café proprietors have stated that the applications are not always as seamless as they are intended be. In the area of staff development, online and video training is increasingly common. Technology can be useful for educating staff with information and procedural updates, such as legislation which might impact on the work environment. There are countless YouTube tutorials on how to make an artisan cup of coffee but, for the professional barista, this method of learning has obvious limitations.

Virtual Reality (VR) barista training has been trialed in an experiment by Google in 2017, with mixed results. Two training methods were compared among two cohorts: those using YouTube and those using VR to learn how to make an espresso coffee with milk. The people who used VR were quicker, but they tended not to follow instructions to the letter and became confused with the myriad pathways involved. The advantage of the virtual model was that it included tactile feedback for touching buttons and other physical steps including tamping (patting down the coffee), although overall the technology was not deemed sufficient to deal with the physical requirements and the potential hazards, such as burning oneself. It is early days in the development of VR, but given the pace of technological change, it is predicted that we will see the introduction of new ways of learning in the near future.[11]

Enthusiastic adoption of technology's affordances, and the benefits it has delivered, initially placed big technology companies at the vanguard of innovation and political acclaim. Moreover, numerous companies adopted the discourse of progressive politics alongside innovation, which generated broad public appeal and social approval. But, more recently, public attitudes to the technology behemoths are shifting, with the realization that many of the larger technical corporations are global, 'economic elites and oligarchs', whose rhetoric is frequently at odds with their corporate behaviour. Concerns around companies' behaviour, which range from antitrust enforcement and wealth redistribution (lack of) to the industry's misogynist workplace culture, evident in certain companies, have generated calls for greater government oversight from both sides of politics. In his book *Radical Technologies: The Design of Everyday Life*, Adam Greenfield argues that the giant technology companies have created 'the colonization of everyday life by information processing', controlling our choices and consequently our decisions. Technology has advanced so explosively since the turn of the century that it is, to some extent, inevitable that regulating bodies find it hard to keep up and lag behind. The borderless, highly technical nature of the internet also makes it something of a regulatory minefield. Concomitantly, a passive and willing army of consumers has readily accepted the benefits that technologies have brought them, while turning a blind eye to incursions of privacy and data mining.

Notwithstanding the global dominance and control of tech companies, it is hard to imagine a world without smartphones, laptops and Wi-Fi. Many people take for granted the ability to communicate, read and write while moving from one place to another. Laptop and Wi-Fi technology, along with industrial re-structuring since the latter part of the 20th century, have produced different ways of working. Mobility and flexibility have become the mantras of contemporary work, afforded in part by the growing 'gig economy', which is underscored by the assumption that people can work online, anytime, anywhere, not least in the spaces of the café. While this might be liberating for some, who are released from the office or the daily routine of the workplace, the shift also signals significant structural problems that are placing greater and greater demands on individuals.

Moreover, while most people in the global north live in a mediated world, the pervasiveness of technology in everyday life can obscure its unequal access globally. World access to the internet is growing, but the digital divide is still significant. Reports vary on numbers, but global access averaged out at around 50% in 2017. Income levels, notoriously unevenly distributed throughout the world, are the key determinants to access, with women and the elderly close behind.[12] A recent shift in global bandwidth access has seen Asia replace North America and Europe as the continents with the greatest concentration of bandwidth. China, with its massive population of 1.4 billion, has double the bandwidth use of the United States. We can be certain that with the rapidity of technological development, greater complexities and inequalities around questions of access and participation will continue to evolve.

Work, technology and the café

J. K. Rowling famously wrote much of her Harry Potter series in an Edinburgh café, The Elephant House, where in the back room she looked out over Edinburgh Castle, allegedly the inspiration for Hogwarts. The café's website claims crime writers Ian Rankin and Alexander McCall-Smith as frequent customers, following a tradition of writers and artists who frequented cafés as part of their creative endeavours. But it is not just independent writers or 'creatives' who are using the café for work or work-related activities in the contemporary city. The term 'coffice' has gained traction to describe the changing face of work. Monumental changes to the workforce over the last few decades, among them the rise of freelancers and contract workers, greater workplace flexibility and the gig economy, has provided another dimension to the café's role.

Today, the world of work and its environment bears little resemblance to that of a few decades ago. Technological innovations, globalization and neo-liberal processes are among the key drivers of change. A decline in manufacturing and subsequent growth in the digital and service industries has produced a plethora of new types of jobs and skills, whose numbers continue their upward trajectory. All this turbulence has led to a host of claims and counter claims about the future of work and what it will look like. Some experts predict that radical transformations will occur on an unprecedented scale, a future in which artificial intelligence and robots will replace many roles that can be automated. Australia's leading scientific research organization, CSIRO, estimates that within ten to fifteen years, approximately 40% of jobs will be replaced by computers.[13] It presents four possible scenarios for the future and identifies several emerging developments that are likely to dramatically change the nature of work. Economic development is diversifying into services, knowledge and innovation exports and the IoT is at the early stages of growth and will impact significantly on jobs and employment markets. To illustrate the scale of technological innovation: in 2006 there were two billion smart connected devices, and by 2020 Intel predicts there will be 200 billion devices.

The world is moving towards greater and greater connectivity, facilitating new modes of work arrangements. The ascendency of online platforms and the peer to peer marketplace (P2P) for job seekers and employers gives ready access to international labour markets for short-term tasks or temporary work. Platforms such as Airtasker, Upwork, Freelancer, Uber and so forth are already transforming traditional labour models. Outsourcing, short-term contracts and freelance work are on the rise in many countries, and the idea of a job for life is no longer either possible or attractive to many employees. Flexible work arrangements are growing steadily, where it is necessary for people to work outside an office with mobile technologies using laptops and the internet.

In this emerging work environment, the café has become a surrogate workplace for the growing army of contractual and freelance workers. On one level, this type of working lifestyle sometimes characterized as the 'digital boheme' or the digital nomad conjures up a somewhat romanticized ontology: an autonomous individual free to work whenever and wherever, liberated from the constraints of middle-class work patterns.[14] They are 'creative' workers but in the broad sense of the word, they are not the artist habitués of 19th century cafés. A current pervasive discourse of autonomy, self-expression and individuality, whose ultimate goal is self-fulfilment, conceals the growing inequality among many countries' labour forces. Contract work is on the rise in the global north and according to the International Labour Organisation, 75% of the world's workers are temporary, casual or self-employed. In an analysis of 180 countries' employment patterns, it was found that the model of permanent full-time employment was 'less and less dominant' in rich, developed economies.[15] The growth of contract and freelance work varies across countries. In Britain casual work is climbing in a steady, consistent pattern with the causal workforce at around 22%.[16] In the United States, one third of the workforce is casual.

The structural inequities of contract labour have contributed to rising job insecurity, particularly in the global north, and subsequently to diminished labour conditions. Critics point out that radically transformed labour conditions since the 1980s have produced the rise of what is termed as the 'precariat' worker. The precariat is defined by so-called flexible labour contracts; temporary jobs; and labour as casuals, part-timers, or intermittently for labour brokers or employment agencies. The precariat has no secure occupational identity, limited access to state-based benefits, and has to constantly re-invent and re-train themselves.[17] She/he is often highly educated and young, as Toby Miller points out:

> We inhabit a world where flexibility is the mega-sign of affluence, and precariousness its flipside: one person's calculated risk is another's burden of labor [sic], inequality is represented as the outcome of a moral test, and the young are supposed to regard insecurity as an opportunity rather than a constraint. What used to be the fate of artists and musicians where "making cool stuff" and working with relative autonomy was meant to outweigh ongoing employment has become a norm across virtually every sector of the economy.[18]

Precariat workers may have found an income stream as eBay power sellers, paid bloggers, people marketing concepts or someone selling homemade clothes online, as well as journalists, artists or computer scientists. The freelance worker will not necessarily have a dedicated office or workstation and has either to make do working at home or in a public or hybrid space such as a library, a café or a co-working space. It may seem liberating for a period of time to have the autonomy of the café as workplace and to keep to one's own timetable, but the precariat's life can be isolating and not least, financially insecure.

The rise of the freelance worker is reflected in the plethora of websites and blogs dedicated to information about work-friendly cafés in cities across the world. Websites such as Workfrom #untethered provide customised information for freelancers about cafés and co-working places in over 200 global cities ranging from Istanbul to Seoul. The site is co-created, and a community of freelancers share information about places to work and freelance jobs available. Online magazines such as *Time Out* or the *theculturetrip.com* produce lists of 'the best cafés to work in' in cities which include Singapore, Sydney, Tokyo, Paris, London and Berlin to name a few. The criteria typically include access to free Wi-Fi, ample table space, work-friendly noise levels and access to power sockets. Of critical importance is the sense that it is alright to occupy a table for a considerable length of time while perhaps only consuming one cup of coffee. Most patrons will acknowledge the tacit understanding not to take advantage of Wi-Fi bandwidth and air-conditioning to the extent that it prevents new customers from finding somewhere to sit. Conversational levels (whether phone, f2f or Skype) are also expected to be low so that the environment remains friendly. Some larger cafés are able to address this potential problem by providing a dedicated work area and charging for the use of co-working space, such as betahaus in Berlin or Timberyard in London, or imposing a time limit on people's use of a table. Some cafés actively discourage technology use with signs such as the one below, by Corner Café in Annapolis Maryland.

Conversely, some cafés appear to actively encourage people to come and plug in their laptops. In these cafés, power sockets are highly visible, placed in rows above table and bench tops, rather than underneath, inviting people to plug in and use them. This was the case in Sourced Market and Cafe, London, a café I visited near Victoria station. The café is one of four in London and is housed in a high-ceilinged, generous space which accommodates long, wide

FIGURE 8.1 Sign outside café in Annapolis Maryland, USA. Photo credit: © iStock.

benchtops adjacent to walls, providing ample space for people to work. Either way, whether facilitating a café working space free of charge, or imposing costs or time limits, the café owner has to negotiate with their customers how best to manage the growing demand for the café to act as a transient workspace. Occupying a table for several hours while sitting on a coffee or two can mean that other customers are turned away. In a small and busy café, this can have financial impact for the business's profitability. Not all cafés supply Wi-Fi for the convenience of their customers, and some have taken an active stance against it. In my interviews with café proprietors, all but one said they had no hesitation in asking people to leave when they'd been sitting on one coffee for a few hours while engaged with their laptop. As Joas of Early Bean Café in Berlin remarked, "It is okay for a long time when they eat and drink. If not, they need to go. This is very strict."

In another commercial solution to the growth of the freelance working life, co-working spaces are on the rise. The number of co-working spaces worldwide has nearly doubled each year since 2006 and in Australia, increased by 156% in 2012 alone (CSIRO 2016, 38). Entire buildings or offices are dedicated to spaces in which a workstation or office can be rented out on a casual basis. This development is disrupting traditional office leasing models. Many co-working companies with offices across the world, recognize the value of social connection that the traditional workplace offers people. Initiatives aimed at nurturing a sense of community through social gatherings, in-house cafés, terraces and 'brain-storming' rooms can also provide those companies with a commercial edge. Costs of co-working spaces vary across cities and companies; in Berlin, for example, a co-working space can be leased for as little as €70 a month depending on location, and a lot more can also be paid. In Australia, costs range from $AU90 to over $AU500 a month depending on facilities and location. Despite the growing take-up of co-working spaces, some people still choose to work in a café. They might use cafés because their work is irregular, or the ambience and location of the café suits them. There are many reasons why the café as a hybrid space fulfils the needs for people with work-related activities.

What is it about the café that is satisfactory for workers?

The history of the café is littered with accounts of its relationship to the creative activity of writers, artists and intellectuals, and the café occupies a lofty role as a place that has nourished creative and intellectual endeavours.[19] As George Steiner observes, 'the bibliography of magnificent books written in cafes is enormous'.[20] Honoré de Balzac, Jean-Paul Sartre, TS Eliot, Franz Kafka, Gertrude Stein and F. Scott Fitzgerald are among many writers and artists whose work was generated in the height of European café culture during the late 19th and early 20th centuries. The artists Édouard Manet and Edgar Degas depicted the bustling and animated life of late-19th-century Parisian cafés in many of their paintings. Cafés of this period were considered to be 'factories of literature, inciters to art and breeding places for new ideas'.[21] From this heyday period, the 'intellectual life' of the café went into a long, slow decline, although it had a brief revival during the 1950s with the introduction of the Espresso Bar to the United States, Australia and Britain. It reached its nadir during the 1960s with the onslaught of consumer culture, mass tourism and the growth of suburbanism.

Today, cafés have reprised their role as places for work and creativity, though in a markedly different way. Twenty-first-century work and creative activity appears, at a glance, to be more atomized than the artistic gatherings of last century suggest, and technology has altered the way we work. The current generation of writers are using laptops and tablets if they write in cafés, as are other 'creatives' who might be employed in the new digital economy as graphic artists, web designers, coders and other roles. For these workers without dedicated workspaces, the café provides a space for short-term work in a convivial environment. Contemporary working conditions have produced the need for independent work-related spaces, but what, or more specifically, *is*, there a connection between creative work and the café as historical accounts suggest?

For historians, it is mostly the café's social characteristic that's regarded as a key promoter of creativity, apparent when people gather and interact to discuss ideas and projects. Creative connections are generated through conversation and interaction with others. But environmental aspects are also considered to help promote creativity. Moving from a static to a dynamic environment such as the café, where you flood the mind with new input, is believed to stimulate creativity. Ambient noise of the café, which registers at around seventy decibels, is regarded as an optimum level to promote creative thought; it is neither too loud or too soft.[22] Kelly, an Australian PhD creative writing student and university tutor finds the ambient noise of the café productive for her creative work. Here she compares working in the café to working at home:

> Sometimes when I'm by myself and it's too quiet, it's too easy for my mind to run wild. I can hear too many of my own thoughts...but when it's the 'white nose' or chatter around me, it's almost as if the resistance makes me work harder...I think just in terms of it (the café) being a neutral, emotional space as well. I mean sometimes at home it's almost as if the walls absorbed the negative feelings and the stress from when I was working last time.

Kelly's reference to the benefits of white noise and the neutral, emotional space of the café is supported by research that suggests that silence or too much solitude can promote procrastination, fuelling non-creative activity. The café environment with its white noise and 'rich, polymorphic sensory experience' is infused with sensual interconnections which, researchers speculate, provide the material conditions for communication and creative output.[23]

Moreover, the importance of being among others, even if undertaking solitary work, is stressed by people who work from home. Kerri Sackville, an Australian writer, describes why she needs to get out of the house to work:

> Most challenging, however, is the isolation. Entire workdays can go by in which my only contact with another adult is my mother's daily phone call...And so I tend to take my laptop to cafes, and sit there to work, sometimes for hours at a time. I love the noise, the people, the busyness of a cafe. I love the sense of being out in the world. Working in cafes can be a joy.[24]

At this point I should declare that while I am writing a book about cafés, I have not written one word of the book in a café, apart from taking hand-written

FIGURE 8.2 Working in cafés with Wi-Fi. Photo credit: © iStock.

observational notes. I prefer the solitude and space of a desk and room and am fortunate to have one to retreat to. There is also something about the singular and private act of writing that's in play here. I'm conscious too of taking up valuable café space while sitting on a cup of coffee for several hours. Every writer has their own needs and some feel more productive in the café, or simply don't have adequate space elsewhere, as was the case for J. K. Rowling. For Kris, an Australian, Brisbane-based journalist and author who often works in cafés, being able to be 'hidden' and unnoticed is among the most important criteria when choosing a café to work in. She discusses how she chooses cafés in which to work:

> A. For the quality of the coffee (and cake!) and B. for their hidey-hole spaces or lack of appeal to other people...Or just a café where I'm pretty sure I won't run into anyone. Happy baristas/staff is important to me... (Merlo Cafe, Cooparooo)...not enough tables inside to be able to hide whereas South Brisbane is big, lots of tables and a bit more anonymous, and the staff know me and know my coffee and leave me alone. No good cake though...Often find myself back in West End where I'd go to Plenty usually – and it's the opposite of the above! Big open warehouse with both individual and communal seating – but a spot upstairs in the rafters where one can hide, and the coffee and cake (and spanakopita) is fabulous. The staff are great, laid-back, welcoming.

While coffee, cake and friendly staff are all a big part of the mix, Kris's repetition of the importance of somewhere to hide in a café is significant as the café assumes a greater role in people's working lives. Hiding is about privacy, not being interrupted and being able to get on with the job at hand. Indeed, historical accounts of writers and artists in early European cafés have claimed that writers are attracted to cafés for the 'seeming tension between the intimate circle of privacy in a comfortable room, on the one hand, and the flow of (perhaps usable) information all around on the other'.[25]

Comfort as a priority was expressed by another Australian writer Nick, who lives in Germany and who has lived and worked in several countries. His criteria for a congenial café to work is:

> Free Wi-Fi and comfortable chairs to work on. This is not always easy to find. I have a little place around the corner from me which is my go-to. The owners are nice, and they know my order. It's always peaceful in there and I usually get quite a bit done.

The sense of familiarity Nick refers to echoes the routines of the workplace. The owners know his coffee preferences and are amiable, and this contributes to the sense that it's okay to work in the café. Nick refers to his productivity, that he's able to get 'quite a lot done', which is supported by research into why people use cafés to work in. The study found that people use cafés to manage their time more effectively, and more pleasantly. Workers often feel that they can 'get more done' in a café away from the distractions of work. Cafés offer an alternative workplace where people seem to be able to focus, or at least feel that they achieve more in the time available. Because managed time has been a force of control in the workplace, self-management of time is also related to a sense of escape and autonomy from the workplace. The ways that employees manage their individual time and place orientations are crucial to the way people use cafés.[26]

Apart from the business of conducting one's own work in the café, through writing or digital communication, the café provides a space for work-related meetings. The neutrality of café space makes it appealing as a place to meet with colleagues, or other people who are in some way connected with work. Academics meet their research students in cafés, consultants and other workers meet potential clients, colleagues meet in cafés to resolve work-related problems or work on projects together. Removed from the social hierarchies and formality of the workplace, the café is a less formal and more ambiguous space, which allows different types of relationships to be forged. Gestures of hospitality are encoded in the cafés' spaces, something that can be beneficial for management and interpersonal work-related strategies aimed at fostering goodwill. Paying for another's drink, although not a great expense, is a simple gesture of hospitality; 'meeting for coffee' has become part of the *lingua franca* of workplace and business culture and relationships.

A New Zealand study found that hospitality is a crucial factor in using cafés for work-related purposes, it sets the scene to express values such as inclusivity and respect:

> Food and drink have a significant but under-understood role to play in organisational life. Food and drink are central to all aspects of culture, and in organisational hospitality rituals of welcoming and belonging. Our study shows organisational agents performing hospitality work for organisations in their appropriation and use of cafes. In various ways, strangers and 'others' are welcomed into the inside of the organisation through the sharing of food and drink, even though these rituals often do not take place anywhere near the physical premises of a business.[27]

As a working space, the informality of the café was highly regarded by customers, and meeting in cafés facilitated the integration of pleasurable social activities with the less pleasurable activities of work, or at least accentuating work's pleasant social aspects. This element of enjoyment for people writing in cafés is expressed by writer Malcolm Gladwell, who on his exchange of an office for the café as a place to write has said: 'Writing seems like a fun activity now…it's more seamlessly integrated into my life and that's made it much more pleasurable.'[28] Meeting in cafés also enables time efficiencies, i.e. to meet for a coffee to catch up and talk work with colleagues who are also friends, or as a reward for task completion.

However, the informality of work-related meetings in cafés can sometimes lead to a deliberate blurring of professional boundaries and services – and therefore charges, which the self-employed or entrepreneur has to be wary of. John, an Australian self-employed architect, says that some of his previous clients will suggest meeting in a café to seek his professional advice, usually on town planning matters. This isn't necessarily related to current or future work and the client expects to receive the advice in exchange for a coffee. As John observes, 'If I was a lawyer, I'd be charging by the minute for the professional advice but going to a café means that the person expects the advice for free'. The ambiguity around what constitutes professional services has the potential to be muddied in

FIGURE 8.3 Espresso cup. Photo credit: © Tricia King.

the café's ambiguous spaces. Codes of hospitality are inscribed in the café, and even the act of buying a coffee may generate a series of expectations. In order to acquire work, the creative or freelancer has to expend time and energy with potential clients, frequently conducted through meetings in cafés.

For places in which to work, differences between independent cafés and chain cafés are underpinned by economies of scale. A preference for coffee chains such as Starbucks and McDonald's as places to work might be due to the relative anonymity of the café, and the reliable standardization of conveniences such as power outlets, Wi-Fi and media resources which are geared towards productivity. By contrast, independently owned coffeehouses, which are usually smaller in scale, may be less organized around technology needs, and instead offer amenities that encourage conversing with others, like seating arrangements designed for socializing, or enjoying a novel atmosphere.[29] The work-related purpose will determine the type of café its patrons choose to attend, and its convenience. And while the physical infrastructure and layout of a café is a determinant of its use, so are less tangible and more subtle elements such as the ambience and atmosphere of the space.

As disruptions wrought by technology continue to transform the nature and patterns of work, the café will maintain its importance as a hybrid, technologically connected space; where we work, meet colleagues, take a break from the office or simply enjoy a reprieve from the next daily demand of our working lives.

In just under two decades, urban life has been radically transformed – and technology is a fundamental driver of this change. If we cast our minds back even twenty years ago, it would have been hard to predict that the way we communicate, work, move around the city and access information would alter as profoundly as it has. The shape-shifting café helps us to manage an increasing array of activities and connections that continue to draw us to into its spaces. What was once principally a meeting space for conviviality is now also a place of work and of virtual interactions. As we negotiate a progressively digital, virtual world, the sensuality of the café environment, its sights and sounds – the aroma of coffee, the taste of the brew, the interaction with people – also attends to some of our more corporeal, earthly and place-bound needs.

Notes

1 Greenfield, Adam. 2017. *Radical Technologies: The Design of Everyday Life*. London: Verso.

2 Houy, Yvone. 2006. "The situationist metro/electro polis: Re-imagining urban spaces in the 21st century." In Christian Emden, Catherine Keen and David Midgley (Eds). *Imagining the City Vol 1: Cultural history and Literary Imagination*. Bern, Switzerland: Peter Lang, pp. 311–333.

3 Laurier, Eric. 2008. "Drinking up endings: Conversational resources of the café." *Language and Communication* Volume 28, pp. 165–181.

4 Boneva, B., Kraut, R. and Frohlich, D. 2001. "Using e-mail for personal relationships: The difference gender makes." *The American Behavioral Scientist* Volume 45, Issue 3, November. Hofkirchner, Wofgang. 2007. "A critical social systems view of the internet." *Philosophy of the Social Sciences* Volume 37, pp. 471–500.

5 Fortunati, L. 2005. "Is body-to-body communication still the protoptype?" *The Information Society* Volume 21, Issue 1, pp. 53–62.

6 Biocca, F, Harms, C and Burgoon, J. K. 2003. "Toward a more robust theory and measure of social presence: review and suggested criteria." *Presence: Teleoperators and Virtual Environments* Volume 12, Issue 5, pp. 456–480.

7 Mantovani, Govani. 2011. "New media, migrations and culture: From multi- to interculture." In Fortunati, L., Pertierra, R. and Vincent, J. (Eds). *Migrations, Diaspora, and Information Technology in Global Societies.* New York: Routledge, pp. 21-35.

8 Current Global State Internet. 2017. https://thenextweb.com/contributors/2017/04/11/current-global-state-internet/#.tnw_Zby8mHxN, April 11. Ret 7.10.17.

9 Bryman, Howard. 2017. *Daily Coffee News.* August 9, 2017. https://dailycoffeenews.com/2014/08/06/coming-soon-a-world-atlas-of-coffee-from-james-hoffman/ Ret. 4.10.17.

10 Russell, Jon. 2017. https://techcrunch.com/2017/02/10/wechat-starbucks/, February 10. Ret. 28.8.17.

11 Bryman, Howard, 2017. "What Google learnt from its experiments in virtual reality barista training." http://dailycoffeenews.com/2017/08/09/what-google-learned-from-its-experiments-in-virtual-reality-barista-training/, August 9. Ret. 3.4.18.

12 ICT Facts and Figures. 2017. *International Telecommunications Union.* https://www.itu.int/en/ITU-D/Statistics/Pages/facts/default.aspx. Ret. 3.4.18.

13 Durrant-Whyte, H., McCalman, L., O'Callaghan, S., Reid, A. and Steinberg, D. 2015. "The Committee for Economic Development of Australia." *Australia's Future Workforce,* Ch. 1.4:60.

14 Friebe, Holm and Lobo, Sascha. 2006. *We Call it Work: The Digital Bohemia or Intelligent Life beyond the Fixed Settings.* Munich: Heyne.

15 International Labor Statistics Report. 2017 http://www.ilo.org/global/statistics-and-databases/lang--en/index.htmIn. Ret. 4.4.18.

16 Booth, Robert. 2016. "More than 7 million Britons in precarious employment." *The Guardian.* https://www.theguardian.com/uk-news/2016/nov/15/more-than-7m-britons-in-precarious-employment, November 15. Ret. 3.8.17.

17 Standing, Guy. 2014. "The precariat." *Contexts* Volume 13, Fall, pp. 10–12.

18 Miller, Toby. 2010. "Culture+labour=precariat." *Communication and Critical/Cultural Studies,* Volume 7, Issue 1, pp. 96–99 (p. 97).

19 Cowan, .Brian. 2005. *The Social Life of Coffee: The Emergence of the British Coffee House.* London: Yale University Press. Ellis, Markman. 2004. *The Coffee House: A Cultural History.* London: Weidenfeld and Nicolson.Hattox, Ralph. 1985. *Coffee and Coffeehouses: The Origins of a Social Beverage in the Medieval Near East.* Seattle, WA: University of Washington Press.

20 Haine, Scott W. and Rittner, Leona. 2013. *The Thinking Space: The Café as a Cultural Institution in Paris, Italy and Vienna.* London and New York: Routledge.

21 Fitch, quoted in McCosker, Anthony and Wilken, Rowan. 2012. "Café space, communication, creativity, and materialism." *M/C Media Culture* Volume 15, Issue 2.

22 Mehta, Ravi, Zhu, Rui (Juliet) and Cheema, Amar. 2012. "Is noise always bad? Exploring the effects of ambient noise on creative cognition." *Journal of Consumer Research* Volume 39, Issue 4, pp. 784–799. JSTOR, www.jstor.org/stable/10.1086/665048.

23 McCosker, Anthony and Wilken, Rowan. 2012. Ibid.

24 Sackville, Kerri. 2018. "How to make a café your office". *Good Food.* https://www.goodfood.com.au/eat-out/cafe/how-to-make-a-cafe-your-office-20180327-h0y0ra, April 9.

25 Fitch, quoted in McCosker, Anthony and Wilken, Rowan. 2012. Ibid.

26 Sayers, Janet. 2009. "Flat whites: How and why people work in cafés." *New Zealand Journal of Employment Relations (Online)* Volume 34, Issue 2, pp. 77–86. Ret. 13.9.17.

27 Sayers, Janet. 2009. Ibid., p. 81.

28 Storey, Robin. 2015. "Why do writers live to write in coffee shops?" *Storey Lines*. http://storey-lines.com/2015/09/14/why-do-writers-love-to-write-in-coffee-shops, September 14. Ret. 30.10.17.

29 Woldoff, Rachael A., Lozzi, Dawn Marie and Dilks, Lisa M. 2013. "The social transformation of coffee houses: The emergence of chain establishments and the private nature of usage." *International Journal of Social Science Studies* Volume 1, Issue 2, October, pp. 205–218.

AFTERWORD

A heady brew

This book has covered a wide range of themes distilled through the filter of the café. Urbanization, technological innovation, population mobility, changes to social structures, work and working conditions, and the rise of the design and knowledge industries – all find expression in the contemporary café. My initial sociological interest, prompted by the constant emergence and overwhelming popularity of new cafés in my own inner-city neighbourhood, was broadened once I began to research and talk about the topic with café patrons and staff.

The café's historical relationship with metropolitan life is well established, so that connection became the first obvious point of enquiry. As indeed my own neighbourhood was gentrifying, confirming that oft-cited link between cafés and gentrification, which has inspired a plethora of media headlines such as *The Guardian's* 'The caffeine curse: Why coffee shops have always signalled urban change' or *The Independent*'s, 'Artisan cafés and luxury flats: How bad can gentrification be?' Cafés have always fuelled the economic life of cities in various ways, but they have also been important places for people to gather and meet. In my enquiry into café culture, which led to an exploration of the myriad technological, social and economic developments occurring at this point in time, I hope that my original questions about the café's popularity – Why now? And in what ways is it different from its historical antecedents? – has to some extent been answered. Aside from those external influences that have reinvigorated the café, the complex business of both café culture and the coffee industry became more and more expansive the further I delved. Since I began my research, new coffee blogs seemed to appear each month, and there are far greater experts writing on the subject of coffee than me. I have only scratched the surface of the topic, as the industry, now thoroughly global, continues to grow and develop in myriad ways.

Much has changed since the last burst of European café culture in the 1920s and 1930s. It is clear that the types of cities we live in now, at the outset of the 21st century, are dramatically different from cities of the last century, only a brief twenty years ago. In a short period of time, our lives have been radically transformed predominantly by technology, but also by increased population mobility and the consequences of globalization, namely the accelerated movement of people, money, objects and ideas. Cities today are more globally connected than they've ever been.

My research took me across the world, visiting cafés and talking to people in cities in the global north and south, seeking out the similarity and differences of café culture. My task was made easy by the assistance of technology, including a plethora of café-finding apps, websites, blogs and of course Google maps, which helped me locate what were often recently opened third-wave cafés, typically clustered around the edges of urban centres – in Melbourne's Fitzroy, London's Bermondsey and Tokyo's Shibuya. The striking commonality was the presence, ubiquity and well-attended nature of cafés in every city I visited.

And while café types are many and varied, the growth of third-wave or specialty cafés, with their attention to the connoisseurship of coffee, is something of a global phenomenon. Technology is the big connector here, – of new developments in coffee and of communities of interest. Technology provides up-to-date information about trends and social connections, as well as visual records of coffee and café life, relaying them around the world in a split second. Find #espresso on Instagram and see nearly six million photographs of coffee. Another commonality is that people involved in specialty coffee, whether as consumers or entrepreneurs, share a passion for coffee, sometimes to the point of obsession. Several of the café owners I spoke with had left other seemingly successful careers – as bankers or artists for instance – to embark on their coffee businesses. They all spoke enthusiastically about how they became immersed in coffee, and how their business was more fulfilling than anything they'd done before.

Like wine and gourmet food, coffee connoisseurship has carved a cultural niche which speaks volumes to contemporary concerns about identity, community and distinction in an increasingly secular and mobile world. The decline and growing scepticism of traditional institutions and the fragmentation of traditional social structures has created a pursuit of meaningful engagement in other arenas. Lifestyle and consumption practices, such as being a foodie, harness a sense of community through shared values and interests. Café culture and the coffee itself offer two points of identification and social connection. The emphasis on coffee *quality* is a distinctive feature of contemporary café culture. In the manner of the grape for wine connoisseurs, the bean's terroir, blend and roasting techniques are paramount. In previous iterations of the café, the fundamental appeal was the social life it offered, and while coffee was a useful stimulant for this purpose, the bean's provenance, brewing practices or blend was of little interest to patrons and owner alike.

The adoption of a standardised aesthetic makes the specialty café, or aspiring specialty café, easy to spot, signalling its lifestyle values to the newcomer: the artisanal, ethical and the authentic. It beckons with the promise of good coffee and like-minded customers, whom one might serendipitously encounter. The aesthetic was recognizable in cafés I visited in cities from Shanghai, Hong Kong to Berlin and Melbourne, but frequently with local variations that lay claim to the vernacular. Globalization works quickly, but it has not completely obliterated the local.

The specialty café provides community as well as distinction, particularly for what can be a young, international crew of café staff who criss-cross the globe finding work and fellowship in cities which they might eventually call home. But the café as a site for community extends to all cafés, not just specialty types. Moreover, communities are not homogenous – they're porous and varied and they appeal to different people at different times. Whatever the café type, as an urban hybrid space it is an important place for people to meet, or simply be alone among others. This is its essential function, and this aspect of its role hasn't changed since its 16th-century origins. In cities of increasing scale and density and often shrinking public facilities, people need places to gather. The wide range of cafés, and their overwhelming popularity, muddies issues around class, urban gentrification and coffee connoisseurship because there are as many styles of cafés as there are café patrons.

If we are to identify inequities in the café industry, it is surely to be found among the coffee-producing nations in the global south, where major inequality still exists, despite the efforts of organizations such as Fair Trade and a growing army of well-intentioned specialty coffee entrepreneurs. New relationships between coffee entrepreneurs in wealthy countries and coffee producers have kick-started multitudinous partnerships and strategies aimed at alleviating poverty and improving working conditions for agricultural workers. Yet coffee's relationship with colonialism and slavery still casts its long shadow. Agricultural labourers, who are mainly women, earn little more in a day than people in wealthy countries pay for a cup of coffee. Café workers in wealthier countries are also not immune from exploitation, particularly as working conditions have become stealthily eroded in many countries. Short-term and contract work with diminishing conditions have paved the way for another role of the café, as a transient workplace.

Technology makes its reappearance here, this time enabling productive endeavour via laptops and tablets. Our devices are a gateway of connectivity – to information, people, data, design, music, film and photography software and word processing. They enable us to span time zones and geographical boundaries; we can work wherever and whenever. The laptop's potential to assist the generation of income through its various applications is accommodated in the café by Wi-Fi, a table, chair and the price of a cup of coffee or two. Outside, the metropolis hums with white noise; the cacophony of the streets obscures the invisible but dizzying array of sensors, pixels and other digital apparatuses which have changed the very fabric of the city and our lives forever, in ways we barely understand. We are just at the brink of the Fourth Industrial Revolution into which we're sliding, quickly, deeply, inexorably. Coffee helps to keep us alert and ready for the next challenge, the next reinvention; and the café is our familiar anchor amidst a rapidly changing world.

REFERENCES

Acoustical Society of America. 2016. "Hearing 'meaningful' sounds decreases performance on cognitive tasks." *ScienceDaily*. www.sciencedaily.com/releases/2016/12/161201163404.htm, December 1. Ret. 21.9.17.

Alexakis, Effy and Janiszewski, Leonard. 2016. *Greek Cafés and Milk Bars of Australia*. Sydney: Halstead Press.

Aldes Wurgaft, Benjamin. 2015. "Writing in cafes." *The Los Angeles Review of Books*. https://lareviewofbooks.org/article/writing-in-cafes-a-personal-history/, September 9. Ret. 3.2.17.

Anderson, Elijah. 2004. "The cosmopolitan canopy." *ANNALS*, AAPS 595, September, pp. 16–30.

Aries, Phillipe. 1977. "The family and the city". *Daedalus*, Volume 106, Issue 2, pp. 227–235.

Bauman, Zygmunt. 1998. *Globalization: The Human Consequences*. New York: Columbia University Press.

Barthes, Roland. 1957. *Mythologies*. Paris: Edition de Seuill.

Bell, David. 2007. "The hospitable city: Social relations in commercial spaces." *Progress in Human Geography* Volume 31, Issue 1, pp. 7–22.

Biocca, Frank, Harms, Chad and Burgoon, Judee K. 2003. "Toward a more robust theory and measure of social presence: Review and suggested criteria." *Presence: Teleoperators and Virtual Environments* Volume 12, Issue 5, pp. 456–480.

Black, Robert. 2012. *The Story of Australia*. Self-published. ISBN: 9781105578298.

Blackman, Allen and Naranjo, Maria O. 2012. "Does eco-certification have environmental benefits? Organic coffee in Costa Rica." *Ecological Economics* Volume 83, November, pp. 58–66.

Bohme, Gernot. 1993. "Atmosphere as the fundamental concept of the new aesthetics". *Thesis Eleven* Volume 36, pp. 113–126.

Boneva, Bonka, Kraut Robert and Frohlich, David 2001. "Using e-mail for personal relationships: The difference gender makes." *The American Behavioral Scientist* Volume 45, Issue 3, November, pp. 530–549.

Bookman, Sonia. 2014. "Brands and urban life: Specialty coffee, consumers, and the co-creation of urban café sociality." *Space and Culture* Volume 17, Issue 1, pp. 85–99.

Booth, Robert. 2016. "More than 7 million Britons in precarious employment." *The Guardian.* https://www.theguardian.com/uk-news/2016/nov/15/more-than-7m-britons-in-precarious-employment, November 15. Ret. 3.8.17.

Bourdieu, Pierre. 1984. *Distinction: A Social Critique of the Judgement of Taste.* Harvard, MA: Harvard University Press.

Brown, Nick. 2017. "Colorados Ink! Coffee apologizes for gentrification focussed marketing." *Coffee News.* https://dailycoffeenews.com/2017/11/24/colorados-ink-coffee-apologizes-for-gentrification-focused-marketing/, November 24. Ret. 17.1.18.

Browne, Talor. 2016. "Smart girls make coffee." http://smartgirlsmakecoffee. tumblr. com/post/142235392500/talorbrowne, April 4. Ret. 26.8.17.

Bryman, Howard. 2015. The many ways in which coffee waste was diverted in 2015. http://dailycoffeenews.com/2015/12/29/the-many-ways-in-which-coffee-waste-was-diverted-in-2015/, 29 December. Ret. 18.8.17.

Chaney, David. 1996. *Lifestyles.* London: Routledge.

Cohen, Luc. 2014. "Starbucks scoops up coffee beans from China for blends in Asia, sales." *Business News.* https://www.reuters.com/article/us-coffee-china-starbucks/starbucks-scoops-up-coffee-beans-from-china-for-blends-asia-sales-idUSKCN0J32 CX20141119, November 19. Ret. 30.6.18.

Cowan, Brian. 2005. *The Social Life of Coffee: The Emergence of the British Coffee House.* London: Yale University Press.

Cuthill, Vivienne. 2007. "Consuming Harrogate: Performing Betty's Café and Revolution Vodka Bar." *Space and Culture* Volume 10, Issue 1, pp. 64–76.

Cunningham, Maura Elizabeth. 2010. "China's coffee culture." *Forbes.* https://www.forbes.com/2010/04/28/starbucks-china-consumers-markets-economy-coffee.html#3a6d872d3a0e, April 28. Ret. 18.8.17.

Davison, Graeme. 1994. "The past and future of the Australian suburb." In L. Johnson (Ed.). *Suburban Dreaming: An Interdisciplinary Approach to Australian Cities.* Geelong, Australia: Deakin University Press.

Diminescu, Dana. 2008. "The connected migrant: An epistemological manifesto." *Social Science Information* Volume 47, pp. 565–579.

Digital Media Research Centre. 2017. *The Creative Economy in Australia.* Queensland: Queensland University of Technology.

Douche Dude Baristas blog. 2017. http://doucheydudebaristas.tumblr.com

Duggan, Jennifer. 2015. "Spilling the beans on China's growing coffee culture." *The Guardian.* https://www.theguardian.com/sustainable-business/2015/may/18/spilling-the-beans-chinas-growing-coffee-culture, May 18. Ret. 4.6.18.

Durrant-Whyte, Hugh, McCalman, Lachlan, O'Callaghan, Simon, Reid, Alistair and Steinberg, Daniel 2015. "Australia's future workforce." *The Committee for Economic Development of Australia.* Ch. 1.4, Pp. 60. http //adminpanel.ceda.com.au/FOLDERS/Service/Files/ Documents/26792~Futureworkforce_June2015.pdf. Ret. 3.10.17.

Ellis, Markman. 2008. "An introduction to the coffee-house: A discursive model." *Language and Communication* Volume 28, Issue 2, April, pp. 156–164.

Ellis, Markman (ed.). 2006. *Eighteenth-Century Coffee-House Culture.* London: Routledge.

Ellis, Markman. 2004. *The Coffee House: A Cultural History.* London: Weidenfeld and Nicolson.

Elliot, Anthony. 1997. "All that is modern melts into postmodern." *Arena Magazine,* June–July 29.

Elliott, Kimberly. 2012. "Is my fair trade coffee really fair? Trends and challenges in fair trade certification." *Center for Global Development,* CGD Policy Paper 017, December.

Emden, Christian; Keen, Catherine and Midgley, David. 2006. *Imagining the City*, Volume 1. Oxford. Peter Lang.

Fairtrade Foundation. 2012. Fairtrade and coffee. Commodity briefing, May. http://www.fairtrade.net/fileadmin/user_upload/content/2009/resources/2012_Fairtrade_and_coffee_Briefing.pdf. Ret. 18.8.17.

Ferreira, Jennifer. 2017. Cafe nation? Exploring the growth of the UK cafe industry. *Area* Volume 49, Issue 1, pp. 69–76.

Fitch, Noël Riley. 2006. *The Grand Literary Cafés of Europe*. London: New Holland Publishers.

Foley, Malcom, McGillivray, David and McPherson, Gayle. 2012. *Event Policy: From Theory to Strategy*. London: Routledge.

Fortunati, Leopoldina; Raul Pertierra and Jane Vincent (eds) 2011. *Migrations, Diaspora and Information Technology in Global Societies*. New York: Routledge.

Fortunati, Leopoldi. 2005. "Is body-to-body communication still the protoptype?" *The Information Society* Volume 21, Issue 1, pp. 53–62.

Fridell, Gavin. 2007. *Fair Trade Coffee: The Prospects and Pitfalls of Market-Driven Social Justice*. Toronto: University of Toronto Press.

Friebe, Holm and Lobo, Sascha. 2006. *We Call It Work: The Digital Bohemia or Intelligent Life beyond the Fixed Settings*. Munich: Heyne.

Gibson, Katie Noah. 2012. Hanging out in cafes alone. https://katieleigh.wordpress.com/2012/08/22/hanging-out-in-cafes-alone/, 22 August. Ret. 25.2.18.

Giddens, Anthony. 1991. *Modernity and Self -Identity: Self and Society in the Late Modern Age*. Stanford, CA: Stanford University Press.

Goffman, Erving. 1971. *Relations in Public: Microstudies of the Public Order*. New York: Basic Books.

Gonzales, Angel 2016. "Starbucks to help pay for China workers housing." *The Seattle Times*. https://www.seattletimes.com/business/retail/starbucks-to-help-pay-for-china-workers-housing/, July 11. Ret. 30.6.18.

Gooding, Sarah. 2015. Helena Holmes, quoted in "Grounds for complaint: Female baristas fail to change café culture." *The Guardian*. https://www.theguardian.com/lifeandstyle/australia-food-blog/2015/aug/19/grounds-for-complaint-female-baristas-struggle-to-change-cafe-culture, August 19. Ret. 17.11.17.

Greenfield, Adam. 2017. *Radical Technologies: The Design of Everyday Life*. London: Verso.

Grinshpun, Helena. 2014. "Deconstructing a global commodity: Coffee culture and consumption in Japan." *Journal of Consumer Culture*, Volume 14, Issue 3, pp. 345–364.

Grodach, Carl and Ehrenfeucht, Renia. 2016. *Urban Revitalization: Remaking Cities in a Changing World*. New York: Routledge.

Guiliana, Elisa, Ciravegna, Luciano, Vezzilli, Andrea and Killan, Bernard. 2017. "Decoupling standards from practice: The impact of in-house certifications on coffee farms' environmental and social conduct. *World Development* Volume 96, August, pp. 294–314.

Haas institute. 2017. *Moving Targets: An Analysis of Forced Global Migration*. Research Report. http://haasinstitute.berkeley.edu/sites/default/files/haasinstitute_moving_targets_globalmigrationreport_publish_web.pdf. Ret. 13.10.17.

Habermas, Jurgen. 1962. *The Structural Transformation of the Public Sphere: An Inquiry into a Category of Bourgeois Society*. Cambridge, UK: Polity Press.

Haine, Scott W. and Rittner, Leona. 2013. *The Thinking Space: The Café as a Cultural Institution in Paris, Italy and Vienna*. London: Routledge.

Hajkowicz, Stefan, Reeson, Andrew, Rudd, Lachlan, Bratanova, Alexandra, Hodgers, Leonie, Mason, Claire and Boughen, Naomi. 2016. "Tomorrow's digitally enabled workforce megatrends and scenarios for jobs and employment in Australia over the coming twenty years." CSIRO. 160026_DATA61_REPORT_TomorrowsDigially EnabledWorkforce_WEB_160204.pdf.

Harrabin, Roger. 2018. "Latte levy of 25pc urged by politicians in bid to cut cup waste. *BBC News*. http://www.bbc.com/news/business-42564948, January 5. Ret. 15.2.18.

Harvey, David. 2008. "The rights to the city". In *New Left Review* Volume 53, September–October, pp. 23–40.

Hassard, Cam. 2017. "Third wave coffee and how Australia is paving the way." *The Upsider*. http://theupsider.com.au/third-wave-coffee-and-how-australia-is-paving-the-way/1766, August 14. Ret. 10.9.17

Hattox, Ralph. 1985. *Coffee and Coffeehouses: The Origins of a Social Beverage in the Medieval Near East*. Seattle, WA: University of Washington Press.

Helmore, Edward. 2017. "Blue Bottle Coffee sells to Nestle: So has it sold out?" *The Guardian*. https://www.theguardian.com/business/2017/sep/16/blue-bottle-coffee-nestle, September 16. Ret. 25.9.17.

Higgs, Peter and Cunningham, Stuart. 2008. "Creative Industries Mapping: Where have we come from and where are we going?" *Creative Industries Journal* Volume 1, Issue 1, pp. 7–30.

Hilbert, Martin. 2016. "The bad news is that the digital access divide is here to stay: Domestically installed bandwidths among 172 countries for 1986–2014. *Telecommunications Policy* Volume 40, Issue 6, pp. 567–581.

Hoffman, James. 2014. *The World Atlas of Coffee: From Beans to Brewing - Coffees Explored, Explained and Enjoyed*. London: Hachette.

Hofkirchner, Wolfgang. 2007. "A critical social systems view of the internet." *Philosophy of the Social Sciences* Volume 37, pp. 471–500.

Houy, Yvonee. 2006. "The situationist metro/electro polis: Re-Imagining urban spaces in the 21st century." In Christian Emden, Catherine Keen and David Midgley (Eds). *Imagining the City Vol 1: Cultural History and Literary Imagination*. Bern, Switzerland: Peter Lang, pp. 311–333.

Huse, Tony. 2014. *Everyday Life in the Gentrifying City: On Displacement, Ethnic privileging and the Right to Stay Put*. Farnham, UK: Ashgate.

Illouz, Eva. 2009. "Emotions, imagination and consumption: A new research agenda." *Journal of Consumer Culture* Volume 9, pp. 377–413.

International Coffee Organization. 2017. Trade statistics. http://www.ico.org/trade_statistics.asp. Ret. 25.3.17.

Jha, Shalene, Bacon, Christopher M., Philpott, Stacy M., Méndez, V. Ernesto, Läderach, Peter, and Rice, Robert A. 2014. "Shade coffee: Update on a disappearing refuge for biodiversity." *BioScience* Volume 64, Issue 5, pp. 416–428.

Johnston, Josee and Baumann, Shyon. 2015. *Foodies: Democracy and Distinction in the Gourmet Foodscape* (second edition). New York: Routledge.

Jones, Hannah, Neal, Sarah, Mohan, Giles, Connell, Kieran, Cochrane, Allan and Bennett, Katy. 2015. "Urban multiculture and everyday encounters in semi-public, franchised cafe spaces." *The Sociological Review* Volume 63, pp. 664–661.

Keane, Michael. 2007. *Created in China: The Great New Leap Forward*. London: Routledge.

Keane, Michael. 2013. *The Creative Industries in China: Art, Design and Media*. Cambridge, UK. Polity Press.

Khamis, Susie. 2009. "'It only takes a jiffy to make': Nestlé, Australia and the convenience of instant coffee." *Food, Culture and Society: An International Journal of Multidisciplinary Research* Volume 12, Issue 2, pp. 217–233.

Kilkenny, Katy 2017. "A brief history of coffee shop as symbol of gentrification." *Pacific Standard*. https://psmag.com/economics/history-of-coffee-shop-as-symbol-for-gentrification, July 26. Ret. 14.10.17.

Kotkin, Joel. 2017. "Big tech finds itself lacking political allies." Orange County Register. http://www.ocregister.com/2017/09/30/big-tech-finds-itself-lacking-political-allies/, Sept 30. Ret. 5.10.17.

Latham, Alan. 2003. "Urbanity, lifestyle and making sense of the new urban economy: notes from Auckland, New Zealand." *Urban Studies* Volume 40, pp. 1699–724.

Laurier, Eric. 2008. "Drinking up endings: Conversational resources of the café." *Language and Communication* Volume 28, pp. 165–181.

Licoppe, Christian. 2009. "Recognizing mutual 'proximity' at a distance: Weaving together mobility, sociality and technology." *Journal of Pragmatics*, Volume 14, Issue 10, pp. 1924–1937.

Low, Tim. 1989. *Bush Tucker: Australia's Wild Food Harvest*. Sydney: Angus and Robertson Publishers.

Low, Tim. 2001. *Feral Future*. Ringwood, Victoria: Penguin.

Lyons, James. 2005. "Think Seattle, act globally." *Cultural Studies* Volume 19, Issue 1, pp. 14–34 (p. 29).

Maffesoli, Michel. 1996. *The Time of the Tribes*. London: Sage Publishers.

Mantovani, Giovani. 2011. "New media, migrations and culture: From multi-to interculture." In Fortunati, L., Pertierra, R. and Vincent, J. (Eds). *Migrations, Diaspora, and Information Technology in Global Societies*. New York: Routledge.

Manzo, John. 2015. "'Third-wave' coffeehouses as venues for sociality: On encounters between employees and customers." *The Qualitative Report* Volume 20, Issue 6, pp. 746–761.

Mehta, Ravi and Cheeha. 2012. "Is noise always bad? Exploring the effects of ambient noise on creative cognition." *Journal of Consumer Research* Volume 39, Issue 4, pp. 784–799.

Miles, Steve and Miles, Malcolm. 2004. *Consuming Cities*. Basingstoke, UK: Palgrave Macmillan.

Miller, Toby. 2010. "Culture+labour=precariat." *Communication and Critical/ Cultural Studies* Volume 7, Issue 1, pp. 96–99.

McCosker, Anthony and Wilken, Rowan. 2012. "Café space, communication, creativity, and materialism." *M/C Media-Culture* Volume 15, Issue 2.

Meyer, Zlati. 2017. "Starbuck's CEO gets off to start on decent earnings." *USA Today*. https://www.usatoday.com/story/money/business/2017/04/27/starbucks/100990396/, April 27. Ret. 4.8.17.

Moat, Justin et al. 2017. "Resilience potential of the Ethiopian coffee sector under climate change." *Nature Plants* (2055-0278), Volume 3, Issue 1708, pp. 1–14.

Moore, Suzanne 2015. "Gentrification means the world is one giant flat white – we have to stand up for sleaze and old dives." *The Guardian*. https://www.theguardian.com/uk-news/commentisfree/2015/nov/18/gentrification-world-giant-flat-white-stand-up-sleaze-old-dives-london, November 15. Ret. 3.10.17.

Mumford, Lewis. 1938. *The Culture of Cities*. New York: Harcourt.

Ndongo Samba Sylla. 2014. (Translated by David Clément Leye.) *The Fair Trade Scandal: Marketing Poverty to Benefit the Rich*. London. Pluto Press.

Nourse, Pat. 2017. "Why Australian coffee is the best in the word and where to drink it." *Aussie Cuisine*. https://aussiecuisine.com.au/2017/07/why-australian-coffee-is-the-best-in-the-world-and-where-to-drink-it/, July 20. Ret. 21.5.18.

Noyce, Diana Christine. 2012. "Coffee palaces in Australia: A pub with no beer." *M/C Media Culture Journal* (online) Volume 15, Issue 2.

O'Connor, Justin. 2009. "Shanghai moderne: Creative economy in a creative city?" In O'Connor, J. and Kong, L. (Eds). *Creative Economies, Creative Cities: Asian European Perspectives*, pp. 175–197. London. Springer.

Partington, Matthew. 2009. "The London coffee bar of the 1950s – teenage occupation of an amateur space?" *Occupation: Negotiations with Constructed Space*. Proceedings of the Conference held at the University of Brighton, July 2–4, 2009. http://arts.brighton.ac.uk/__data/assets/pdf_file/0004/44842/33_Matthew-Partington_The-London-Coffee-Bar-of-the-1950s-.pdf. Ret. 5.5.18.

Payal, MGM. 2016. "MICE 2016: 3 days of specialty coffee heaven in Australia. " *Perfect Daily Grind*. https://www.perfectdailygrind.com/2016/05/mice-2016-3-days-specialty-coffee-heaven-australia/, May 6. Ret. 10.9.17.

Peck, Jamie and Tickell, Adam. 2002. "Neoliberalizing urban space." *Antipode* Volume 34, Issue 3, July, pp. 380–384.

Pendergrast, Mark. 2010. *Uncommon Grounds: The History of Coffee and How It Transformed Our World*. New York: Basic Books.

Piekut, A. 2013. "You've got a Starbuck's and Coffee Heaven…I can do this!" Spaces of social adaption of highly skilled migrants in Warsaw. *Central and Eastern European Migration Review* Volume 2, Issue 1, pp. 117–138.

Piekut, A and Valentine, Gill. 2017. "Spaces of encounter and attitudes towards difference: A comparative study of two European Cities." *Social Science Research* Volume 62, February, pp. 175–188.

Pow, Choon Piew. 2015. Do Singapore neighbourhoods risk death by cappuccino? *The Straits Times*. https://www.straitstimes.com/opinion/do-singapore-neighbourhoods-risk-death-by-cappuccino, January 30. Ret. 3.10.17.

Raban, Jonathan. 1974. *Soft City*. London: Penguin.

Rice, Charles. 2007. *The Emergence of the Interior: Architecture, Modernity, Domesticity*. London: Routledge.

Rosenstein, Carole. 2011. Cultural development and city neighbourhoods. *City, Culture and Society* Volume 2, Issue 1, March, pp. 9–15.

Russell, Jon. 2017. WeChat users in China can now gift friends a Starbucks coffee via chat. https://techcrunch.com/2017/02/10/wechat-starbucks/, February 10. Ret. 28.8.17.

Sackville, Kerri. 2018. "How to make a café your office". *Good Food*. https://www.goodfood.com.au/eat-out/cafe/how-to-make-a-cafe-your-office-20180327-h0y0ra, April 9.

Samper, Luis and Quiñones-Ruiz, Xiomara F. 2017. "Towards a balanced sustainability vision for the coffee industry." *Resources (Basel)* (2079-9276), Volume 6, Issue 2, p. 17.

Sayers, Janet. 2009. "Flat whites: How and why people work in cafés." *New Zealand Journal of Employment Relations*, Volume 34, Issue 2, pp. 77–86.

Schivelbusch, Wolfgang. (Translated David Jacobsen.) 1992. *Tastes: A Social History of Spices, Stimulants and Intoxicants*. New York: Random House.

Selwyn, Neil. 2004. "Reconsidering political and popular understandings of the digital divide." *New Media and Society* Volume 6, Issue 3, pp. 341–362.

Sennett, Richard. 1992. *The Conscience of the Eye: The Design and Social Life of Cities*. New York: W.W. Norton and Co.

Sheller, Mimi and Urry, John. 2016. "The new mobilities paradigm." *Environment and Planning A: Economy and Space* Volume 38, Issue 2, pp. 207–226.

Simmel, Georg. 1950. The Metropolis and Mental Life by Kurt Wolff (Trans.) *The Sociology of Georg Simmel*, New York: Free Press.

Sinclair, Iain. 2010. *Classic Cafes*. http://www.classiccafes.co.uk/Psy.html. Ret. 15.5.17.

Smith Maguire, Jennifer and Hu, Dan. 2013. "Not a simple coffee shop: Local, global and glocal dimensions of the consumption of Starbucks in China." *Social Identities* Volume 19, Issue 5, pp. 670–684.

Sorokowska, Agnieszka, Sorokowski, Piotr, Hilpert, Peter, Cantarero, Katarzyna, Frackowiak, Tomasz, Ahmadi, Khodabakhsh, Alghraibeh, Ahmad M., Aryeetey, Richmond, Bertoni, Anna, Bettache, Karim et al. 2017. "Preferred interpersonal distances: A global comparison." *Journal of Cross-Cultural Psychology* Volume 48, Issue 4, pp. 577–592.

Spencer, James, H. 2014. *Globalization and Urbanization: The Global Urban Ecosystem*. New York: Rowman and Littlefield.

Standing, Guy. 2011. *The Precariat: The New Dangerous Class*. London: Bloomsbury Academic.

Standing, Guy. 2014. "The precariat." *Contexts* Volume 13, pp. 10–12.

Stevenson, Deborah. 2013. *The City: Key Concepts*. Cambridge, UK: Polity Press.

Storey, Robin. 2015. "Why do writers live to write in coffee shops?" *Storey Lines*. http://storey-lines.com/2015/09/14/why-do-writers-love-to-write-in-coffee-shops, September 2014. Ret. 30.10.17.

Summers, Chris. 2014. "How Vietnam became a coffee giant." *BBC News*. http://www.bbc.com/news/magazine-25811724, January 25. Ret. 31.3.17.

Sunderland, Sophie. 2012. "Trading the happy object: Colonialism, coffee and the friendly feeling." *MC Online Journal of Media and Culture* Volume 15, Issue 2, pp. 473–481.

Symonds, Michael. 2007. *One Continuous Picnic: A Gastronomic History of Australia*. Melbourne: Melbourne University Press.

Taylor, Peter Leigh, Murray, Douglas L. and Raynolds, Laura T. 2005. "Keeping trade fair: Governance challenges in the fair trade coffee initiative." *Sustainable Development* Volume 13, pp. 199–208.

Teisser, Eric. 2017. "Tokyo coffee profiles: Kojima Kenji of Fuglen Coffee Roasters." Daily Coffee News. http://dailycoffeenews.com/2016/04/07/tokyo-coffee-profile-kojima-kenji-of-fuglen-coffee-roasters/, April 7. Ret. 8.8.17.

Tonkiss, Fran. 2005. *Space, the City and Social Theory: Social Relations and Urban Forms*. Cambridge, UK: Polity Press.

Torres Quintão, Ronan and Zamith Brito, Eliane Pereira. 2016. Connoisseurship consumption and market evolution: An institutional theory perspective on the growth of specialty coffee consumption in the USA. *REMark* Volume 15, Issue 1, p. 1. http://gateway.library.qut.edu.au/login?url=https://search-proquest-com.ezp01.library.qut.edu.au/docview/1792806779?accountid=13380

Valkila, Joni. 2014. "Do fair trade pricing policies reduce inequalities in coffee production and trade?" *Development Policy Review*. Vol. 32 Issue 4: 475–493.

Wang, Jeng. 2012. "The coffee/cafe scape in Chinese cities." *MC Online Journal of Media and Culture* Volume 15, Issue 2.

Wasserstrom, Jeffrey. 2008. "Sipping Starbucks from Bloomington, Indiana to Shanghai, China." *World Hum*. http://www.worldhum.com/features/speakers-corner/sipping_starbucks_from_bloomington_indiana_to_shanghai_20080128. Ret. 30.1.18.

Waters, Cara. 2017. "Turning specialty coffee into a $50 million business at Veneziano Coffee." *Sydney Morning Herald*. http://www.smh.com.au/small-business/bold-businesses-podcast-turning-specialty-coffee-into-a-50-million-business-at-veneziano-coffee-20170925-gyo37y.html, September 27. Ret. 25.9.17.

Waxman, Lisa. 2006. "The coffee shop: Social and physical factors influencing place attachment." *Journal of Interior Design* Volume 31, Issue 3, pp. 35–53.

Wellman, Barry and Haythornwaite, Carolyn. 2002. *The Internet in Everyday Life*. Malden, MA and Oxford: Blackwell.
White, Merry. 2012. *Coffee Life in Japan*. Berkeley, CA: University of California Press.
Witz, Anne, Warhurst, Chris and Nickson, Dennis. 2003. "The labour of aesthetics and the aesthetics of organization." *Organization* Volume 10, Issue 1, pp. 33–54.
Woldoff, Rachael A., Lozzi, Dawn Marie and Dilks, Lisa M. 2013. "The social transformation of coffee houses: The emergence of chain establishments and the private nature of usage. "*International Journal of Social Science Studies* Volume 1, Issue 2, October, pp. 206–218.
Wild, Anthony. 2005. *Coffee: A Dark History*. New York. W.W. Norton and Company.
Wilson, Elizabeth. 1991. *The Sphinx in the City: Urban Life, the Control of Disorder, and Women*. Oakland, CA: University of California Press.
Zeller, Manfred and Beuchelt, Tina May. 2011. "Profits and poverty: Certification's troubled link for Nicaragua's organic and fairtrade coffee producers." *Ecological Economics* Volume 70, Issue 7, pp. 1316–1324.
Zukin, Sharon. 2010. *The Naked City*. New York: Oxford University Press.
Zukin, Sharon. 1999. *The Culture of Cities*. Malden, MA: Blackwell.

Websites and blogs

AnzaCoffee.com. Ret. 21.6.17. https://blog.beanhunter.com/melbournes-coffee-history/.
Australian Food Timeline. http://australianfoodtimeline.com.au/espresso-machine/.
Barista Basics. http://www.baristabasics.com.au/?Half-a-Century-of-Austalian-Espresso,-Bean-Scene,-Winter,-2006;News;112.
Browne, Talor. blog:http://smartgirlsmakecoffee.tumblr.com/post/142235392500/talor browne.
Daily Coffee News. https://dailycoffeenews.com/.
Douche Dude Baristas blog. 2017. http://doucheydudebaristas.tumblr.com
Eater.com. https://www.eater.com/drinks/2016/2/19/11059310/australian-coffee-culture-america. Ret. 28.6.17.
Christiaan Van Vuuren and Nick Boshier. 2016. http://www.dailymail.co.uk/video/tvshowbiz/video-1146492/The-Bondi-Hipsters-introduce-The-Closed-Caf.html.
Current Global State Internet. 2017. https://thenextweb.com/contributors/2017/04/11/current-global-state-internet/#.tnw_Zby8mHxN. Ret 7.10.17.
Signature Book Lover's Guide to Coffee. http://www.signature-reads.com/guides/the-book-lovers-guide-to-coffee/.
Sprudge, Coffee Industry website. www.sprudge.com.
The Largest Cities. *New Geography*. http://www.newgeography.com/content/005593-the-largest-cities-demographia-world-urban-areas-2017. Ret. 3.10.17.
Ibis World Report. "Cafes and Coffee Shops Australia Market Research Report". *Ibis World*. https://www.ibisworld.com.au/industry-trends/market-research-reports/accommodation-food-services/cafes-coffee-shops.html. January 2018. Ret. 29.6.18.
Taste Australia. http://tasteaustralia.biz/bushfood/wattleseed/. Ret. 13.7.17.
The Design Economy Report. 2015. United Kingdom Design Council. http://www.designcouncil.org.uk/resources/report/design-economy-report. Ret. 8.4.18.
Tumbler post. http://68.media.tumblr.com/ce1afa626674c59d25be3686cde7b373/tumblr_inline_o7z1sim5Rn1scwanp_500.png. Ret. 17.11.17.

INDEX

Page numbers in **bold** denote figures.